Modern Managerial Decision Making

Modern Managerial Decision Making

K. J. Radford
Chairman
Department of Administrative Studies
Atkinson College
York University
Downsview, Ontario

Reston Publishing Company, Inc.
A Prentice-Hall Company
Reston, Virginia

Library of Congress Cataloging in Publication Data

Radford, K J
    Modern managerial decision making.

    Includes bibliographies and index.
    1. Decision-making.   2. Management.   I. Title.
HD30.23.R32   658.4′03   80-24406
ISBN 0-8359-4571-5

© 1981 by
Reston Publishing Company, Inc.
A Prentice-Hall Company
Reston, Virginia

10 9 8 7 6 5 4 3 2 1

Printed in the United States of America

Table of Contents

Preface

There have been many approaches to decision making in recent years. These approaches range from that of creating a mathematic model of the decision situation, as in operations research and other forms of mathematical decision analysis, to those based on human and organizational behavior. It is only recently that those working in the field have begun to combine approaches in the study of the decision making problems that arise in modern organizations. This book is an attempt to assist those concerned with managerial decision making in this combination of approaches.

Decision problems have been classified in the past according to the conditions under which they arise, and, to some extent, in terms of the approach that is taken to their resolution. Mathematically-oriented writers have used the classifications of certainty, uncertainty, risk, and competition, which appear to have been derived primarily from the type of mathematics used in the methods that they suggest for resolution of the decision problems. For example, deterministic methods of operational research have been put forward as means of treating decisions under conditions of certainty. Statistical decision theory has been applied to decision making under conditions of uncertainty and risk. Some attempts have been made to treat decisions under conditions of competition by methods derived from game theory. The behaviorists are concerned with the differences between the resolution process that an individual uses and that are experienced in a group.

The position taken in this book is that these methods of classifying decision situations are no longer completely satisfactory, for a number of reasons. For example, the naming of categories in terms of certainty, uncertainty, risk, and competition tends to give the impression that these conditions are mutually exclusive. In actual practice many of the most complex decision situations encountered in modern organizations contain a combination of these conditions.

It is proposed, therefore, that decision problems be considered in terms of four major characteristics that have a major effect on methods of resolution, rather than in other categories that have been used frequently in the past. The four characteristics are the following:

1. whether the power to make the decision is in the hands of a single individual, organization or entity, or whether many such participants in the problem have the power to influence the outcome;
2. whether a single objective is involved (and therefore a unique criterion of decision can be used), or whether the participant or participants have multiple objectives;
3. whether or not the benefits and costs resulting from the implementation of available courses of action can truly be measured in quantitative terms (including possibly a quantitative expression of utility);
4. whether or not uncertainty exists in the decision situation being considered.

Combinations of the presence or absence of the above characteristics is therefore used in this book as the basis for discussion of different types of decision situations. The advantage of this approach is that practical decision situations can be readily identified in terms of the characteristics that affect the choice of methods of resolution.

The text starts with a general review of procedures for dealing with various types of decision situations. This review is followed in Chapter 2 by a discussion of methods that can be used in the resolution of well structured decision situations involving one participant, a single objective, quantitative measures of benefits and costs, and no uncertainty. The task of establishment of quantitative measures in situations in which such measures are not readily apparent is discussed in Chapter 3. Chapter 4 covers methods of dealing with uncertainty in practical decision situations and Chapter 5 is devoted to situations involving multiple objectives. The remainder of the text is concerned with decision situations in which two or more participants are involved, ranging from situations in which the participants are anxious to reach a mutual understanding to those in which there is open confrontation among the parties.

The book is based on my earlier text *Managerial Decision Making* published in 1965. Additions have been made covering subjects such as multiple objective situations more thoroughly and in some cases including more explanatory material. A number of practical decision situations have been added at the end of the chapters to provide the reader with an opportunity to use the methods described in the resolution of real-life situations.

Considerable care has been taken to maintain the material presented in as readable form as possible, considering the complexity of the subject.

Although the whole work is mathematically based, a minimum of mathematics is included in the text. Where necessary, mathematical derivations have been referenced or included in exhibits accompanying the description of the decision process to which they refer.

The book has been designed to be suitable for senior undergraduate and graduate courses in business, commerce, and management science, as well as for similar courses in technical and community colleges. The extensive referencing makes it possible to use the book as reading for courses of greater or lesser depth as required. Managers engaged in day-to-day decision making will also find the material useful to them in their work.

Acknowledgments

I would like to express my thanks to my many colleagues who have contributed suggestions regarding the content of this book. Special thanks are due to Martin Giesen who has worked on many of the aspects of the present text, especially on the practical decision situations. Terry Spier made a major contribution in the preparation and modification of the many drafts that were necessary before the final text was prepared. The book could not have been produced without the help of all these great people.

K. J. Radford

 *Chapter One*

The Nature of the Decision Process

INTRODUCTION

Situations in which a decision must be made arise continually in our daily lives, in the organizations in which we work, and in the communities in which we live. Dealing with these decisions is a major part of the work of individuals at all levels in a modern organization. Some of the decision situations encountered occur repetitively and in essentially the same form on each occasion. These decisions can be approached effectively by following rules and patterns of behavior that have been established as a result of previous experience. Other decision situations encountered may be similar to situations that have been experienced in the past. However, a particular characteristic of the newly arising problem may make it different in some important aspect. Still other situations are new and unique in every respect. The intuition and judgment of persons who have had experience with similar types of problems is the most important resource available in an organization to deal with situations of these latter types.

The essence of decision making is in the formulation of alternative courses of action to meet the situation under consideration and in the choice between these alternatives after an evaluation of their effectiveness in achieving the decision maker's objectives.[1, 2] One of the most important components of the decision-making process is the gathering of information from which an appreciation of the decision situation can be made. If

1

sufficient information can be gathered to obtain a complete specification of all of the alternatives and of their effectiveness in the situation under consideration, the decision making process is relatively straightforward. However, it may be impossible in practice to assemble all of the information and material that bears upon a given decision situation in view of the limited amounts of time and resources available for the task. Furthermore, it may not be possible in some cases to determine exactly what constitutes all of the relevant information, even if sufficient time and resources are available to collect it. An element of uncertainty then enters into the decision process, because of the lack of complete information. Under these circumstances, the decision maker may be unsure about the nature of the alternatives available and about the effectiveness of these alternatives in the achievement of his objectives. Uncertainty is one of the most pervasive characteristics of the decision situations encountered by modern management. It is also one of the factors causing the greatest difficulty in practical decision making.

In many decision situations, the responsibility for the choice between alternatives lies with one individual who makes the decision with respect to his or her own interests or those of the organization that he or she represents. In other cases, the decision must be taken by a number of individuals acting as members of a group, as in the management committee of an organization. Part of the decision process in such circumstances consists of a period of discussion, in which there may be some modification of the opinions of one or more of the group members. The process may lead to a consensus among those involved and to a mutually agreed evaluation of the alternatives in the decision situation under consideration. If this is the case, the agreed evaluation can be used as a basis for choice on behalf of the group as if it were a single decision maker.

A much more complex situation arises if the individuals concerned cannot arrive at an agreed position that represents the views of the group. This may occur when some or all of the individual members are pursuing different and conflicting objectives. In these circumstances, subgroups may form with differing opinions and evaluations of alternatives. The conflict between these opinions and evaluations may require a considerable period of interaction and negotiation between the subgroups before the decision situation under consideration can be resolved.

A similar condition arises in a decision situation in which a number of independent participants with conflicting interests are involved. For example, a proposal to build an airport or a power station may be opposed by citizens' groups and local government. It may, however, be supported by local contractors and the authority making the proposal. In situations of this sort, each of the participants envisages an outcome that is most preferred in relation to his or her own interests. For example, the citizens' groups may prefer that no facility be built because of the disruption that it would bring to their neighborhood. The contractors and the proposing authority may each prefer that the facility be built, but for somewhat different reasons. In situations in which the participants' initial preferences are different, the ultimate resolution takes place only after a period of interaction and negotiation between the participants. During this process, the views and preferences of some of the participants may change and a compromise may emerge. The passage of time often brings pressure on one or more of the participants to agree to an outcome that was not initially the most preferred. Nevertheless, all the participants may eventually accept this outcome in preference to a continuation of the confrontation. If the move towards a resolution of the decision situation does not occur and if the participants remain committed to the outcomes they preferred initially, a stalemate is reached which may take a considerable time to resolve.

The subject of decision making is concerned with a wide range of situations, each of which has a number of unique characteristics. The purpose of this book is to present a discussion of each of these situations and to demonstrate methods and techniques of decision making that may be helpful to those involved in the choice between alternatives. The first step in this discussion is to consider the background of a decision situation. This subject is covered in the next section of the text.

THE BACKGROUND TO A DECISION

It is interesting and helpful in the discussion of decision making to regard the organizations, individuals, and groups of individuals involved in terms of systems theory.[3, 4] In this theory, a system is envisaged as a set of elements or components that are bound together by some form of relationship. The behavior of the system is determined by the relationship between its elements. An organization is seen, for example, as a system that consists of a number of individuals, groups of individuals, or departments working together to achieve a set of common objectives. The behavior of the organization depends to a large extent on the behavior of its component parts and on the relationships between them.

Systems exist at a number of different levels. At a lower hierarchical level each of the elements of a system can be considered as a system in its own right. For example, the departments of an organization each exhibit all the characteristics of a complete system. At a higher level, the original organization might be regarded as only an element of an even more comprehensive system. Hierarchical arrangements of this nature are familiar in daily life. They appear in many forms of human activity. Generally speaking, there is no logical end to the process of dividing systems into elements. In practice, however, the process is usually carried no further than is necessary to serve the considerations at hand.

The Environment of a Decision Situation

Organizations and individuals that are involved in modern decision making operate in an environment and react to stimuli that impinge upon them in that environment. The external environment of an organization or of an individual may contain other organizations and individuals that compete for benefits from that environment. It may also contain elements that place constraints on the manner in which the participants in the environment can operate. These elements may be social, technological, natural, or quasi-natural.[5] The social elements are those that refer to or result from relationships with other systems in the environment. They include commitments, laws, policies, guidelines, and other factors that arise in interactions between the systems in the environment. Technological elements are concerned with economic, physical, human, and organizational factors. Natural elements consist of events in which there is no discernible involvement by humans. Quasi-natural events result from the unintentional effects of one situation on the actions of individuals and organizations that are pursuing their own interests in other unrelated situations.

An organization has an internal as well as an external environment. The internal environment consists of all its component parts and of the set of social, technological, and natural elements that constitute the fabric of the organization. A particular decision situation may exist wholly within the external environment of an organization, wholly within its internal environment, or partially in the external and partially in the internal environments. The portions of the external and internal environments that relate to a particular decision situation constitute the environment of that decision situation.

The Objectives of an Organization, Individual, or Group

Individuals, organizations, and groups have ideals, objectives, and goals related to their functions, as expressed, for example, in their terms of reference or their charters under law. What is described as an objective by one person is often called an ideal or a goal by others. It may be helpful, therefore, to differentiate between ideals, objectives, and goals by means of the following definitions. These definitions are not unique and many might argue for a different distinction between the ideas conveyed by the words. However, for the purposes of this text, let us regard an *ideal* as something that is ultimately desirable but not necessarily ever attainable; an *objective* as something that is desired to attain, but not necessarily in a given time period; and a *goal* as an outcome to be obtained within a particular time period. For simplicity in what follows, the word "objective" will be used to cover the meaning of the three terms. The individual terms will be used only when it is necessary to emphasize the time period over which the desired condition is to be attained.

Covert and Overt Objectives

Statements of objectives prepared for organizations sometimes contain only those items that management is prepared to see published. Other objectives that management wants to keep confidential are not included in statements prepared for publication. This practice is understandable in the case of a business organization that does not wish to alert a possible competitor to its future activities. Under these circumstances, the statement that is published contains what may be called the *overt* objectives of the organization. There is in addition a supplementary list of *covert* objectives that remains in the minds of managers or in the company confidential files. In some cases, the overt and covert objectives may be mildly contradictory. They may even be in direct conflict with each other. Both types of objectives are important in establishing the background for decisions in the organization. Management policies and the decisions that spring from them are necessarily related to all of the objectives of the organization.

Multiple Objectives

Most modern organizations have many objectives. Some of these objectives may conflict with one another with respect to some activities of an organization. For example, a business enterprise may have an objective to attain a particular return on investment, but at the same time have objectives related to its social responsibility to the community in which it operates. Satisfying the social objectives of the organization may reduce to some extent the degree of achievement of the return on investment. Even if the sole objective of an organization were to maximize its return on investment, there might be some discussion and conflict over whether this maximization should take place over the short, medium, or long terms. Nonprofit organizations do not often have the same economic objectives as those that operate in a competitive business environment. Nevertheless, such organizations often have objectives related to their primary mission that are in conflict with others that refer to their secondary roles and missions. Individuals and groups also pursue many objectives. Achievement of one of these objectives often detracts temporarily from pursuit of one or more of the others.

It is necessary, therefore, to consider the range of objectives of the organization, individual, or group of individuals involved as a background to decision making. Furthermore, priorities must be established between the members of a set of multiple objectives. It may be possible to assess this priority in numerical form, so that a quantitative weighting factor can be applied to each of them. In many cases, however, it is not possible to express the priority between objectives in terms of a single number. In these circumstances, the objectives may be placed in a qualitative order of importance as a guide to those who may be involved in decision making.

It is particularly desirable in establishing priorities between objectives to distinguish between those that contribute to the achievement of short-term missions and those that relate to the maintenance of freedom of action in the longer term.[6] It may be, for example, that the asignment of very high priority to the achievement of short-term objectives detracts from the longer-term strategic capability of an organization. It can be argued that all such considerations ultimately reduce to the single issue of the future survival of the organization, group or individual in a form acceptable to those involved. The relative priority assigned to the individual objectives in a multiple set may therefore be directly related to the perceptions of those engaged in the objective-setting activity with respect to this overriding consideration.

Objectives of Individual Members of an Organization

Individuals who work in organizations also have ideals, objectives, and goals that may or may not coincide completely with those of the organization. Cyert and March have suggested that an organization or group be viewed as a coalition of the individual members.[7] In a manner consistent with systems theory, they see the conditions existing within the coalition as being a major factor affecting the behavior of the organization. They point out, further, that the relationship between the objectives of the organization and those of individual members or subgroups is often determined by a form of bargaining process. In the course of this process, a series of side payments are negotiated as a means of facilitating agreement and of overcoming potential areas of conflict. These side payments may take the form of monetary compensation, other employee benefits, or adjustments of working conditions. They are designed to satisfy (at least partially) the desires of the individual members to achieve their own objectives, while allowing progress towards the objectives of the organization at the same time.

WELL STRUCTURED AND ILL STRUCTURED DECISIONS

A number of authors have made a distinction between two types of decision situations. Herbert A. Simon was among the first to do so when he referred to decisions that are "programmed" and those that are "nonprogrammed."[8] He described programmed decisions as those that are met repetitively and that become routine as a result of many encounters with the same situation. These decisions are "programmable" because a specific procedure can be worked out by which they can be resolved. This procedure is based on experience in a number of situations of the same type. Once it has been established, all like situations can be treated by use of the standard procedure. The only innovative activity with respect to situations of this nature is a check that it is appropriate to employ the usual procedure for resolution.

Programmed decisions usually occur in the routine operational and administrative activities of an organization. They are found mostly at the middle and lower levels of management. The input data used in making a decision of this type is usually complete and well defined. Details of the procedures involved in resolving a programed decision are well known and are agreed upon by all who are concerned with the problem. Senior management is usually not involved with particular decisions of this kind. However, the results of a series of such decisions over a period of time may be of interest to senior managers. Sometimes many relatively straightforward programed decisions can be linked together in a logical progression that forms the basis for resolution of a very complex problem. The use of mathematical models to provide the basis for decisions in scheduling the use of resources, distribution of products, inventory control, and handling of queues provides many examples of the use of a progression of programmable decisions in dealing with very complex situations. These examples are often comparable to the use of process control routines in industrial production.

By contrast, nonprogrammed decisions are not repetitive. They appear to be new and unique to the decision maker in one or more respects when they occur. No complete and well established procedure exists for dealing with nonprogrammed decisions, mainly because no direct experience has been obtained from previous encounters with a decision situation of exactly the same sort. In comparison to programmed decisions, the data available concerning a nonprogrammed decision is usually incomplete and ill defined. The means of dealing with situations of this nature are not unique nor are they usually agreed upon by all concerned. Different persons may have different perceptions of a particular situation and of the manner in which it should be handled. Nonprogrammable decisions are mostly found at the middle and senior levels of management and are often related to the policy making and planning activities of an organization.

The distinction between "programmed" and "nonprogrammed" decisions refers to the procedure that can be adopted in the process of resolution of the decision situation. Programmed decisions are seen as having a well defined and recognizable structure, so that new occurrences of a well known type of situation can be immediately placed in a category and processed routinely. Nonprogrammed decisions, on the other hand, are those for which no routine procedure or structure can be applied. Each nonprogrammable decision appears to those involved to have characteristics that do not fit into any of the structures that have been formulated for the routine treatment of decision situations. This emphasis on structure has resulted in the use of the terms "well structured" and "ill structured" (or "unstructured") to replace "programmed" and "nonprogrammed" in the recent technical literature.[9, 10] The fact that a complete and comprehensive specification can be written to describe the procedure for resolving a programmed or well structured decision situation has also suggested the terms "completely specified" to describe this sort of situation and "non-completely specified" to refer to nonprogrammed or ill structured decisions.[11] None of these sets of terms describes the distinction between the two sorts of decision situations completely satisfactorily. However, authors have recently tended towards the use of well structured and ill structured to refer to this distinction and this practice will therefore be adopted in this text.

The use of two such terms to describe the distinction between decision situations may give the impression that only two types of decision situations are ever encountered. In practice, a continuum of situations exists, ranging from those that are well structured at one end of the spectrum to those that are ill structured at the other end. The decision situations in between have been called "partially structured" or "partially specified." An illustration of this spectrum of decisions and a brief description of the characteristics of each sort of decision is shown in Fig. 1-1.

Partially structured decision situations are those in which only a part can be well structured or completely specified. Typically, they consist of decision situations in which a great deal of data or a number of supplementary decisions can be processed according to a well structured routine. However, the final choice between alternatives is not as well structured. A number of matters that cannot be represented completely by a formal specification are involved in this final choice. It is therefore left to the decision maker to make the ultimate selection between alternatives on the basis of the data and supplementary factors that have been assembled, using judgment and experience in dealing with the ill structured parts of the decision. For example, consider the decision involved in filling a senior position in an organization. The individual who is to make the choice would probably agree to writing some broad specifications describing the staff member required and including necessary characteristics such as age, experience, and education. These specifications can be used to select from the personnel files all those who meet the general requirements for the job. The manager is thus relieved of the routine work of scanning all the personnel files. The final choice is made by the individual involved using the results of the well structured portion of the decision process, further information obtained during the interviews, and intuition and judgment gained from experience in similar situations in the past.

FIG. 1-1:   Range of Decision Situations in an Organization

SPECTRUM OF DECISION SITUATIONS

Well structured (Programmed or Completely Specified)	Partially Structured	Ill-Structured (Nonprogrammed or Non-completely-Specified)
1. Specification of decision procedure agreed in advance of resolution.	1. Only a part of decision process can be completely specified and structured.	1. Decision procedure cannot be completely structured in advance of resolution.
2. Little managerial involvement at time of each resolution.	2. Manager makes final resolution using results from structured portion and his experience and intuition.	2. Individuals resolve each situation on basis of experience, beliefs, and judgment.
3. Repeated resolutions with same data produce same result.	3. Two different managers may agree on certain relevant data but reach different conclusions.	3. Two different managers may reach different conclusions.

THE DECISION MAKING PROCESS

The nature of decision making has been studied intensively in recent years. The conclusions drawn from individual studies have been different in many respects. All agree, however, that decision making is a process involving a number of interwoven stages, rather than a single, isolated act. One of the first authors to describe the decision making process as a series of phases was John Dewey. Writing in 1910, he suggested that the process of problem solving could be thought of as consisting of three phases, namely, answering these questions: (1) What is the problem? (2) What are the alternatives? (3) Which alternative is best?[12]

A number of other models of the decision making process follow the same general approach as that proposed by Dewey. Perhaps the best known is that of Herbert A. Simon.[13] His model consists of three stages that may be described as follows:

Intelligence: The internal and external environments of the decision maker are searched for conditions requiring a decision, and information is gathered about these conditions.

Design: The courses of action available to the decision maker are determined and analyzed as possible solutions to the decision problems that have been detected.

Choice: One of the available courses of action is selected for implementation on the basis of an evaluation of their effectiveness relative to the achievement of objectives.

In his later work, Simon added a fourth phase which he called *review*. This review phase consists of a process of assessment of past choices during which possible modifications to the approaches used are considered in preparation for further decision making activity. This fourth phase represents a revision of general decision making techniques rather than a part of the process applicable to any one situation.

A somewhat more detailed description of the decision making process has been provided by Eilon in an article that seeks to explore a number of aspects of the nature of decisions.[14] Eilon's description of the decision process consists of eight steps that can be listed briefly as follows:

1. Information input
2. Analysis of the available information
3. Specification of measures of performance and cost
4. Creation of a model of the decision situation
5. Formulation of alternatives (or strategies) available to the decision maker
6. Predictions of outcomes of the alternatives
7. Specification of criteria of choice between alternatives
8. Resolution of the decision situation

Both Simon's and Eilon's models provide an initial framework for consideration of the decision process and an idea of the progression of steps that may be necessary before the decision situation can be resolved. In practice, the steps described may take place in a somewhat different order. Some may be undertaken implicitly and some concurrently. Furthermore, the actual decision process often consists of a series of iterations through some or all of the steps described, rather than a single run through a process consisting of a simple series of phases.

A PROCEDURE FOR DEALING WITH WELL STRUCTURED SITUATIONS

A procedure for resolution of well structured decision problems can be constructed from a combination of the Simon and Eilon models of the decision process. Remembering that the objectives of the decision maker constitute the background to the decision process, the steps in this procedure can be described as follows:

1. Intelligence

(a) *Perception and formulation of the situation:* The identification of a decision situation and the definition of its main characteristics.

(b) *Construction of a model of the situation:* A model provides a vehicle for estimating the possible outcomes of a decision situation over a range of possible conditions.[15]

(c) *Determination of such quantitative measures of costs and benefits as are appropriate to the situation under consideration:* Uniform measurement systems facilitate comparisons between the alternate ways of resolving the decision problem.

2. Design

(a) *Specification of available alternatives:* Possible courses of action are identified and clearly formulated.

3. Choice

(a) *Evaluation of the benefits and costs of the available alternative courses of action:* The effect of the implementation of each course of action is assessed in terms of the measures of costs and benefits specified earlier.

(b) *Establishment of a criterion for choice between courses of action:* Rules are established by which outcomes can be related to the objectives of the party making the choice.

(c) *Resolution of the decision situation:* A choice is made from among the available courses of action on the basis of an acceptable criterion.

As before, these steps need not necessarily be taken in the exact order shown. Also, in practice, the procedure may consist of a series of repetitions of all or some of the above steps before the decision situation is finally resolved. The individual steps can be described in more detail as follows:

Perception and formulation of the situation.   This first step in the decision making procedure consists of (1) searching the environment of the organization concerned for conditions that call for a decision; (2) collecting as much information as appears necessary and as available time and resources allow on situations that are detected; (3) forming a perception of each situation on the basis of the information at hand; and (4) placing each situation in a category consistent with its perceived characteristics. Drucker has described four different conditions that the decision maker may detect at this stage:[16]

1. An event that is truly one of a type that is met repetitively by the individual or organization concerned and that may be classified as well-structured after further investigation.

2. An event that is new to the particular organization or department in which the individual is working, but which is in fact well structured and met repetitively in other similar organizations or departments.

3. An event that appears to be unique, but that is in reality the first manifestation of a situation that can be well structured and which will be met repetitively in the future.

4. A truly unique event that is unlikely to occur again in the same form in the foreseeable future.

Correct initial identification of the observed conditions and accurate perception of the symptoms are essential to effective resolution of the decision situation. Treatment of a routine and repetitive situation as new and unique most always results in inefficiency and wasted effort. On the other hand, misperception of a new and unique problem as one that can be handled routinely is likely to cause even greater difficulty. There is no prescription for accurate diagnosis better than persistence and dogged determination to explain the observed phenomena. This persistence involves repeated inquiry as to whether the perception and formulation of the problem explain all the observed events. It is important to establish whether some event has been ignored or forgotten that is not compatible with the proposed formulation. If that is the case, a modification of the problem definition may be necessary.

Construction of a model of the situation. Perception and formulation of the decision situation is the basis for the construction of a model, giving full details of the factors involved and the relationships between them. This model is used to explore the effects of actions that might be taken to resolve the decision situations. In some of the more routine situations, it may be appropriate to describe the relationships between the factors in a situation by mathematical formulations. Such expressions provide a convenient method of description in a format for which rules of manipulation of the parameters involved have already been established. However, the attractiveness of mathematical models should not be a source of temptation to use them without considerable thought. In particular, many such models involve assumptions that are clearly stated in their formulation. The applicability of these assumptions to the decision situation at hand must be checked thoroughly before any such model is adopted.

John D. C. Little states in a recent article that a model of a decision situation should be "... simple, robust, easy to control, adaptive, as complete as possible and easy to communicate with."[17] In addition, it should contain a complete statement of the constraints or boundary conditions existing in the situation. A solution to a decision situation that does not satisfy the existing constraints is, in fact, a solution to the wrong problem. Tannenbaum has listed five types of constraints that may exist in a typical decision situation:[18]

- *Authoritative constraints*, which result from policies or directives within an organization.
- *Biological constraints*, which arise from the limitations of individuals who may be affected by the decision.
- *Physical constraints*, including such factors as geography, climate, physical resources, and characteristics of man made objects.
- *Technological constraints*, involved with the state of the art in relevant technological development.
- *Economic constraints*, concerned with the money or other resources available to implement the chosen alternative.

These constraints are the result of the social and technological elements of the environment described earlier in the text. One of these constraints, or a combination of them, may limit the number of alternatives available to the decision maker. Since the time frame of the decision situation normally extends into the future, it is necessary in many cases that the estimated future behavior of the constraints and boundary conditions be included in the model.

Determination of quantitative measures of costs and benefits. The task of the decision maker is considerably easier if the results of each of the alternatives that must be considered can be expressed in terms of quantitative measures of costs and benefits. When maximization of monetary gain is the objective, there is little difficulty in choosing between two alternatives if one is estimated to produce more profit (measured in dollars) than the other. The search for quantitative measures that are true representations of the benefits and costs of the alternatives is therefore an important part of the decision making process. These measures must be directly related to the objectives that form the background to the decision situation under consideration.

Specification of available alternatives. The individual dealing with a decision situation must list the alternative courses of action that he considers to be available within the boundary conditions of the situation as it is perceived and formulated. The effect of constraints existing in the environment of the decision must be taken into account and the limitations on available alternatives that are caused by these constraints must also be studied. Care should be taken to list as many of the available alternatives as possible, including some that may not come immediately to mind. It is often useful to seek the opinions of persons with substantially different backgrounds and experience before being satisfied that the listing is as complete as possible.

Estimation of the outcomes from available alternatives. Given a list of available alternatives and a model of the decision situation, it is possible in well structured situations to estimate the outcomes that would be expected from implementation of each of the alternatives in terms of the chosen measures of benefits and costs.

Establishment of a criterion of choice between outcomes. Having estimated the benefits and costs of the available alternatives, it is necessary to establish a criterion of choice between them. This criterion must be closely linked to the objectives that form the background to the decision situation. Maximization of benefits for a given cost or minimization of cost for a given benefit are criteria of choice often found in situations in which the economic welfare of an organization is the prime objective.

Resolution of the decision situation. Resolution of the decision situation is the final stage of the decision process. It consists of the choice of a course of action after completion of all the above steps. In many cases the process consists of a number of cycles through all or some of these steps. Once resolution has been achieved, implementation of the chosen alternative course of action can begin.

The above procedure provides a means of dealing with well structured decision situations. In fact, a typical characteristic of a well structured decision situation is that it can be resolved by the application of a logical sequence of steps such as that described above. It is interesting to note that in practice, there is no unique quality that determines that a decision situation is well structured. It is necessary only that the individuals, organizations, or groups involved in the decision situation agree that it be considered to be well structured. Such agreement is often based on expediency. It is sometimes economic in time and resources to agree to a specification of a decision situation that is admittedly not perfect, but that is nevertheless adequate for the purposes at hand. For example, most payroll systems do not provide payments to employees that represent the exact amount due to them in a given time period. The amount paid is usually an approximation to this exact amount. The approximation is nevertheless acceptable to the employees who do not argue over minor discrepancies in the amount received. They have some faith that these deviations from their exact entitlement will be corrected in due course. In the same way, some models used to evaluate operational systems do not consist of an exact representation of those systems. These models often neglect characteristics that are judged to have only a minor effect on the operation of the system. They do, however, provide a representation that is regarded as accurate enough by the individuals who are involved in the decision situation under consideration.

Resolution of a well structured decision situation by an agreed procedure has been called *impersonalistic* by Eilon.[19] His reasoning is that adoption of an agreed procedure precludes the insertion of individual decision makers' beliefs, attitudes, and value judgments into the decision process once the agreement on the procedure has been reached. The outcome of the decision process under these circumstances is the same for all decision makers who use the procedure. It is interesting to note that the writing of an agreed specification for resolution of an operational or administrative process is a necessary step in preparing that process for computer support. The decision situations that we delegate completely to a computer are therefore necessarily well structured and the resolution of these situations is carried out by the computer in an impersonalistic and well structured fashion.

Use of an agreed procedure to resolve a well structured situation can be said to contribute to rational decision making. The notion of rationality is one of the most contentious in the technical literature of decision making. The dictionary definition of the word rational as "endowed with reason" is not adequate for our purposes. A broader concept of rationality is that a rational decision maker is one who, after consideration of alternatives, chooses that which is most preferred relative to stated objectives. To do otherwise can be called irrational. Choice of the most preferred alternative after application of a well structured and agreed procedure can therefore be regarded as rational. This view is supported by Diesing in his review of the role of rationality in society and of the many forms that it can take.[20] However, later in his work he seeks to broaden the concept of rationality by applying it solely to the selection of a decision making procedure rather than to the choice between alternatives. The choice of a well defined step-wise procedure in the case of a well structured decision situation would in this way of thinking be regarded as rational and as leading to a rational choice between alternatives. We will return to this subject later in the text as we ponder the question of what constitutes rational behavior in decision situations that are not well structured.

DECISION MAKING IN AN ILL-STRUCTURED SITUATION

Decision situations are classified as ill structured when conditions in their environment preclude the possibility of resolution using a routine procedure such as that described above. There are four main characteristics of ill structured situations, some or all of which may be present in practical circumstances. These characteristics are:

1. Lack of complete information regarding the decision situation and its environment.
2. Lack of quantitative measures that truly and completely describe the costs and benefits of the available alternatives.
3. The existence of multiple objectives on the part of the organization, individual, or group concerned.
4. The existence of more than one participant in the decision situation with power to influence the outcome.

These four characteristics are now discussed in turn.

Lack of Complete Information

Lack of complete information about a decision situation leads to uncertainty among those involved in its resolution with regard to many of its characteristics. This uncertainty has three main effects. First, it is usually impossible with incomplete information to construct a comprehensive model of the decision situation that includes all the relevant factors and the relationships between them. With an incomplete model of the situation, those involved may feel that some of the more important aspects of the situation are beyond their immediate comprehension. Furthermore, much of the information available may consist only of symptoms of a need for action (such as an increase in absenteeism in a factory or an increase in violent crime in a city) rather than being a detailed description and formulation of all the vital aspects of the situation. In these circumstances, a great deal of time and effort may need to be spent in identifying the nature of the situation under consideration. Without complete information, it cannot be certain at any time that a correct identification has been made.

Second, under conditions of limited information, different individuals involved in a decision situation may form different impressions of its characteristics. Each individual's perceptions of the situation are based on the information available viewed against his previous experience and factors relating to spheres of competence, judgment, and motivation.

It may be very difficult, therefore, for two or more individuals to agree to a specification and formulation of the problem. In these circumstances, it is unlikely that complete agreement can be reached between the individuals involved on such matters as alternative courses of action, quantitative measures of costs and benefits, and criteria for choice between alternatives.

Third, lack of complete information leads to uncertainty about the exact conditions in the environment of the decision situation. There may be a considerable period of time between the choice and the completion of the implementation of a course of action. There is a possibility therefore that conditions in the environment of the decision when the course of action has been implemented will have deviated from those that had been predicted. The effects of a course of action chosen in an attempt to resolve a decision situation may therefore be different from that estimated at the time of its selection. The longer the implementation time, the greater is the risk that the outcome of a course of action will be different from that estimated during the decision process.

Lack of Appropriate Quantitative Measures of Benefits and Costs

Choice between alternatives is considerably easier when the comparison between them can be made in terms of well understood benefits and costs. This condition, which is often found in well structured situations, allows the alternatives to be compared in like terms. In many situations, however, the assignment of purely quantitative measures to the benefits and costs of alternative courses of action is very difficult. This difficulty arises particularly in situations in which the health, happiness, and welfare of a segment of the population is affected. Measurement of these factors is not easily accomplished and there is a danger that vital aspects of benefits or costs will be neglected by an inappropriate choice of measures. The same problem arises in business decision situations also. For example, it is difficult to suggest a truly appropriate measure of the public image of a corporation or of the manner in which a company meets its social responsibilities.

There is a temptation in these circumstances to assign quantitative measures of benefits and costs even if they do not relate exactly to the factors involved in progress towards achievement of the objectives that form the background to the decision situation. This temptation arises from the simplification of the decision process if the choice between alternatives can be made in quantitative terms. However, this simplification may involve a considerable distortion of the decision situation. Conclusions reached after analysis of the distorted situation are frequently misleading when applied to the conditions that are actually facing the individuals involved. Unfortunately, such conclusions often have an aura of validity purely from having been derived by an apparently logical process. Individuals who are not familiar with the analysis and with the effects of the assumptions that have been made may therefore be seriously misled.

When the individuals involved have different perceptions of a decision situation and its characteristics, they may also have different views with respect to the measures of benefits and costs that should be employed in the decision process. This possible difference in views is a further reason why a completely agreed upon specification of the process of resolution of an ill structured decision situation cannot be obtained.

The Existence of Multiple Objectives

Most organizations, individuals, and groups have more than one objective. In such cases, adoption of a course of action that provides satisfactory achievement of one objective may result in less progress towards satisfying some or all of the others. There may be no means of selecting an alternative that is unequivocally best in these circumstances. The choice between alternatives is more easily handled if progress towards achievement of each of the objectives can be measured in the same well understood unit (such as dollars) and when the priority between objectives can be expressed in terms of numeric weighting factors. However, these conditions often do not exist in ill structured decision situations. Individuals involved in such a decision situation may disagree regarding the priority to be assigned to each of the objectives and on the manner of evaluating alternatives with respect to them. In such cases, the choice between alternatives is made using the intuition and judgment of experienced individuals rather than by the adoption of a well structured decision making routine.

The Existence of Many Participants

In many of the ill structured decision situations encountered today the power to bring about an outcome does not lie with a single decision maker. A basic characteristic of such situations is that two or more participants each have the capability to influence the outcome. These participants may have conflicting interests and intentions. They may each have in mind outcomes that they feel they can achieve and that they think will be most appropriate to the achievement of their objectives. However, no one participant has the power at the outset of the decision situation to bring about by unilateral action the outcome that he or she most prefers. Satisfactory resolution of a decision situation of this kind can be achieved only by agreement between participants that retain the power to influence the outcome. For example, in an industrial relations dispute, management cannot obtain the settlement that it wishes as long as the union has in mind an outcome that it considers to be more in its interests and as long as management has no means of forcing the union to accept its will.

The actual outcomes of situations of this nature are usually determined as a result of an open or implicit process of negotiation between the participants.[21] The objective of each of the participants during this process of negotiation is to persuade the others to accept the outcome that he or she most prefers. Often, the outcome that emerges is not one that was originally seen as most preferred by any participant, but one that each is prepared to accept after the process of negotiation as preferable to a continuation of the confrontation. In industrial relations disputes, for example, the outcome of negotiations is often a compromise that is eventually accepted by both parties in order that the dispute can be resolved without further passage of time.

Complex decision situations such as those described above do not lend themselves to resolution by a routine procedure such as can be applied to well structured situations. A logical process of this sort may well be useful in determining an order of preference of a particular participant for possible outcomes of a decision situation. However, the actual outcome results from a process of negotiation between participants for which no well structured procedure has yet been devised. Even if a completely structured process of resolution of these complex situations could be devised, it would probably be unacceptable as a basis of resolution by participants with different interests, objectives, and perceptions of the situation in which they are involved.

THE RESOLUTION OF ILL STRUCTURED SITUATIONS

A pervasive feature of ill structured decision situations is the lack of complete information concerning their characteristics. There can therefore be no unique and undisputable formulation of such a decision situation and no unequivocal method of resolution that is acceptable to all. Individual decision makers form their perceptions of a decision situation and of the means by which it can be resolved on the basis of the information available to them at the time. In the absence of a well structured and agreed model of the process of resolution, the experience and intuition of those involved in a decision situation becomes a major factor in the choice between alternative courses of action and between outcomes. Under these circumstances, decision making is personalistic, as contrasted to the impersonal nature of the use of a well structured and logical procedure.[22] Nevertheless, some aspects of the well structured procedure can be retained. The logical sequence of steps provides at least a guide to the considerations that are important in a first approach to a decision situation. The three-stage model of Simon (intelligence, design, and choice) is applicable to many ill structured situations in which a single decision maker is charged with the choice between alternatives.

Some modification of the original Simon model is necessary, however, in approaching decision situations in which there are two or more participants. This modification is required to take account of the process of negotiation between the participants that is essential to the determination of the outcome. The modification consists of a redefinition of the three phases of the decision making process, as follows:

Information gathering: The internal and external environments of the organization are searched for incipient decision situations, information gathered about each situation that is detected, and alternative courses of action listed for each of them.

Analysis: Possible outcomes of a decision situation that may be brought about by a combination of courses of action taken by the participants are analyzed and placed in an order of preference. Tactics designed to bring about preferred outcomes are considered in this phase.

Interaction: Preferences and intentions are communicated explicitly or implicitly to other participants with the objective of persuading or coercing them to agree to a most-preferred outcome.

The question remains as to what constitutes rational behavior in the resolution of ill structured decision situations. The concept of rationality is relatively straightforward in well structured situations in which there is complete information, a single objective, the ability to evaluate benefits and costs in quantitative terms, and a single decision maker. In these circumstances, all possible alternatives can be envisaged and evaluated. Rational behavior consists of choosing the alternative that is seen as best (or most preferred) in terms of a criterion related to the objective. Any other choice can be seen to be against the interests of the decision maker and can be called irrational.

The concept of rationality in ill structured situations is not as clear-cut. Lack of a simple decision making rule is possibly one reason why these situations have been called "wicked" as compared with the "tame" and more tractable well structured kind.[23, 24] Without complete information, any list of the alternatives available to the decision maker is necessarily incomplete. There is no guarantee that another course of action that is preferable to those considered would not be revealed if more information were available. In these circumstances no choice between alternatives can be said unequivocally to be the best and therefore to be uniquely rational. Furthermore, two individuals involved in the same decision situation might have different information and consequently different perceptions of that situation. In these circumstances, the two individuals might recommend different courses of action for resolution of the same decision situation, each claiming, however, that he had acted rationally in the choice between alternatives.

Some qualification of the concept of rationality is clearly needed in the case of ill structured decision situations. This qualification can be introduced in the following manner. Choice of the alternative or outcome that is most preferred relative to an objective under conditions of complete information is termed *objectively rational.* An objectively rational choice is unique and optimal under the conditions stated. A choice between alternatives when information is not complete and under other conditions found in ill structured decision situations is called *subjectively rational.* A subjectively rational choice is not unique. Two individuals may reach different conclusions and each be subjectively rational in the circumstances as they perceive them. Subjective rationality can be considered in some cases to be more related to the approach to the decision situation than to the actual choice between alternatives. A subjectively rational approach may be one that, in Diesing's words, ". . . yields adequate decisions for complex situations with some regularity."[25]

A further extension of the idea of rationality is necessary when two or more participants are involved in an ill structured decision situation. In these circumstances, the outcome is often reached only after a process of negotiation between the participants. This outcome may be viewed as being *jointly rational,* insomuch that it permits resolution of the decision situation and is preferred by all participants to a continuation of the confrontation.

CATEGORIES OF DECISION SITUATIONS

The division of decision situations into well- and ill-structured categories serves as a first step in identifying their characteristics. A more detailed differentiation is necessary, however, in discussing methods by which each of the various decision situations that are encountered by modern organizations and individuals can be approached. It has been conventional in the technical literature to divide decision situations into categories depending on whether they exist under conditions of certainty, risk, uncertainty, and competition. These conditions are defined as follows:

- *Certainty*—when all possible alternative courses of action are known and when there is only one consequence or outcome of each of these courses of action.
- *Risk*—when there is more than one possible consequence or outcome of each of the alternatives and the decision maker is assumed to know the probability of occurrence of these consequences or outcomes.
- *Uncertainty*—when neither the number of possible consequences or outcomes nor the probability of their occurrence is known to the decision maker.
- *Competition*—when an identified opponent to the decision maker exists, whose objectives, intentions, and choices may be in direct or indirect conflict to those of the decision maker.

These categories are derived to some extent from the types of mathematical approaches to decision making that have been devised in the past forty years. However, this classification has a number of deficiencies in the light of more recent work on the characteristics of decision situations. It does not, for example, take explicit account of the existence of multiple objectives or the lack of truly appropriate quantitative measures of benefits and costs, which are important features of many modern decision situations. Furthermore, the naming of the categories tends to give the impression that uncertainty and competition are mutually exclusive, whereas much of the complexity of many decision situations derives from a combination of these and other factors.

It has recently been suggested that the four characteristics that have a major effect on the process of resolution of a decision situation should be used to construct a new series of categories for the purpose of detailed study of these situations.[26] These characteristics are:

1.   whether or not uncertainty exists in the decision situation being considered;

2.   whether or not the benefits and costs resulting from the implementation of available courses of action can be truly represented in quantitative terms;

3.   whether a single objective is involved or whether multiple objectives must be taken into account;

4.   whether the power to make the decision lies in the hands of one organization, individual, or group or whether many such participants have power to influence the outcome of the situation.

Combination of the two states of each of the above characteristics leads to sixteen categories of decision situations. These sixteen categories can be condensed into five as shown in Table 1-1.

The first category shown in the left hand column consists of decision situations in which there is (or there is assumed to be) no uncertainty. A single decision maker with a single objective must make a choice between alternatives on the basis of an evaluation of these alternatives in quantitative terms. Examples of decision situations in this category occur in many routine operational and administrative processes. These situations are well structured. They refer to problems such as the following:

1.   The need to find the mix of products in a production line that provides the most profit in meeting a demand in situations where there are constraints on the availability of the necessary resources.
2.   The need to supply points at which there is a demand (such as retail

TABLE 1-1. Types of Decision Situations

	Category 1	Category 2	Category 3	Category 4	Category 5
Certainty or Uncertainty	Certainty	Certainty or Uncertainty	Uncertainty	Certainty or Uncertainty	Certainty or Uncertainty
Quantitative or Non-Quantitative Measures of Benefits and Costs	Quantitative	Non-quantitative	Quantitative	Quantitative or Non-quantitative	Quantitative or Non-quantitative
Single or Multiple Objectives	Single Objective	Single Objective	Single Objective	Multiple Objectives	Single or Multiple Objectives
Single or Many Participants	Single Participant	Single Participant	Single Participant	Single Participant	Many Participants
Examples	Optimum use of resources in a production process: optimum distribution from warehouses to retail points: optimal flow through networks	Do I choose 5 apples or 4 oranges: *or* a chance of obtaining 5 apples or a different chance of obtaining 4 apples?	30% chance of $10,000 profit *versus* 60% chance of $6,000 profit	Should I buy a new set of golf clubs, go on an ocean cruise or buy a new suit?	Should we built an airport or develop the land as a recreational facility?

outlets) from points at which there is a supply (warehouses) in a manner that incurs least cost.

3. Means for ensuring maximal flow or the shortest route through a network leading from a point of supply to a point of consumption.

These problems and others like them can often be treated by use of deterministic models that have been developed in the discipline of operations research. The solution point has a unique optimum value at which maximum benefit is obtained for a particular cost, or a particular benefit is reserved for a minimum cost.

In Category 2 in Table 1-1, no quantitative measures of benefits and costs of courses of action are available. The choice in situations in this category is typified by that between five apples and four oranges. Since no well defined measures of benefits and costs that are equally applicable to all alternatives are available, no unequivocal basis of choice is available in decision situations of this sort. The choice is complicated in Category 2 under conditions of uncertainty. This further element in the choice is illustrated by the alternatives of a chance of obtaining five apples and a different chance of obtaining four oranges.

Estimates of probability are often used to express uncertainty in quantitative terms. Situations in which this is done are represented in Category 3. This category corresponds closely to circumstances that have previously been described as conditions of risk. For example, suppose that there are two alternatives: (1) a 30% chance of obtaining a $10,000 profit (with the corresponding 70% chance of no profit at all), and (2) a 60% chance of obtaining a $6000 profit (with the corresponding 40% chance of no profit at all). If the opportunity described occurs many times, the decision can be made on the basis of the expected benefits (probability × amount) of the two alternatives. In these circumstances, the alternative with a 60% chance of obtaining a $6000 profit is that which provides the greatest benefit. However, if the situation occurs only once, this basis for choice is not appropriate. The choice between alternatives in single occurrence situations of this sort depends upon the attitude of the decision maker to risk rather than on a multiplication of probability and profits of the type used above.

The decision situation is further complicated in Category 4 by the introduction of multiple objectives. In the light-hearted, but practical, example shown, the decision maker must choose either a new set of golf clubs, an ocean cruise, or a new suit of clothes. He can afford to take only one of the alternatives. Three objectives are involved:

(1) to improve performance in a recreational activity;
(2) to improve health and well-being; and
(3) to present an improved image to the world.

Neither the benefits of adopting any one course of action nor the chance that the benefits envisaged can be attained can necessarily be expressed in quantitative terms. No well structured and completely specified model of decision making can be applied to a situation of this kind. The ultimate choice between alternatives is personalistic. The individual involved uses judgment and intuition on the basis of all the information available at the time of decision.

The decision situations in Category 5 are the most complex of those with which we are faced today. Their identifying characteristic is the involvement of two or more participants each with his own objectives and intentions and each endeavoring to bring about an outcome that he sees as most preferred. These situations are encountered in planning and policy making in a large corporation, in public policy making such as in the construction of a regional development plan, and in many other considerations of issues of much less import. They occur *within* organizations and communities and *between* them. They are often interlinked with other situations of the same sort involving many of the same participants. The key element in these situations is the conflict of interests and objectives of the many participants. The choice between alternatives is highly personalistic and the eventual outcome is usually one that is jointly (not individually) rational for all the participants.

THE PLAN OF THE BOOK

The plan of the book follows generally the categories of decision situations shown in Table 1-1. The development of the text runs from the single participant, single objective, well structured decision situations of Category 1 to the ill structured, multiparticipant situations of Category 5. A brief description of the content of the chapters related to the categories of decision situation is as follows:

Chapter 2:   Quantitative techniques that can be applied to well structured, single participant, single objective situations under conditions of certainty.

Chapter 3:   A discussion of the treatment of situations in which appropriate quantitative measures of benefits and costs are not immediately available, including an analysis of the subject of utility.

Chapter 4:   Methods of dealing with single participant, single objective decision situations under conditions of uncertainty and risk.

Chapter 5:   Treatment of single participant, multiple objective decision situations.

Chapter 6: A discussion of multiparticipant decision situations under conditions in which resolution may result from the formation of consensus.

Chapter 7: Treatment of the background to multiparticipant decision situations with conflict of interests and objectives.

Chapter 8: Practical methods of dealing with the complex multiparticipant decision situations.

The text of each of the chapters is illustrated by examples of the techniques and models discussed applied to real-life decision situations. A series of exercises that allows practice in the application of the techniques and models is given at the end of each chapter.

SUMMARY

Decision situations encountered by modern organizations, individuals, and groups range from those that occur repetitively in essentially the same form to those that are new and unique. Repetitive decision situations can be approached by following rules and patterns of behavior that have been established as a result of previous experience. The approach to new and unique situations relies much more on the intuition and judgment of those involved.

The essence of decision making is the choice between alternatives. This choice is made against a background of the objectives of the decision maker and after as much information has been gathered as seems necessary and as time and available resources allow. Organizations, individuals, and groups involved in decision making can be regarded as systems operating in an external environment and having an internal environment of their own. The portions of these environments that relate to a particular decision situation constitute the environment of that situation. Decision makers may have more than one objective. Organizations and groups can be regarded as coalitions of components, each of which may have objectives that are to some extent in competition with those of the overall entity.

Decision situations can be divided into those that are "well structured" and those that are "ill structured." Well structured decision situations are those that have become well understood as a result of many encounters with situations of the same kind. Resolution of well structured decisions can usually be achieved by application of a standard procedure. In contrast, each ill structured decision situation that is encountered appears to have characteristics that make it not exactly like any other that has been met in the past. Some decision situations have only a part that can be regarded as well structured. These situations are called "partially structured".

Early descriptions of the decision making process divided it into three phases called *intelligence* (or search for information), *design* of alternatives, and *choice* between these alternatives. A step-by-step procedure can be devised from these three phases that can be applied to the resolution of well structured decision situations. Decision making using such a procedure has been called impersonalistic because none of the decision maker's beliefs, attitudes, and value judgments enter into the process, once the procedure has been established. Choice of the alternative that is seen as most preferred after application of such a procedure can be regarded as rational.

There are four conditions characteristic of ill-structured decision situations that preclude the possibility of resolution using an impersonalistic, step-by-step procedure:

1. Lack of complete information concerning the situation.
2. Lack of appropriate quantitative measures of benefits and costs.
3. The existence of multiple objectives.
4. The existence of many participants with power to influence the outcome of the decision situation.

Lack of complete information dictates that there cannot be a unique and indisputable formulation of an ill structured decision situation. Individual decision makers often have different perceptions of the situation and of the means of resolution. The decision process therefore becomes personalistic and resolution depends upon the intuition and judgment of those involved and on negotiation between them. These conditions require a modification of the three-phase decision process so that it consists of the following:

1. Information gathering (as before).
2. Analysis of possible outcomes, with each participant placing these outcomes in an order of preference and the design of tactics by each participant designed to bring about his or her most preferred outcome, and
3. Interaction between participants during which the actual outcome is determined by a process of negotiation.

The concept of rationality requires some modification in the light of conditions in ill structured decision situations. Choice of a most-preferred alternative under conditions of complete information can be called *objec-*

tively rational. However, when information is not complete, decision makers can hope only to be *subjectively rational.* Two different individuals can recommend different alternative solutions to an ill structured decision situation and each can claim to be subjectively rational. Rationality, in such situations, is perhaps best applied to the choice of an approach to decision making. A rational approach might be regarded as one that yields adequate decisions for complex situations with some regularity. A further extension of the concept of rationality is needed when two or more participants are involved in a decision situation. In these circumstances, an outcome that is accepted by all participants can be regarded as *jointly rational.*

Until recently, approaches to resolution of decision situations have been considered in categories related to conditions of certainty, risk, uncertainty, and competition. However, this classification does not take explicit account of the features of many modern decision situations. A more comprehensive classification can be based on the following four characteristics:

1. Whether or not uncertainty exists in the decision situation.
2. Whether or not benefits and costs can be truly represented in quantitative terms.
3. Whether or not multiple objectives are involved.
4. Whether the power to influence the outcome lies with one or more than one participant.

DISCUSSION TOPICS

1. Herbert A. Simon has said that management is synonymous with decision making. Do you agree with that? Give your reasons.

2. Most organizations can be thought of as purposeful systems. How is the nature and the quality of decision making in an organization related to its purposefulness?

3. Can you think of an organization that has only a single objective? If not, are there organizations that you know with multiple objectives for which one objective is far more important than all the others? Take an organization that you know well and write a list of what you consider its objectives to be.

4. Do you think that any organizations, individuals, or groups with which you have had contact have any covert objectives? If they have, why are the objectives that you have identified kept confidential?

5. What are the more important state-maintaining components or

processes in an organization that you know? Are these components supported by standard procedures designed to undertake the routine and repetitive decision making that is involved?

6.   How would you ensure that decision processes that are repetitive in your organization are not treated as new decisions each time they occur? What is the relationship of standard operating procedures to these decision processes?

7.   Do you consider the idea of an organization as a coalition to be a useful concept? If so, what are the important factors concerned with the formation and maintenance of the coalition? If not, what other models of organizational behavior do you consider provide a suitable background for the study of decision making?

8.   Do you think the concept of an organization as a group of component systems is applicable in the study of decision making? How is the behavior of an organization affected by the relationships between its component parts?

9.   What proportion of the decision situations in an organization that you know are well structured? Where do these well structured situations occur and to what activities do they relate? Where in the organization do ill structured decision situations occur and to what organizational activities are they related?

10.   Can you give examples of any partially structured decision situations in a typical organization?

11.   How would you define rationality in the context of decision making? Is the resolution of a well structured decision situation using a standard procedure necessarily rational? What constitutes rational behavior in dealing with an ill structured decision situation?

12.   What are the effects on decision making of the lack of complete information about the situation under consideration? How does the lack of information affect the concept of rationality in decision making?

13.   Can you give examples of situations in which the benefits and costs of alternative courses of action (1) can and (2) cannot be measured in appropriate quantitative terms? What might be the effects of an inappropriate choice of units for the measurement of benefits and costs?

14.   Can the situation of an individual with multiple objectives be likened to that of two participants each with their own objectives? What are the similarities and differences in the two cases? How might the process of resolution differ between the two cases?

15.   What are the characteristics of the process of negotiation between participants in the resolution of a decision situation? Do you agree that communication is an essential element of negotiation? What part does the relative power of the participants play in the resolution process?

16. Can the step-by-step process used in the resolution of well structured situations be applied (at least in part) to ill structured situations? What parts of the process are inapplicable in the case of ill structured situations and why are they not applicable?

17. Diesing has suggested that the concept of rationality should be applied to the choice of a decision making process rather than to the choice between alternatives. Do you agree with this idea? Give your views for and against Diesing's proposal.

18. Do you think that classification of decision situations in terms of the four characteristics described in this chapter is preferable to the previous certainty, risk, uncertainty, and competition categories? Give your reasons for and against the two classifications.

REFERENCES

1. Ofstad, H., *An Enquiry into the Freedom of Decision*, Allen and Unwin, 1961.
2. Churchman, C. W., *Challenge to Reason*, McGraw Hill, 1968.
3. Boulding, K. E., "General Systems Theory", *Management Science*, Vol 2, 1956, pp 197–208.
4. Radford, K. J., *Complex Decision Problems: an Integrated Strategy for Resolution*, Reston, 1977, Chapter 2.
5. Ackoff, R. L., "Towards a System of Systems Concepts", *Management Science*, Vol 17, No 11, July 1971, pp 661–671.
6. Ansoff, H. I., *Corporate Strategy*, McGraw Hill, 1965, pp 29–74.
7. Cyert, R. M. and March, J. G., *A Behavioral Theory of the Firm*, Prentice Hall, 1963, pp 27–32.
8. Simon, Herbert A., *The New Science of Management Decision*, Harper & Row, 1960: Second Edition, Prentice Hall, 1977, Chapter 2.
9. Simon, Herbert A., "The Structure of Ill-Structured Problems", *Artificial Intelligence*, Vol 4, 1973, pp 181–202.
10. Mintzberg, H., Raisinghani, D. and Theoret, A., "The Structure of 'Unstructured' Decision Processes", *Administrative Quarterly*, Vol 21, June 1976, pp 246–274.
11. Radford, K. J., *Information Systems in Management*, Reston 1973, pp 36–40.
12. Dewey, John, *How We Think*, New York, D. C. Heath & Co., 1910, Chapter 8.
13. Simon, Herbert A., *The New Science of Management Decision, op cit*, p 2.
14. Eilon, S., "What is a Decision?" *Management Science*, Vol 16, No 4, December 1969, pp B172–189.

15. Little, John D. C., "Models and Managers: the Concept of a Decision Calculus," *Management Science,* Vol 16, Apr 1970.

16. Drucker, Peter F., "The Effective Decision," *Harvard Business Review,* January-February 1967, pp 92–98.

17. Little, John D. C., *op cit.*

18. Tannenbaum, R., "Managerial Decision Making", *Journal of Business,* Vol 23–24, 1950–51, pp 22–39.

19. Eilon, S., *op cit,* p B178.

20. Diesing, Paul, *Reason in Society,* University of Illinois Press, 1962.

21. Murray, Edwin A., "Strategic Choice as a Negotiated Outcome," *Management Science,* Vol 24, No 9, May 1978, pp 960–972.

22. Eilon, S., *op cit,* p B178.

23. Churchman, C. W., "Wicked Problems," *Management Science,* Vol 14, No 4, December 1967, pp B141–42.

24. Rittel, H. W. J. and Webber, M. M., "Dilemmas in a General Theory of Planning," *Policy Sciences,* Vol 4, 1973, pp 155–169.

25. Diesing, Paul, *op cit,* p. 178.

26. Radford, K. J., "Categories of Decision Problems and their Resolution" *INFOR,* The Canadian Journal of Operational Research and Information Processing, Vol 18, No 1, February 1980.

 *Chapter Two*

Well Structured Decision Situations

INTRODUCTION

Well structured decision situations are those that have become well understood as a result of many encounters with situations of the same kind. The experience gained in these many encounters leads to the construction of a standard procedure for dealing with situations of a particular type. Most well structured decision situations contain little or no uncertainty about their characteristics. Sometimes the minor uncertainty that exists in an otherwise well structured situation is neglected in the interests of obtaining a solution to a problem that is sufficiently close to reality for all practical puposes.

The decision situations described in this chapter can usually be formulated in terms of well understood measures of benefits and costs, such as profit from a production process or the cost of performing a service. The single participant involved in these decision situations has the sole objective of maximizing benefit for a given cost or of minimizing cost for a particular benefit. These situations fall into Category 1 of Table 1-1.

Models that can be used to represent decision situations of this nature have been described in great detail in the technical literature.[1,2,3] It is not the purpose in this chapter to repeat these technical expositions. Rather, the approach will be taken of describing the types of situations that are amenable to treatment by models of this sort and of discussing the results that can be obtained by this type of analysis. The objective is to provide a means of recognizing practical situations of the various types as they occur as well as the manner in which they can be treated.

OPTIMIZATION IN PRODUCTION PROCESSES

Many operational decision situations arise in the management of production processes that have the following general characteristics:

- A product or a service is being produced to meet a demand.
- The product or service results from a mix of ingredients or resources.
- The product or service can be produced in a number of alternative ways each of which has a different profitability or efficiency.
- There are certain conditions or constraints usually concerned with the resources that affect the way the product or service can be produced.
- There is a desire to optimize a payoff or an "objective function" which usually concerns cost or profit.

Consider, for example, the following fertilizer-mix problem. A particular fertilizer has two main ingredients A and B in a 50/50 mix. It can be made by mixing the ingredients directly. However it can also be made from two other mixes that are alread on hand. These mixes are a by-product from another operation. They contain the same ingredients but in proportions that are different from those required in the fertilizer. Mix 1 has two parts of ingredient A and one part of B. Mix 2 has one part of ingredient A and three parts of B. Furthermore, for each ton of mix 1 that is used, a saving of $50 is made over the use of pure ingredients. A saving of $100 is realized for each ton of mix 2 that is used. There are 70 tons of mix 1 available and 60 tons of mix 2 available for each 100 tons of the fertilizer that must be produced.

Situations of this type can be analyzed by use of the linear programming model. The first step in the analysis is to formulate the situation in terms of an objective function and some constraints. The objective function is a statement of the factor that we wish to maximize (for profit) or minimize (for cost). In the present case the objective is to maximize the saving that can be obtained by the use of the by-product mixes. From the above description of the situation, a saving of $50 per ton can be made by using mix 1 and $100 per ton by using mix 2. If X_1 and X_2 represent the number of tons of mix 1 and mix 2 used respectively, the total saving can be written as $50X_1 + 100X_2$. The objective function is therefore:

Maximize $\qquad\qquad 50X_1 + 100X_2$

There are, however, some restrictions or constraints on this maximization process. First, each 100 tons of the required fertilizer (which is 50% ingredient A and 50% ingredient B) cannot contain more than 50 tons of each ingredient derived from the by-product mixes. Taking into account the different contents of mix 1 and mix 2, these constraints can be written as:

Ingredient A $\frac{2}{3}X_1 + \frac{1}{4}X_2 \leqslant 50$

Ingredient B $\frac{1}{3}X_1 + \frac{3}{4}X_2 \leqslant 50$

In addition, only 70 tons of mix 1 and 60 tons of mix 2 are available. The constraints representing these availabilities can be written:

$$X_1 \leqslant 70 \qquad : \qquad X_2 \leqslant 60$$

The whole situation can now be summarized as:

Maximize $50X_1 + 100X_2$

Subject to $\frac{2}{3}X_1 + \frac{1}{4}X_2 \leqslant 50$

$$\frac{1}{3}X_1 + \frac{3}{4}X_2 \leqslant 50$$

$$X_1 \leqslant 70$$

$$X_2 \leqslant 60$$

$$X_1, \quad X_2 \geqslant 0$$

The latter two (non-negativity) constraints recognize the fact that negative amounts of the two mixes cannot be used.

The linear programming model provides a method of obtaining a solution to a formulation of the simple resource allocation problem described above. The solution in this case shows that maximum saving is made by using 60 tons of mix 1 and 40 tons of mix 2. No pure ingredients A or B are necessary. The 100 tons of fertilizer with the required 50/50 content can be made entirely from the by-product mixes. In the above case, a graphical solution is possible and that solution is described in Appendix A to this chapter. In most other circumstances, a graphical solution is not possible because the analysis involves more than two variables such as X_1 and X_2. In these cases, significant amounts of computation are necessary to obtain the desired results. Fortunately, however, simple and effective computer packaged routines are available for such work. Once the formulation of the situation is accomplished, the resolution of even the most complex problem can be done easily and cheaply using these computer packages.

A Product Mix Problem

As a further example of the application of the linear programming model to the optimization of production processes, suppose that a company has the option of using one or more of four types of production process to manufacture a product from certain materials. Suppose, further, that:

1. each unit of production by the four processes yields a net profit of 4, 5, 9, and 11 dollars respectively;
2. the resources from which the product is made consist of three materials A, B, and C of which there are 15, 120, and 100 units respectively available;
3. the four processes require different amounts of each of the three materials as shown in Table 2-1.

TABLE 2-1. Units of Materials Required in the Product Mix Problem

	Process 1	Process 2	Process 3	Process 4
Material A	1	1	1	1
Material B	7	5	3	2
Material C	3	5	10	15

Management wishes to know which of the processes or which combination of processes results in the maximum profit under the above conditions.

Formulation of the Product Mix Problem

Application of the linear programming model requires that the problem situation be formulated in a manner that specifies (1) the objective function; and (2) the constraints inherent in the situation. The formulation of the Product Mix problem is shown in Table 2-2. The objective function is an expression of the desire to maximize profit. Suppose that X_1, X_2, X_3, and X_4 are the numbers of units of product made by each of the processes respectively. Since the net profit obtained from each unit produced by using each of these processes is 4, 5, 9, and 11 dollars respectively, the total profit can be written as: $4X_1 + 5X_2 + 9X_3 + 11X_4$. The objective function is therefore the maximization of this expression, namely,

Maximize $\qquad\qquad 4X_1 + 5X_2 + 9X_3 + 11X_4$

The constraints in the situation arise from the amounts of materials available. Three materials are used so that there are three main constraints. These constraints express the necessary conditions that the total

TABLE 2-2. Formulation of the Product-Mix Problem

Description	Formulation
Objective Function	
The total profit from production of product from each of the four processes should be maximized	Maximize $4X_1 + 5X_2 + 9X_3 + 11X_4$
Constraints	
The amount of Material A used cannot exceed 15 units	$1X_1 + 1X_2 + 1X_3 + 1X_4 \leqslant 15$
The amount of Material B used cannot exceed 120 units	$7X_1 + 5X_2 + 3X_3 + 2X_4 \leqslant 120$
The amount of Material C used cannot exceed 100 units	$3X_1 + 5X_2 + 10X_3 + 15X_4 \leqslant 100$
Other Conditions	
No negative amounts of product can be made by any process	$X_1, X_2, X_3, X_4 \geqslant 0$

amount of material used in the production of the number of units by each process cannot exceed the amount of materials available. The three constraints can be written as:

Material A	$1X_1 + 1X_2 + 1X_3 + 1X_4 \leqslant 15$
Material B	$7X_1 + 5X_2 + 3X_3 + 2X_4 \leqslant 120$
Material C	$3X_1 + 5X_2 + 10X_3 + 15X_4 \leqslant 100$

The coefficients of X_1, X_2, X_3, and X_4 in the Material A constraint are written as 1 in order to maintain consistency of the format in which these conditions are expressed. One further condition requires that X_1, X_2, X_3, and X_4 must all be non-negative. This condition expresses the obvious fact that negative amounts of the product cannot be manufactured by any of the processes.

Further examples of the formulation of situations using the linear programming model are given in the practical decision situations section at the end of this chapter.

Limitations on the Use of the Linear Programming Model

A number of conditions must be met in a problem situation before the linear programming model can be applied without reservation.[4] These conditions refer to the nature of the relationships that are expressed in the formulation of the problem.

First, the linear programming model demands that the objective function and every constraint function be linear. This condition requires that the measure of effectiveness contained in the objective function and the measures of resource usage contained in the constraints must be strictly proportional to the level of each activity conducted individually. For example, in the Product Mix situation just described, it is necessary for truly appropriate application of the model that the amount of profit realized by the additional production of one unit by each of the processes be the same over the entire range of production levels considered. Similarly, the change in use of resources for increases or decreases in production level in each of the processes must be constant over the range of activity covered in the situation.

Clearly, these conditions are not always met in situations to which the linear programming model may seem to be applicable. In many practical situations, for example, the unit profitability or the amount of resources needed for additional production changes as the level of production changes. In these circumstances, either the objective function, or some of the constraint functions, or both may not be exactly linear. The linear model may not therefore be strictly appropriate. It may be justifiable in such cases to assume a condition of linearity as a first approximation to the practical situation. However, assumptions of this nature can lead to serious misrepresentations of the practical conditions and consequently to incorrect analytical results. The temptation to fit the practical situation to the model (rather than the other way round) for reasons of analytical convenience should always be resisted.

Second, a form of nonlinearity arises if there are interactions between the activities in terms of profitability or the use of resources. For the linear model to be strictly applicable, the total measure of effectiveness represented in the objective function and the total resource usage represented in the constraints must equal the respective sums of these quantities resulting from the component activities being conducted independently. For example, in the Product-Mix situation, the profitability of production by process 1 must be unaffected by the level of production by processes 2, 3, or 4. Similarly, the use of resources in any one process must be unaffected by the level of production in any other process. These conditions are usually referred to as the requirement for *additivity* with respect to the objective function and the constraints.

Third, even if all the values of the parameters contained in the formulation of a practical solution are integers, the optimal solution obtained by the model may contain fractional values of some of them. However, it may not be possible in many practical situations for some of the parameters to take fractional values. For example, certain resources may be available only in integer amounts. Production processes may need to operate only at nonfractional levels. It is tempting in these circumstances to round the results emanating from the anlysis to the nearest integer values. However, there is no guarantee that the situation described after such rounding of results is close to optimal or even a feasible solution to the problem as formulated. Arrival at an optimal integer value solution may require considerably more analysis using more complex techniques. The requirement that fractional values of the variables be admissible in an analytical solution is usually referred to as the condition of *divisibility.*

It is rare that a practical situation meets all of the conditions necessary for unreserved application of the linear programming model. It may be possible, however, to obtain useful information from such an application in cases in which all the necessary conditions are not met. In such cases, it is wise to be aware of all the assumptions implicit in the use of the model, so that any reservations arising from these assumptions can be taken into account in the consideration of the analytical results.

Results in the Product Mix Situation

With the foregoing matters in mind, it is interesting to consider the nature of the results obtained in the analysis of the Product-Mix situation described earlier. The analysis of this situation can be done by hand calculation[5] or by the use of a packaged computer program. In each case, the analytical procedure defines a set of values of X_1, X_2, X_3, and X_4 that determines levels of production in each of the four processes. The conditions under which the profit defined by the objective function is a maximum are as follows:

Number of units produced in each process

Process 1 $X_1 = 50/7$
Process 2 $X_2 = 0$
Process 3 $X_3 = 55/7$
Process 4 $X_4 = 9$

Amount of available resources unused in the optimal feasible solution

Material A   all used
Material B   325/7 units unused
Material C   all used

Profit obtained from the optimal solution

Value of the objective function $4X_1 + 5X_2 + 9X_3 + 11X_4$
at the optimal feasible solution = 695/7

The analytical procedure yields two other useful results. The first of these results concerns *shadow costs.* In the above situation, a shadow cost is the cost of production of a unit by the processes from which no units are required in the optimal solution. It can be shown, for example, from the complete solution of the Product Mix situation, that if one unit were produced by process 2, the maximum profit would be decreased by 3/7. This information is useful in estimating the inefficiencies that might arise in the region of the optimal production situation if the number of units produced by certain processes were marginally changed.

A similar measure is available in the complete solution of a linear program concerning the resources that are used. This measure is called the *shadow price*. It is defined as the unit worth of each resource in the region of the optimal solution of the linear program. In the Product Mix situation, the solution shows that the profit level can be increased by 13/7 for each additional unit of material A and by 5/7 for each additional unit of material C that is made available. This information is useful in deciding whether to bring in more material in order to increase the profitability of the production process. Shadow prices and shadow costs are usually presented in the output from computer-supported linear programming packages. They can be obtained also from hand calculated solutions to the linear programming model.

COMPLEMENTARY OPTIMIZATION PROBLEMS

Situations sometimes arise in which two participants take different but complementary views of the same circumstances. Consider, for example, the situation in which a farming cooperative plans to buy fertilizer in bulk for the following crop year. It is necessary that the fertilizer purchased contain four basic ingredients in the following amounts:

4014.4 units of ingredient 1
366.0 units of ingredient 2
648.5 units of ingredient 3
329.0 units of ingredient 4

The cooperative knows that it can purchase any amounts of three standard fertilizer mixes (F_1, F_2, F_3) at prices of \$18.50, \$24.00, and \$38.50 per bulk loading. Each bulk load of the three mixes contains the number of units of the required basic ingredients shown in the following table.

TABLE 2-3.   Units of Ingredients in Each Bulk Load of Fertilizer Mix

		Units of Ingredients			
		1	2	3	4
	F_1	3.92	0.20	0.15	0.30
Mix	F_2	1.30	0.65	0.12	0.44
	F_3	1.32	0.80	2.30	0.20

The cooperative wishes to know how much of each fertilizer mix it would need to buy to satisfy its needs for the required ingredients at minimum cost. This problem can be formulated as in the left hand side of Table 2-4. The optimal solution to the cooperative's problem is that it should buy

950 bulk loads of mix F_1
0 bulk loads of mix F_2
220 bulk loads of mix F_3

The minimum cost of these purchases while still allowing the needs for ingredients to be satisfied is $26,045.

However, an independent supplier has heard of the cooperative's situation. He proposes to deliver to the cooperative the basic ingredients from which the required fertilizer mixes could be prepared. The cooperative stipulates and the supplier agrees that the costs of the mixes under this arrangement should not exceed those already quoted ($18.50, $24.00, and $38.50 per bulk loading respectively). The supplier would like to know the prices he should quote per unit of each ingredient so that the above cost of the three fertilizer mixes should not be exceeded but at the same time his total contract price should be the maximum possible under these conditions. The supplier's problem can be formulated as in the right hand side of Table 2-4. The optimum solution is that the supplier should charge

$ 2.50 per unit of ingredient 1
$21.00 per unit of ingredient 2
$ 7.00 per unit of ingredient 3
$11.50 per unit of ingredient 4

for a maximum total revenue under these conditions of $26,045.

Reference to Table 2-4 shows that there are a number of links between the cooperative's problem (which can be called the primal situation) and the supplier's problem (which can be called the dual situation). Each constraint in the primal situations corresponds to a variable (Y_1, Y_2, Y_3, Y_4) in the dual. Each variable (X_1, X_2, X_3) in the primal corresponds to a constraint in the dual. The right-hand-side values in the constraints of the primal are the coefficients of Y_1, Y_2, and Y_3 in the objective function of the dual, and vice versa. Minimization in the primal situation corresponds to maximization in the dual and vice versa. It is entirely arbitrary which of the two solutions is called the primal and which the dual (the dual of the dual is, in fact, the primal). The desire of the decision maker in the primal in the above example is to minimize costs while ensuring that certain needs for ingredients are met. The objective in the dual is to maximize benefits to the supplier without exceeding cost constraints imposed by the customer. The solution point in each problem is at the same figure, namely $26,045.

Many situations in which two participants are in opposing and competi-

TABLE 2-4. Formulation of the Fertilizer Mix Problem and of its Dual

The Cooperative's Problem
(Primal)

Minimize $\quad 18.5X_1 + 24.0X_2 + 38.5X_3$

Subject to: $\quad 3.92X_1 + 1.30X_2 + 1.32X_3 \geqslant 4014.4$

$\qquad\qquad 0.20X_1 + 0.65X_2 + 0.80X_3 \geqslant 366.0$

$\qquad\qquad 0.15X_1 + 0.12X_2 + 2.30X_3 \geqslant 648.5$

$\qquad\qquad 0.30X_1 + 0.44X_2 + 0.20X_3 \geqslant 329.0$

where X_1, X_2, X_3 are the amounts of fertilizer mixes F_1, F_2, F_3 purchased.

Optimal Solution

$\quad X_1 = 950$ units of F_1

$\quad X_2 = \quad 0$ units of F_2

$\quad X_3 = 220$ units of F_3

$\qquad$ Total cost = \$26,045

The Supplier's Problem
(Dual)

Maximize $\quad 4014.4Y_1 + 366.0Y_2 + 648.5Y_3 + 329.0Y_4$

Subject to: $\quad 3.92Y_1 + 0.20Y_2 + 0.15Y_3 + 0.30Y_4 \leqslant 18.5$

$\qquad\qquad 1.30Y_1 + 0.65Y_2 + 0.12Y_3 + 0.44Y_4 \leqslant 24.0$

$\qquad\qquad 1.32Y_1 + 0.80Y_2 + 2.30Y_3 + 0.20Y_4 \leqslant 38.5$

where Y_1, Y_2, Y_3, Y_4 are the prices quoted per unit of the four ingredients respectively.

Optimal Solution

$\quad Y_1 = \$2.50$ per unit of ingredient 1

$\quad Y_2 = \$21.00$ per unit of ingredient 2

$\quad Y_3 = \$7.00$ per unit of ingredient 3

$\quad Y_4 = \$11.50$ per unit of ingredient 4

$\qquad$ Total revenue = \$26,045

tive positions can be represented either by a primal formulation or by its dual. The choice of which form of representation is used for analysis is often a matter of analytical convenience. In particular, a case in which an objective function contains more than two variables but in which only two constraints are present can be solved graphically in the dual format (see Appendix A to this chapter). It is interesting to note that the strictly competitive situation in which two participants are involved in a two-person, zero-sum game can be formulated in the primal and the dual from the point of view of each of the participants (see Exhibit 7-1, Chapter 7).

SITUATIONS IN WHICH THERE ARE SPECIFIC STAGES

A number of different types of situation arise that have the characteristic that they may be studied by reference to a series of stages or time periods. Consider, for example, the situation in which customers requiring a certain item are supplied from inventory. The inventory can be replenished from time to time from production or by ordering from a supplier. There are certain set-up (or ordering) and deliver costs which make it desirable to replenish the inventory by larger rather than smaller amounts. However, if production or reordering is done in larger quantities there is a greater chance of the inventory of the item being reduced to zero before replenishment. On the other hand, the costs of maintaining the inventory may be greater if it is replenished in larger rather than smaller quantities. A situation of this type in which demand and inventory levels are assessed on a weekly basis is illustrated in Fig. 2-1. Situations of this nature have been studied extensively in the technical literature.[6] The objective in all the analytical approaches has been to minimize the cost of maintaining the inventory whilst at the same time meeting certain conditions with respect to the demand.

Situations of this sort have a number of characteristics that can be summarized as follows:

1.   The situation can be divided into stages and a decision is required at each stage. In the example shown in Fig. 2-1, the stages are the weeks and the decision is whether or not to replenish the inventory during the current week.

2.   Each stage has a state associated with it—in Fig. 2-1, the state is defined as the inventory level associated with a possible replenishment situation.

3.   The effect of a decision at each stage is to transform the current state into a state associated with the next stage. A decision to replenish the inventory affects the level in the next stage.

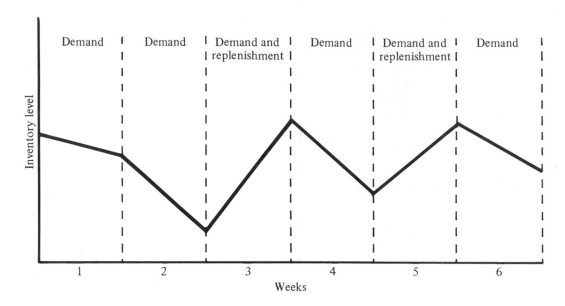

FIG. 2-1. Demand and replenishment in an inventory situation.

4. The current state of the system is totally derived from all previous states and the optimal policy in remaining stages is independent of previous policy decisions. The present inventory level is derived entirely from previous replenishment decisions, and future decisions regarding optimal replenishment policies are not dependent on past decisions.

The analytical procedure associated with such decision situations is called *dynamic programming.* The first step in that procedure is to establish:

1. The stages in the situation, for example the weeks referred to in Fig. 2-1.
2. The variables that determine the "state" in each stage, for example, the demand and the replenishment costs and conditions resulting in an inventory level and a cost in each stage.
3. The manner in which an optimal decision can be made with respect to each stage; for example, what constitutes an optimal decision with respect to inventory replenishment in each stage.

The analysis then proceeds by defining the number of stages to be considered. For the situation illustrated in Fig. 2-1, the number of stages could be, for example, the eight weeks. The analysis procedure then continues by finding the optimal policy that can be adopted in the *last* of these stages. It then works backwards and identifies the optimal policy with n

stages remaining given that the optimal policy with n-1 stages remaining is known. For example, the policy in week 7 (one stage remaining) is determined with a knowledge of the optimal policy in week 8 (no stages remaining). The result is a listing of optimal policies for all stages of the situation. Suitable routines are available that allow these calculations to be done once the situation has been described in the appropriate terms. As in the case of application of the linear programming model, the most important aspect of the treatment of such situations is the recognition of the type of problem and the formulation of the situation in a manner suitable for analytical treatment by dynamic programming. Practice in formulation can be obtained by reference to the practical decision situations included at the end of this chapter.

The dynamic programming technique has an application to situations that are not immediately identifiable as having the above characteristics. Consider, for example, the situation in which a grocery chain has purchased six truckloads of fresh strawberries for distribution among its four stores.[7] Unless the strawberries are sold quickly, losses from spoilage will be experienced. Sales and therefore spoilage losses are expected to be different among the four stores. The policy is not to split truckloads among stores although it is allowable to deliver no strawberries to one or more of the four locations. The estimated total profit as a result of the delivery of certain numbers of truckloads to each of the four stores is shown in Table 2-5. This situation can be formulated simply in the following form. If X_1, X_2, X_3, X_4 are the number of truckloads delivered to each store and P_1, P_2, P_3, P_4 are the profits made at each store as a result of these deliveries:

Maximize

Subject to:

$$P_1X_1 + P_2X_2 + P_3X_3 + P_4X_4$$
$$X_1 + X_2 + X_3 + X_4 \leqslant 6$$
$$X_1, X_2, X_3, X_4 \geqslant 0$$

TABLE 2-5. Profit from Numbers of Truckloads Delivered to Four Stores

		Store			
		1	2	3	4
Number of	0	0	0	0	0
Truckloads	1	4	2	6	2
	2	6	4	8	3
	3	7	6	8	4
	4	7	8	8	4
	5	7	9	8	4
	6	7	10	8	4

It might at first sight be thought that this situation could be analyzed by the linear programming model. However, it is immediately apparent that some of the relationships are not linear. For example, in all stores, profit is not directly proportional to the number of truckloads delivered. The linear programming model cannot therefore be used. A situation of this nature can, however, be analyzed using the dynamic programming model in the following way.

Consider the stages to be the four stores in some arbitrary order. The decision variable that determines the state in each stage is the numbers of truckloads that are allocated to the *n-th* stage from the end of the process. The state in each stage is concerned with the amount of profit that can be made in each store. Application of the dynamic programming model results in the identification of eight alternative optimal solutions yielding a total profit of 18 including, for example, allocations to the four stages of (1, 4, 1, 0) and (2, 1, 2, 1).

The dynamic programming model, therefore, offers a means of treating situations of the sort similar to those approachable by linear programming but that do not meet the restriction that all relationships in the situation must be linear. No such restriction applies to the use of dynamic programming. The only requirement is that the situation can be described in a number of stages, that variables describing the state in each of the stages can be identified and that a basis for deciding an optimal policy in each of the stages can be determined.

DISTRIBUTION PROBLEMS

Many operational situations are concerned with the distribution of a commodity (goods or materials) from a number of sources (production or storage points) to a number of destinations. Each source has a limited supply in a given time period and each destination has a limited requirement in that same period. The cost of transporting one unit of the commodity from a source to a destination is known. The objective is to meet the demands of the destinations within the supply restrictions of the sources in a manner which minimizes the total cost of transportation of the commodity between the sources and the destination points. The situation can be illustrated as in Table 2-6. The figures in parentheses in this table represent the cost of transportation between the respective destinations and sources. Such situations are often referred to as transportation or distribution problems.

Problems of this nature can be treated by application of the linear programming model as long as the conditions specified earlier for the use of this model are satisfied. In addition, it is necessary that the total supply be equal to the total demand as it is in Table 2-6. However, if the supply is

TABLE 2-6. A Typical Distribution Situation

		Destinations				
		1	2	3	4	Supply
	1	(25)	(23)	(8)	(25)	15
	2	(40)	(40)	(45)	(7)	12
Sources	3	(9)	(14)	(28)	(27)	40
	4	(5)	(7)	(31)	(30)	25
Demand		7	30	20	35	92

greater than the demand, the problem can be "balanced" and the model applied by the creation of a "dummy" destination to which the excess supply is transported at zero unit cost. If the demand is greater than the supply, a dummy source is used in much the same way.

North-West Corner Rule

Use of the linear programming model provides a method of determining a minimum total transportation cost in such situations. However, a number of simple techniques exist by which feasible, but not necessarily optimum, distribution arrangements can be determined. The best known of these techniques is called the North-West Corner Rule. Using this rule, the analyst starts at the top left of the table (as in Table 2-7) and inserts the maximum supply or demand figure allowed by the requirement of the destination or the capacity of the source. The analyst then moves to the space below or to the right and once again inserts the maximum figure allowed by the characteristics of the problem. The movement is continued until supply is exhausted or demand is satisfied, after which a right-angled turn is made and the process is continued. The completed process is shown in Table 2-7. The numbers in this table following the format of 7(25) indicate 7 units distributed at a cost of 25 for each unit. It is easy to confirm that the total cost of the distribution plan determined in this manner is 2559. This distribution is at least feasible in that demands are met within the supply restrictions. However, it is not necessarily optimal. In this particular case it is far from the minimum cost distribution mode.

Least Cost Rule

Other heuristic rules often give much improved (but not necessarily near-optimal) distribution plans. For example, in the above case, the Least Cost Rule can be applied with advantage. In using this rule, the greatest possible amount of the commodity is shipped by the lowest-cost route and

TABLE 2-7. Use of the North-West Corner Rule

Destinations

		1	2	3	4	Supply
	1	7(25)	8(23)			15
Sources	2		12(40)			12
	3		10(14)	20(28)	10(27)	40
	4				25(30)	25
Demands		7	30	20	35	

TABLE 2-8. Use of the Least-Cost Rule

Destinations

		1	2	3	4	Supply
	1			15(8)		15
Sources	2				12(7)	12
	3		12(14)	5(28)	23(27)	40
	4	7(5)	18(7)			25
Demands		7	30	20	35	92

TABLE 2-9. Optimal Distribution Plan

Destinations

		1	2	3	4	Supply
	1			15(8)		15
Sources	2				12(7)	12
	3	7(9)	5(14)	5(28)	23(27)	40
	4		25(7)			25
Demands		7	30	20	35	92

then the greatest possible amount by the next cheapest route and so on until all demands are met within the supply restrictions.

Application of this rule provides the distribution plan shown in Table 2-8. The total cost for this plan is 1294, a figure considerably below that obtained by the North-West Corner Rule.

It is interesting to note that the optimum distribution is as shown in Table 2-9. This distribution obtained by use of the linear programming model has a minimum cost of 1273, 21 units of cost below that obtained by the Least Cost Rule.

ASSIGNMENT PROBLEMS

There is a special class of distribution situations that has come to be known as "assignment" problems. These situations arise when there are a certain number of tasks to be undertaken and an equal number of ways in which each task can be completed. For example, a number of production tasks may need to be assigned to a like number of machines. The cost incurred, the time taken, or the profit realized may vary according to which task is assigned to which machine. The problem for the analyst is to determine an assignment plan that minimizes cost or time or maximizes profit. The methodology by which situations of this nature can be treated is a special case of the distribution model in which the number of sources (machines) is equal to the number of destinations (tasks) and the supply and demand at each source and destination respectively is one unit. It can be noted in passing that a distribution problem can be converted into an assignment problem by ascribing a separate source and destination to each unit of the commodity to be distributed.

As an example of an assignment situation, consider an electronic manufacturing company that has orders for six different designs of printed circuits. Each design can be manufactured on each of six machines, but the costs of production depend on the design being produced on a particular machine, in the manner shown in Table 2-10. The company wishes to determine the pattern of assignment of designs to machines to minimize production costs. Similar situations arise in the assignment of aircrews to airline flights and trucks to haulage contracts. A nonoptimal solution to the situation shown in Table 2-10 can be obtained by simply assigning Design 1 to Machine 1 and so on. The cost of this assignment plan is $56,000. The

TABLE 2-10. Production Costs in an Assignment Problem (thousands of dollars)

			Design			
	1	2	3	4	5	6
1	10	11	(6)	7.5	9	13
2	9	(9.5)	7.5	7.5	8	11
3	15	16	10	(11)	12.5	17
4	(7)	8	4	6	6.5	9
5	12	12	10	11.5	11.5	(12)
6	7.5	8.5	6.5	7	(6.5)	9

optimal assignment plan in which Designs 1, 2, 3, 4, 5, and 6 are located on Machines 4, 2, 1, 3, 6, and 5 respectively costs only $52,000. This optimal assignment is indicated in Table 2-10 by the circled positions.

SHORTEST ROUTE SITUATIONS

Shortest route situations are those in which it is desired to find the shortest route between two points when a number of alternate routes exist. The situations from which this type of problem got its name are concerned with distance or time to travel between two points. However, the same considerations apply to minimizing cost in processes consisting of a number of steps that can be achieved in a number of alternative ways. The situations can be illustrated by means of a network diagram. The

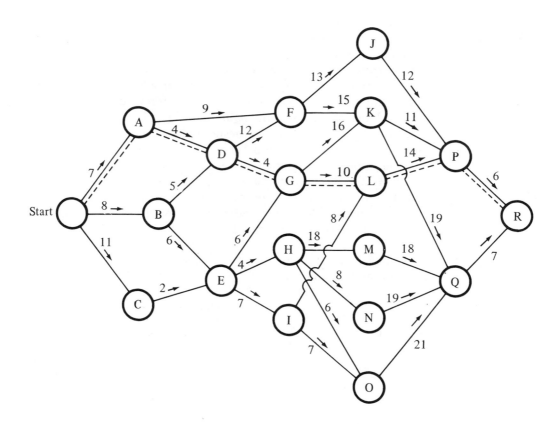

FIG. 2-2. Network diagram for a shortest-route situation.

shortest route can be found by a special version of the assignment model.

Suppose, as an example, that a company manufacturing electronic microchips must pass each item through a number of processes. These processes can be carried out in many different ways. The total production cost depends upon the route that each unit takes from the start of the process to the end. The situation can be illustrated as in Fig. 2-2. In this diagram, points A through R represent machines at which the various stages in the production process can be completed. A, B, and C are alternative machines for the first stage of the process, D and E for the second stage, (but note that it is possible to proceed directly from A to F). Machines F, G, H, and I are alternatives for the third stage, and so on. Not all routes are possible. For example, it is impossible to proceed from E to F. The cost of each additional stage in the process is shown on the links between the individual machines.

The analytical model that can be applied to shortest route situations can be described as follows. Start at the last machine R. Determine the cost (distance or time) from R to all previous machines. It is 6 from P to R and 7 from Q to R. Place these "values" on machines P and Q. Then, examine all routes to P and Q. Determine the total cost to R by all routes from machines that are one stage earlier in the process than P and Q. For example, the "value" placed on J is 18 and on K 17. Note that the value of K is 17 because this value is the minimum of 17 for K→P→R and 26 for K→Q→R. Continue the process backwards to "Start." The minimum cost route in this situation is from Start →A→D→G→L→P→R for a total cost of 45.

MAXIMAL FLOW SITUATIONS

Maximal flow situations are closely related to shortest route problems and to the linear programming model. They arise when the supply of a commodity (oil, gas, or electric power, for example) can be obtained by means of a number of alternative routes through a network consisting of connections between certain modes. Flow through each component of the network is limited to a certain maximum level. The flow may be possible in both directions, but the maximum flow in any component may not be the same for each direction.

Suppose, for example, that a mining company intends to build a new smelting facility. The company will need a large amount of electric power at the facility. It has asked the electric supply company to estimate the maximum current flow that could be expected to the facility from the existing grid. The situation is illustrated in Fig. 2-3. The numbers on each component of the grid represent the maximum spare current capacity for that component. It is assumed that the supplying station can generate sufficient power to satisfy the maximal flow characteristics of, any route through the network.

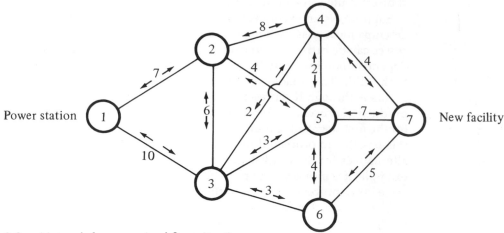

FIG. 2-3. Network for a maximal-flow situation.

This situation can be stated in a form suitable for treatment by the linear programming model as follows:

Objective function: Maximize total current flow through the network = (I)
Constraints:

1. The total flow in components 1→2 and 1→3 (in-flow to the network) must be equal to I.
2. The total flow in components 4→7, 5→7, and 6→7 (outflow from the network) must be equal to I.
3. The amount of flow into each node must equal the amount of flow out of that node.
4. The capacity constraints of each component cannot be exceeded.

The maximal flow diagram for this situation is illustrated in Fig. 2-4. The optimal flow in each component compared with the capacity in that segment is shown thus: 4(8). The maximal flow is seen to be 16. It is interesting to note that not all segments are used to full capacity. There would be little point, for example, in expanding the capacity of the segment 2→4. Any effort in increasing the capacities of the links should clearly be concentrated on 3→4, 3→5, 3→6, and subsequent segments in the network.

CRITICAL PATH SITUATIONS

Critical path situations are typically those in which specific activities necessary to complete a project must be scheduled so as to minimize the time between the beginning and end of the project.[8] Suppose for example that a

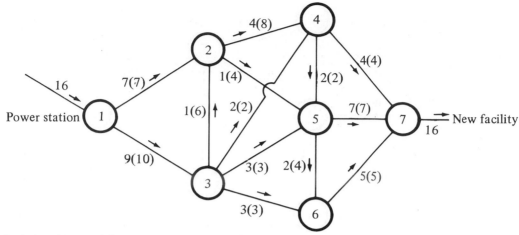

FIG. 2-4.   Maximal-flow pattern in a network.

building project requires work by various contractors. Each job has an estimated duration. Some jobs can be carried out simultaneously while
some cannot be started until others have been finished. The relationships
between eight jobs (A to H) comprising the total project can be stated as in
Table 2-11. The information in this table can be shown in network form as
in Fig. 2-5. The dotted lines in this diagram (for example between node 6
and node 5) represent "dummy" activities that have been inserted to
express a particular precedence relationship between some of the other
activities. Note for example that G cannot start before D, E, and F are finished, so that a dummy activity with duration zero is necessary between
node 6 and node 5.

TABLE 2-11.   Jobs in a Critical Path Situation

Job (Activity)	Immediate Predecessor	Estimated Duration
A	—	2
B	—	8
C	—	6
D	A	14
E	B	6
F	B, C	9
G	D, E, F	7
H	F	4
Termination	G, H	—

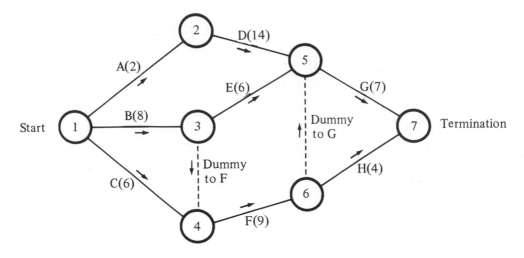

FIG. 2-5. Network representation of a critical-path situation.

The architect in charge of the project would like to know the minimum time necessary to complete the project. He would also like to know which of the jobs has a duration that is critical to the completion of the project in that minimum time. The analysis of a situation of this nature is conducted in terms of two factors: (1) the earliest starting time (ES) of an activity; and (2) the latest finishing time of the activity (LF).

The first of these times is the earliest possible starting time taking into account any work that must be completed prior to starting the activity. The second time is the latest finishing time of the activity without extending the overall duration of the project. If, for any activity, the earliest starting time plus the duration of the activity is equal to the latest finishing time, this activity is called *critical*. A critical activity is one for which no increase in duration and no delay in starting is possible without increasing the overall project duration. An activity that is not critical is said to have *slack*. The amount of slack may be defined as the total of the delay in starting and extension of the duration that is possible before the activity becomes critical. In the analysis, the earliest starting time for each activity is found by determining the maximum of the sum of the earliest starting time and the duration for each of the predecessor activities. The latest finishing time for each activity is found by determining the minimum of the sum of the latest finishing times of the following activities minus their durations. The results of an analysis of this sort are shown in Table 2-12 for earliest starting times and Table 2-13 for latest finishing times. The information in Tables 2-12 and 2-13 can be combined to show the slack present in each activity, as in Table 2-14. The activities with zero slack are critical. The critical path

TABLE 2-12. Earliest Starting Times of Activities in a Critical Path Analysis

Activity	Predecessor	Earliest Starting Time of Predecessor	Duration of Predecessor	Total = ES (Pred) + Dur. (Pred)	Earliest Starting Time of Activity
A	—	—	—	—	0
B	—	—	—	—	0
C	—	—	—	—	0
D	A	0	2	2	max = 2
E	B	0	8	8	max = 8
Dummy to F	B	0	8	8	max = 8
F	{ Dummy to F	8	0	8	max = 8
	{ C	0	6	6	
Dummy to G	{ F	8	9	17	max = 17
	{ D	2	14	16	
G	{ E	8	6	14	max = 17
	{ Dummy to G	17	0	17	
H	F	8	9	17	max = 17
Terminals	{ G	17	7	24	max = 24
	{ H	17	4	21	

through the network is B→dummy→F→dummy→G. The dummy part of this path is of no significance, since these activities are introduced only to ensure continuity in the analysis.

Critical path analysis forces a thorough preplanning of a project. It defines activities that are likely sources of slippage in completion of the project. If slippage takes place, it allows the overall plan to be revised in the best way to meet the changed circumstances. The method is equally applicable to the control of cost as it is to the planning of a time schedule. It is possible also to use a form of the analysis in situations in which only estimated durations or costs of activities are available and in which variations on both these factors express uncertainty about these estimates.[9]

INVENTORY MANAGEMENT

Inventories contain a stock of items held against future needs. If items that are sold or used could be replaced immediately, there would be no

TABLE 2-13. Latest Finishing Times of Activities in a Critical Path Analysis

Activity	Following Activity	Latest Finishing Time of Following Activity	Duration of Following Activity	Total = LF (F) − Dur (F)	Latest Finishing Time of Activity
H	Termination	—	—	—	24
G	Termination	—	—	—	24
Dummy to G	G	24	7	17	min = 17
F	H	24	4	20	min = 17
	Dummy to G	17	0	17	
E	G	24	7	17	min = 17
D	G	24	7	17	min = 17
Dummy to F	F	17	9	8	min = 8
C	F	17	9	8	min = 8
B	E	17	6	11	min = 8
	Dummy to F	8	0	8	
A	D	17	14	3	min = 3
Start	A	3	2	1	
	B	8	8	0	min = 0
	C	8	6	2	

need for substantial inventories. Because it usually takes time to order and replace such items, stocks must be held to avoid disappointing customers or to prevent processes dependent on these items being delayed. Maintenance of an inventory requires capital that might otherwise be put to other productive uses. The cost of providing this capital must therefore be balanced against the costs that would arise if an item were temporarily out of stock.

Complex inventory replenishment situations are best treated by the dynamic programming model as discussed earlier in this chapter. There is, however, a simple formula that can be used in situations in which certain assumptions can be said to apply. This formula determines the optimum reorder quantity as a function of the rate of depletion of an inventory, the cost of reordering, the costs of holding items in inventory, and the cost of

TABLE 2-14.   Slack in Each Activity in a Critical Path Analysis

Activity	Earliest Starting Time of Activity	Duration of Activity	Earliest Starting Time + Duration	Latest Finishing Time of Activity	Slack
A	0	2	2	3	3
B	0	8	8	8	0 (critical)
C	0	6	6	8	2
D	2	16	16	17	1
E	8	16	14	17	3
[Dummy to F	8	8	8	8	0 (critical)]
F	8	17	17	17	0 (critical)
[Dummy to G	17	17	17	17	0 (critical)]
G	17	24	24	24	0 (critical)
H	17	21	21	24	3

any shortage. Suppose that the level of an item in inventory varies as shown in Fig. 2-6. Suppose also that

a = rate of depletion of inventory (demand rate) in items per unit time
k = fixed cost per replenishment of inventory
c = per item cost of replenishment
h = holding cost of items in inventory in dollars/item/unit time
u = penalty costs for shortages in dollars/item/unit time

It can be shown[10] that the optimal reorder quantity (EOQ) is Q^* where

$$Q^* = \sqrt{2ak/h} \ \sqrt{(u+h)/u}$$

If no shortages are allowed (i.e., $u \to \infty$),

$$Q^* = \sqrt{2ak/h}$$

Consider the situation of a retail drugstore that sells 1000 packages of disposable diapers each week. Demand is very predictable. The store can at no time be without stock. The company replenishes its inventory by making a trip to the manufacturer's plant. The cost of each such trip is $900. Goods not immediately sold are held in the stores until sold. The total cost of holding unsold goods is 5 cents per package per week. Application of the above formula shows that the optimal reorder policy would be to pick up 6000 packages per trip to the manufacturer. With a demand of 1000 packages per week, the trip would need to be undertaken every six weeks on the average.

Suppose now that the store is prepared to risk being sold out of the dia-

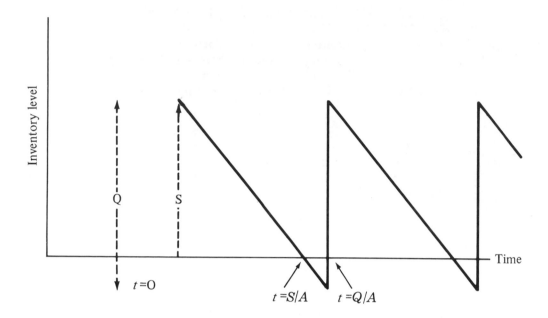

FIG. 2-6. Variation of inventory level with demand and replenishment.

pers for one quarter of the time and that the cost of such shortages is 15 cents per package per week. The optimal delivery policy given by the first of the two formulae above is to obtain 6928 (or 7000) packages per delivery every seven weeks. The quantity S shown in Fig 2-6 as the upper level of the inventory is given by the formula

$$S^* = \sqrt{2ak/h}\ \sqrt{u/(u+h)}$$

providing a figure of 5196 in the above case. Thus, a maximum shortage of 1804 packages would be experienced approximately every seven weeks.

Calculations of this nature can be used by managers as a guide to decision making rather than as an unbreakable rule. Duckworth has argued that the use of the popular square root economic order quantity rule almost certainly results in an inflated level of stock being carried in circumstances in which no shortages are allowed.[11] The basis of his argument is that the marginal rate of return on capital employed in inventory replenishment near the optimum reorder quantity is very close to the marginal cost of capital. It seems therefore that an organization without unlimited resources could find other uses for capital with a much greater return than that obtained by keeping high levels of inventory. The EOQ formula should therefore be used with care and with a constant reference to the practical decision situation in which any choices will be applied.

SUMMARY

There are a number of analytical models that can be used to study well structured decision situations. The best known of these models is called linear programming. This technique can be used to find the best way to produce a product or service in the presence of certain constraints. The model requires that the practical situation be formulated in terms of a single objective function and a series of constraints. The objective function is usually a statement of the desired maximization of profit or minimization of cost. The constraints usually refer to the availability of the resources necessary to the production process. A number of conditions must be met before the linear programming model is strictly applicable to a practical decision situation. These conditions, usually called linearity, additivity, and divisibility, may not be met in many practical decision situations. In such cases, it is wise to be aware of all the assumptions implicit in the model, so that any reservations arising from the assumptions can be taken into account in consideration of the analytical results.

Some situations in which two participants are in opposing and competitive positions can be represented by the linear programming model. In these cases, the positions of the two participants can be formulated by use of two complementary and interconnected versions of the model called the primal and the dual.

Some decision situations are naturally divided into stages of time, with a decision required at each stage. These situations can be analyzed by use of the dynamic programming model. This model studies the state of the situation in each stage and allows an optimum policy to be determined over all stages. The dynamic programming model does not require relationships among the factors involved to be linear. This model may therefore be used to analyze situations of the sort that can be treated by linear programming, but that do not meet the conditions of linearity necessary for the use of that technique.

The linear programming model is applicable also to situations in which goods or materials must be distributed from a number of originating points (such as warehouses) to a number of destinations (such as retail outlets). The model provides a method of determining the minimum cost of such distribution within the conditions imposed by the supply or demand at each point. Situations in which there is a certain number of tasks to be undertaken and an equal number of ways in which they can be completed are a special class of distribution situations. Similarly, situations in which it is required to find the shortest route between two points on a network that has a number of alternative routes, and those in which the maximal flow through a network is desired can be treated by variations of the linear programming model.

Critical path situations are typically those in which specific activities that are necessary to complete a project must be scheduled in such a way as to minimize the time between the beginning and the end of the project. The critical path model determines the earliest starting time and latest finishing time for each of the interrelated activities. Activities for which the earliest starting time plus the duration of the activity are equal to the latest finishing time are called critical activities. These activities are those in which a delay in starting or an increase in duration can cause an extension of overall project duration. The linking of critical activities throughout the project is called the critical path.

Complex inventory management decisions can be treated by use of the dynamic programming model. However, a simple formula can be derived to determine the economic order quantity as a function of the demand rate, the replenishment cost, the holding costs of inventory items, and the penalty costs for shortages. Results from use of this formula should be used as a guide to decision making rather than as a hard and fast rule. There is reason to believe that the use of the formula may result in inflated levels of stock, particularly in situations in which unlimited amounts of capital are not available.

PRACTICAL DECISION SITUATIONS

2.1 The T-Shirt Printing Company

A small company prints designs on T-shirts. It is planned to add two new designs A and B to the current range. Both of these designs can be printed on a single machine which is available for a total of 30 hours a week for use with either or both designs. Production costs for a shirt with a design A are $3.25 per shirt and for design B they are $4.70 per shirt. It takes a total of 1.4 minutes to print each shirt with design A and 2.6 minutes for design B.

The management of the company has arranged for delivery of at least 400 additional unprinted shirts per week at a price of $3.50 per shirt. There is no limit to the number of such shirts that could be delivered to the plant, but no unprinted shirts are kept in inventory for more than part of a week. The packing department can handle an additional load of only 800 newly printed shirts per week. The retail price of the printed shirts is $7.85 for design A and $8.90 for design B, so that the profit for each design A shirt sold is $1.10 and that for each design B shirt is $0.70.

Management would like to know the levels of production of shirts with the two designs that would maximize total contribution to profit on the assumption that up to 400 shirts printed with design A and up to 650 shirts with design B can be sold each week. Management would also like to know if the profit could be increased by increasing the availability of the production machine to 32 hours per week.

2.2 The Plywood Supply Company

A manufacturer of plywood has the following orders for sheets of plywood all of the same thickness:

130 sheets	40 cm × 80 cm
400 sheets	50 cm × 70 cm
190 sheets	60 cm × 60 cm

He must cut these sheets out of production sheets that are 100 cm × 130 cm. Any material not part of the final sheet sizes is waste. He realizes that he can cut the 100 cm × 130 cm sheets in one or more of eight ways if he is to make the best use of each of these sheets. An example of eight ways of cutting the sheets is shown in the following table:

Pattern number	Final Sheet Sizes		
	40 cm × 80 cm	50 cm × 70 cm	60 cm × 60 cm
1	1	1	1
2	2	1	0
3	2	0	1
4	1	2	0
5	0	2	1
6	1	0	2
7	3	0	0
8	0	3	0

The manufacturer wishes to know the number of sheets to cut in each pattern in order to fill the above order and minimize the number of 100 cm × 130 cm sheets cut.

2.3 The Steel Products Manufacturing Company

A manufacturer makes three products from steel tubing and extruded parts. The major costs in production arise from materials and labor. The following linear program has been devised to describe the problem of maximizing profit from the manufacturing operation. If X_1, X_2, and X_3 are the number of units produced per week for the three products 1, 2, and 3 respectively:

Maximize $\qquad$ $20X_1 + 15X_2 + 15X_3$

Subject to $\qquad$ $10X_1 + 3X_2 + 10X_3 \leqslant 100$

$\qquad\qquad\qquad\qquad\quad 5X_1 + 5X_2 + 5X_3 \leqslant 60$

$\qquad\qquad\qquad\qquad\quad X_1, X_2, X_3 \geqslant 0$

Explain the situation represented by this formulation and write down the dual complementary formulation. Use the dual to find the maximum profit obtainable in the situation described by the above formulation.

2.4 The Oil Sands Mining Company

A company engaged in mining oil sands uses giant bucketwheel reclaimers that are very costly and that wear out quickly. The total installed cost of a new bucketwheel reclaimer is $550,000. Operating costs in each of the first five months of usage are $300,000, $400,000, $600,000, $850,-000, and $925,000 respectively. Maximum life of the bucketwheel is five months but a new one can be installed at the end of any month. After 1, 2, 3, 4, and 5 months' use, a used bucketwheel can be sold for $300,000, $200,000, $125,000, $75,000, and $45,000 respectively. The company wishes to develop a program for replacement of the bucketwheels that minimizes costs during the 5-month period.

2.5 The Antique Furniture Company

A one-person company specializes in the hand-crafted manufacture of a particular item of furniture. The company has the following orders on hand:

3 units to be delivered by the end of March
2 units to be delivered by the end of June
4 units to be delivered by the end of September
1 unit to be delivered by the end of December

Some parts of each unit are produced on machines. The set-up cost for these machines is $300 per production run. It costs an additional $400 to complete each unit. Storage costs for completed units are $90 per unit per quarter. This amount is charged at the beginning of each quarter during which a unit is produced and stored. There is currently no inventory of units, nor does the company want to have any units left over at the end of the year. It is required to schedule production so that total costs are a minimum.

2.6 The Computer Manufacturing Company

A manufacturer of desktop computers has three assembly facilities A_1, A_2, A_3 from which completed units are sent to four warehouses W_1, W_2,

W_3, W_4 for regional distribution. The assembly costs for units produced at A_1, A_2, and A_3 are $1200, $1050, and $1225 per unit respectively. The maximum capacities at the three assembly facilities are 600, 400, and 800 units per week respectively. The selling prices from the warehouses W_1, W_2, W_3, and W_4 are $1300, $1250, $1400, and $1350 per unit respectively and the demand on each of these warehouses is 300, 500, 150, and 400 units per week respectively. The transportation costs from the assembly points to the warehouses are shown in the following table:

		Warehouses			
		W_1	W_2	W_3	W_4
Assembly Facilities	A_1	12	14	70	75
	A_2	15	10	50	40
	A_3	90	60	40	65

The company wishes to set up a distribution plan by means of which profit (defined as selling price less assembly and transportation costs) is maximized. Note that supply and demand are not in balance and that a dummy warehouse with zero transportation cost must be set up to absorb the excess of supply over demand.

2.7 The Oil Exploration Company

A company engaged in oil exploration consulting has contracts to carry out tests on six different sites at some time during a 4-month period. A test at any one site takes approximately 1 month to complete. The company has two crews (A and B) that can carry out the tests. Crew B is better equipped for operations in the high arctic than the other. Both crews are entitled to a month's vacation at some time during the 4-month period in question.

The costs depend on three factors:

1. Which crew carries out the test.
2. The exploration area in question.
3. The time of the year during which the tests are carried out; some of the exploration areas are in the high arctic, thus requiring special winter equipment.

The cost information has been summarized as follows:

Costs in Thousands of Dollars if Crew A Carries Out the Tests

Exploration Area

		1	2	3	4	5	6	Vacations
	1	15	14	16	20	25	12	10
Month	2	15	18	16	25	40	12	10
	3	15	22	17	35	impossible	12	10
	4	15	22	18	35	impossible	12	10

Costs in Thousands of Dollars if Crew B Carries Out the Tests

Exploration Area

		1	2	3	4	5	6	Vacations
	1	20	17	17	19	25	18	11
Month	2	20	18	17	23	35	18	11
	3	20	19	18	30	50	18	11
	4	20	20	18	30	50	18	11

The company wishes to construct an assignment model that would allow the tests to be done at least cost while accommodating the vacation entitlements of the crews.

2.8 The Oil Sands Mining Company Revisited

Can the bucketwheel replacement problem of situation 2.3 be formulated as a shortest route situation? If so, what would be the appropriate network diagram? Can you derive the optimal replacement policy which was the result of the application of other analysis models from the shortest route formulation?

2.9 The Project Management Company

A project management company has been engaged to supervise completion of a project consisting of eighteen separate activities (lettered A through R). The relationships between the activities and the estimated durations are shown in the following table:

Job	Immediate Predecessor	Estimated Duration
A	—	17
B	—	23
C	—	14
D	A	6
E	A	12
F	C	21
G	C	6
H	D	8
I	D	5
J	E, B	10
K	B	6
L	H, K, F	12
M	I, J	10
N	K, F	7
O	D, G	2
P	L	9
Q	L, M	6
R	I, J, N, O	13
Termination	P, Q, R	—

The company wishes to conduct an analysis to determine the overall time for completion of the project and which activities are critical.

2.10 The Plastics Manufacturing Company

The purchasing manager of a plastics manufacturing company wishes to determine a policy for ordering raw materials used in production processes. The production line requires 15 tons, 8 tons, and 1 ton per day of three materials A, B, and C respectively. Materials A and B are delivered by rail and each delivery has a fixed cost of $1176 in addition to the cost of the materials. Material C is delivered by road with a fixed cost of $450 per delivery. Holding costs in inventory of the three materials are $0.80, $1.50, and $4.00 per ton per day. Demands for materials A and B must always be met. Shortage of material C are possible, since half-finished products can be stored at a cost of $2 per day per ton shortage of material C.

DISCUSSION TOPICS

1. Make a list of the well structured decision situations in a company or organization that is known to you. Can you identify any of these situations that are supported by models of the type discussed in this chapter?

2. Well structured decision situations contain little or no uncertainty. If uncertainty exists, it is often neglected in the interests of obtaining a solution that is sufficiently close to reality for practical purposes. Can you think of any situations in which uncertainty is neglected in this manner in an organization that is known to you?

3. There are some restrictions on the use of the linear programming model that are called linearity, additivity, and divisibility. How do these restrictions affect the use of the model in practical situations?

4. What is the usefulness of the derivation of shadow costs and shadow prices in a situation studied by use of the linear programming model? What decisions would you make using these results?

5. What is the relationship between the primal and the dual in a linear programming application? How do the objectives of the participant in the primal relate to those of the participant in the dual?

6. Which of the well-structured decision situations in your organization do you think could be treated by the dynamic programming model? What characteristics of these situations make this model particularly appropriate in studying them?

7. How can dynamic programming be applied to a situation that might seem to be appropriate for use of the linear programming model? What limitations to the use of the linear model can be overcome by use of the dynamic programming model?

8. Can you provide a rationale for the fact that distribution and assignment situations can be treated by the linear programming model? What characteristics of these situations make the use of this model appropriate?

9. How are network situations related to the linear programming model? Can you formulate a network situation in the same terms as, say, a product mix problem?

10. What are the factors that require caution in the use of the optimal order quantity formula for inventory replenishment? How does the availability of capital affect decisions of this nature?

REFERENCES

1. Wagner, Harvey M., *Principles of Operations Research*, 2nd Ed., Prentice Hall, 1975.
2. Hillier, F. S. and Lieberman, G. J., *Introduction to Operations Research*, Holden-Day, 1st Ed., 1967, 2nd Ed., 1975.
3. Lapin, L., *Quantitative Methods for Business Decisions*, Harcourt Brace Jovanovich, 1976.
4. Hillier, F. S. and Lieberman, G. J., *op cit*, 1st Ed., pp 135–138.
5. Wagner, H. M., *op cit*, pp 98–110.
6. Peterson, R. and Silver, E. A., *Decision Systems for Inventory Management and Production Planning*, Wiley, 1978.
7. Example based on a situation described in Hillier, F. S. and Lieberman, G. J., *op cit*, 1st Ed., pp 245–247.
8. Levy, F. K., Thompson, G. L., Weist, J. D., "The ABC's of the Critical Path Method" *Harvard Business Review*, September/October 1963.
9. Battersby, A., *Network Analysis for Planning and Scheduling*, St. Martins Press, 2nd Ed., 1967.
10. Duckworth, E., *A Guide to Operational Research*, Methuen University Paperbacks, UP120, 1965, pp 58–64.
11. *Ibid*, p 64.

APPENDIX TO CHAPTER 2

Graphical Solution of the Fertilizer-Mix Problem

The problem has been formulated in the text as

Objective Function $\qquad\qquad\qquad\qquad$ *Maximize* $50X_1 + 100X_2$

Constraints

1. No more than 50 tons of ingredient A
    in 100 tons of product $\qquad\qquad\qquad\qquad \frac{2}{3}X_1 + \frac{1}{4}X_2 \leqslant 50$
2. No more than 50 tons of ingredient B
    in 100 tons of product $\qquad\qquad\qquad\qquad \frac{1}{3}X_1 + \frac{3}{4}X_2 \leqslant 50$
3. Only 70 tons of mix 1 available $\qquad\qquad\qquad\qquad X_1 \leqslant 70$
4. Only 60 tons of mix 2 available $\qquad\qquad\qquad\qquad X_2 \leqslant 60$
5. Negative amounts of mix 1 and mix 2
    are not possible $\qquad\qquad\qquad\qquad X_1, X_2 \geqslant 0$

Constraints 1 and 2 may be illustrated as shown in Figures 2A-1 and 2A-2.

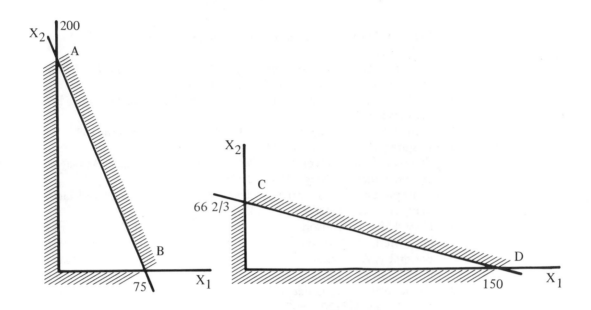

FIG. 2A-1

AB is the line
$\frac{2}{3}X_1 + \frac{1}{4}X_2 = 50$

FIG. 2A-2

CD is the line
$\frac{1}{3}X_1 + \frac{3}{4}X_2 = 50$

The unshaded region in each case is the region in which the constraint is met. Constraints 3 and 4 can be illustrated by Fig. 2A-3. Superimposing all the constraint diagrams results in Fig. 2A-4.

The unshaded area is the area of all *feasible* solutions to the formulation. The line EF is a line with equation $50X_1 + 100X_2 = $ constant, i.e., the objective function. The optimum solution is obtained by allowing this line to move as far up and to the right as it can while remaining in the feasible area. The optimum occurs at the point (60, 40).

Note that the above problem can be illustrated in two-dimensional diagrams because the objective function can be expressed as a function of two variables. The number of constraints is immaterial in this respect. Note also that a situation in which there are only two constraints can be illustrated in two dimensions irrespective of the number of variables in the objective function by considering the dual of the original problem. An original problem in which there are only two constraints has a dual in which there are only two variables in the objective function.

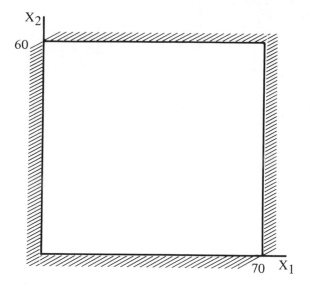

FIG. 2A-3

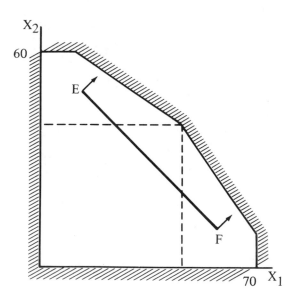

FIG. 2A-4

 *Chapter Three*

Quantitative Measures of Benefits and Costs

INTRODUCTION

The decision situations examined in Chapter 2 were well structured and clearly defined. They involved a single individual with the power to make the decision. This individual had a single, well defined objective, such as maximizing profit, minimizing cost, maximizing flow, or minimizing the duration of a project. Success in achieving this objective was assessed in terms of a single, well defined measure expressed in easily understood units such as dollars, barrels of oil, or days. Situations of this nature are well understood. They can be treated in most instances by a well structured analytical procedure.

Simple, well defined measures of the benefits and disbenefits of courses of action may not be available in many practical decision situations. This chapter contains, therefore, a discussion of the problems of establishing quantitative measures and of the manner in which decision makers can proceed if such measures cannot be used. In the text that follows, the term "disbenefits" is taken to mean not only dollar costs, but also any disadvantages that may arise from a course of action that do not immediately appear to be measurable in terms of dollars. Examples of such disbenefits include loss of public image of a corporation, reduction in the standard of living of a person or a community, and reduction in the aesthetic value of an object or of a geographic location.

The early part of this chapter concentrates on the problems of establishing quantitative measures of benefits and costs in a number of types of practical decision situations. The discussion proceeds from situations in which there is a choice between alternative quantitative measures to those in which no such measures are immediately apparent. This development leads to the introduction of utility as a quantity in which the preferences of decision makers between alternatives might possibly be expressed. The chapter ends with a short account of the limitations imposed on the decision making process if these preferences cannot be represented in quantitative terms. The decision situations treated in this chapter are those included in Category 2 of Table 1-1 and those in Categories 4 and 5 in which there are some benefits and disbenefits that cannot necessarily be measured in quantitative terms.

ESTABLISHMENT OF QUANTITATIVE MEASURES OF BENEFITS AND COSTS

The purpose of establishing quantitative measures of benefits and costs is to facilitate comparison of the effectiveness of alternative courses of action in a decision situation. We need quantitative measures so that comparisons between numbers are easy to comprehend and unequivocal. We are all used to the idea that 5 units of a benefit are better than 3 units. Comparisons of the profit or costs arising from each of several alternatives are easily made in this fashion, as was demonstrated in Chapter 2. It is extremely important, however, in establishing such quantitative measures to ensure that the basic objectives of the decision maker are known and understood. In situations involving maximization of profit or minimization of costs, there may be no major problem in this respect. However, in other situations in which objectives are less well defined, it may be more difficult to establish quantitative measures that relate to the true purpose expressed in the objective. The chance that a measure is suggested that does not represent exactly the nature of the objective of the decision maker is correspondingly increased. For example, the objective of a corporation which is commonly expressed as "being a good corporate citizen" is open to a number of interpretations. One such interpretation may be in terms of the corporation's dealings with the community in which it operates and its relations with the people in that community. Another interpretation might be with respect to the percentage of gross earnings devoted to the public good. Very different measures of achievement might apply to these two interpretations.

In other cases, alternatives may need to be considered against a range of objectives, and quantitative measures may need to be established for each of these objectives. For example, in consideration of alternative proposals to meet a transportation need, the desires for shorter travel time, safe travel, and low cost are frequently expressed. The effects of the proposals on the environment, on service to industry, on recreational areas, and on the disruption of neighborhoods may also have to be taken into account. The measures of benefits and disbenefits relating to these factors are different and each must be established before the evaluation of alternatives can start.

Efficiency and Effectiveness

Two particular types of measurement in common use in practical situations are concerned with *efficiency* and *effectiveness*. In general, efficiency relates to the best use of resources used in a process or in carrying out a course of action. An alternative that results in the greatest amount of output for a given amount of resources used (or the least amount of resources for a given amount of output) is regarded as the most efficient. A measure of efficiency might be concerned, for example, with the greatest amount of flow through a pipeline or the maximum use of space in a building. Measures of effectiveness, on the other hand, relate to the degree of achievement of objectives. Such a measure might be concerned, for example, with the degree to which a particular course of action contributes to an objective of diversification of the activities of a company.

Efficiency and effectiveness sometimes coincide. For example, if the sole objective of a company were to make a profit, maximum efficiency would result in maximum effectiveness. However, the two concepts do not always run in parallel. In the administration of a health care unit, for instance, maximum efficiency might be thought of in terms of the number of patients treated in a given period. Pursuit of maximum efficiency in these terms might lead to a situation in which the amount of time devoted to each patient was insufficient to provide satisfactory health care. The effectiveness of the unit might therefore be jeopardized by adherence to the concept of maximum efficiency. On the other hand, if standards of health care could be established, it might be possible to define situations of maximum efficiency while ensuring that the prescribed standards are met.

Measurements of workload that are possibly good indicators of efficiency are not necessarily equally good indications of effectiveness. A report of the number of purchasing departments visited by a sales representative is not always an indication of the potential effectiveness of that individual in increasing sales. A record of the number of inspections made of manufacturing plants is not necessarily an indication of the effectiveness of the visits in increasing safety at these locations. In similar fashion, the establishment of standards such as are frequently used in government planning agencies does not necessarily indicate a certain level of effectiveness unless these standards are related to products that are directly concerned with objectives.[1] For example, that a community has a certain number of dentists per 1000 of the population does not necessarily imply a particular level of effectiveness of dental health for the community.

The aim in most decision situations is to choose an alternative that provides the greatest effectiveness relative to the objective or objectives of the decision maker. If the alternative chosen also provides the greatest efficiency in the use of resources, this is well and good. However, it is possible to be effective while not operating at maximum efficiency. It is also possible to be not at all effective while being very efficient. Furthermore, it is possible for the relationship between effectiveness and efficiency to change as conditions change. Consider, for example, a manufacturing plant that makes a product from certain ingredients. The objective is to make maximum profit consistent with meeting certain standards in production. If the market for the product is very good, high efficiency contributes to high effectiveness in meeting the objective. Suppose, however, that the market for the product disappears, as happened, for example, when certain types of pesticide were banned for general use. The plant may continue to work at high efficiency, but the effectiveness of the operation drops to zero because no profit can be made from the sale of the product.

Situations with No Immediately Apparent Quantitative Measures of Benefits and Disbenefits

Many practical decision situations exist in which there are no immediately apparent quantitative measures of benefits and disbenefits. The objectives in these situations are such that well understood quantitative measures relating to money, time, and effort do not describe completely the results of progress towards their achievement. Many of these situations are in the public sector and have to do with health, welfare, and the provision of services to the public. It is frequently very difficult, for example, to describe in simple quantitative terms, the benefit of a course of action that leads to an improvement in the health or quality of life of a segment of the population. However these problems are not confined to the public sector. Similar difficulties arise in measuring the degree of success of a corporation in achieving a desired level of social responsibility or public image.

The natural tendency in such situations is to try to represent the benefits of a course of action in terms of easily measurable items such as money. This practice is often justified by the premise that the usefulness of an article or a situation to an individual is directly measurable by the amount of money he is prepared to pay to obtain or achieve it. This argument is tenable only as long as a market exists for the article or situation being considered. In many cases, however, such a market does not exist. It is very difficult, for example, to put a price on good health or public esteem.

Attempts to represent benefits in easily measurable terms have been reported in a number of studies.[2, 3] The most frequently referenced of these studies is that of the Roskill Commission on the Third London Airport.[4] In this study, the research team appears to have established quantitative measures of benefits and disbenefits with little thought for the consequences or the implications with respect to the results of analysis. For example, the team placed a value of about $25,000 on each human life likely to be lost in an aircraft accident. Furthermore, it is explained in this report, that approximately $13,000 of the total represents the effects of the loss in terms of such factors as the grief of the next-of-kin, and the remainder accounts for the economic loss to society of the individual's premature death.[5] The team made similar assumptions with respect to measurement of the convenience of an airport site to the traveling public. In this respect, it assumed that convenience could be measured in terms of the value of the time taken to travel to the airport by the users. In order to arrive at this figure, business travel time was valued at £2.32 per hour and leisure travel time at 23 pence per hour for adults and 5 *pence per hour for children*. At this distance from the study, it is hard to imagine how such assumptions could have been adopted by a research team. Possibly the use of these assumptions was due to a desire to use any quantitative form of benefits and disbenefits in order to arrive at a basis for numerical comparison.

Defenders of this type of quantification make the point that a choice between alternatives implicitly puts a value on such factors as human life. It is argued that an openly discussed process of quantification is no worse than an implicit valuation. It may, in fact, be preferable, insomuch as some of the major factors involved are at least brought out in explicit discussion. There is some validity to this argument. A municipal authority allocating funds to ambulance and rescue services or to the removal of grade crossings implicitly puts a value on human life. If human life were priceless, there would be no alternative but to allocate an infinite amount of money to services that would save just one individual. However, practical considerations always dictate that a finite sum be assigned in such circumstances.

There are many situations in which readily available measures of benefits and disbenefits (such as dollars for cost) cannot be used. In such cases, it may be possible to conceive of a *proxy measure* that can be used instead. A proxy measure is one which does not measure a benefit or disbenefit directly but does measure something closely enough related to it to provide an indication of the value of a course of action. Hatry has suggested, for example, that the response time of an ambulance service might be a suitable proxy measure for assessing alternative proposals for such services.[6] Similarly, the street price of a narcotic might be a proxy by which to measure the effectiveness of efforts to reduce the flow of drugs to the consumer.

Good analytical practice requires that proxy measures of benefits and disbenefits represent as faithfully as possible the effects of courses of action in relation to the objectives in the decision situation. Furthermore, it is essential that no significant aspect of the benefits and disbenefits be left unrepresented by the proxy measures that are adopted. Particular care must be taken in assigning proxy measures in situations in which the health, safety, welfare, or quality of life of persons or segments of the population are concerned. There has been a tendency, for example, in some of the literature on cost-benefit analysis to measure the benefits of programs affecting individuals in terms of their production on behalf of society (in dollar terms) less the dollar cost of their consumption.[7] An assumption of this nature neglects altogether considerations of human happiness and nonmonetary aspects of the welfare of the individuals involved. It can lead to conclusions from analysis that certain segments of the population should receive less attention because of their relatively smaller contributions and relatively greater needs. Further extension of the arguments based on these premises could lead to the conclusion that society would be better off if certain elements of the population were eliminated. This position not only is morally indefensible; it also demonstrates a strong discrepancy between the results of some analytical studies and decisions that are reached by responsible administrators.

It is most important therefore in dealing with proxy measures to avoid choices that automatically build undesirable bias into the analysis on which decisions are based. It has been common in analysis of health care programs, for example, to use the dollar value of contribution lost to society as a factor to be minimized in seeking the most efficient courses of action. However, selection of this proxy measure may introduce a bias into the analysis against programs that are beneficial to women, because women are generally paid less than men in today's society. It is important also to consider the effect that selection of different proxy measures can have upon the conclusions drawn from analysis. For example, in a comprehensive analysis of courses of action against conditions that lead to death and disability for U.S. citizens, the Department of Health, Education, and Welfare derived detailed analytical results that are illustrated in Table 3-1.[8] Programs against these conditions are listed in Table 3-1 in descending order of effectiveness in terms of two proxy measures; the program cost per death averted and a calculation of direct and indirect savings to the community.

Leaving aside for the moment the appropriateness of the second measure, the two criteria are seen to provide very different orderings between the programs. Arthritis and syphilis, diseases that result in crippling rather than in early death, appear high in the ordering against a measure of cost to the community, but not at all in the list in terms of deaths averted. On the other hand, uterine cervical and breast cancer are high on the deaths averted listing but lower on the cost to the community ordering, primarily

TABLE 3-1. Effectiveness of Programs Against Killing and Disabling Factors Judged in Terms of Two Proxy Measures

	Order	Program Cost Per Death Averted	Direct and Indirect Savings to the Community
Highest	1	Seat belt use	Seat belt use
	2	Uterine cervical cancer	Arthritis
	3	Reduce drinking driving	Reduce drinking driving
	4	Lung cancer	Syphilis
	5	Breast cancer	Uterine cervical cancer
	6	Tuberculosis	Lung cancer
Lowest	7	Head and neck cancer	Breast cancer

because those affected by these conditions are women. This differentiation brings into question once again the validity of measures in which gross earnings by members of the population are a factor.

UTILITY

The desire for a quantitative basis of comparison of alternatives has led to the development of the concept of utility. The basic premise of this concept is that if an individual demonstrates a preference for one alternative over another, that person can be said to have a greater utility for the chosen alternative than for the other. There is little basis for argument against this idea. Problems arise, however, when an attempt is made to measure utility in quantitative terms. Such measurement is necessary to much of the recently developed techniques of decision theory. It is appropriate, therefore, to investigate the nature of utility as it has been described over the past two hundred years and the more recent attempts that have been made to measure it as the basis of comparisons between alternatives. These matters will be the subject of the following sections of the text.

The word utility has been used in the technical literature to describe a number of different but related concepts. The question of the utility of money was considered in the early eighteenth century by the Swiss mathematicians Cramer and Bernoulli. Their basic premise was that the usefulness of an additional amount of money decreases with the amount of money possessed. Under this premise the value of an additional dollar to an individual having one thousand dollars is less than that to a person having only ten dollars. This concept has come to be known as *Bernoullian Utility.*[9]

In line with the philosophy of his day, Bernoulli assumed that all men, being rational, would behave in the same way. He therefore proposed a fundamental law which he maintained governed such behavior. This law stated that the utility of money to an individual could be measured in terms of the logarithm (to any base) of the amount of money. Both Cramer and a French scientist named Buffon argued in favor of different laws (Cramer for the square root and Buffon for the reciprocal of the amount of money) as a measure of utility. However, each of the proposals resulted in a curve of utility for money plotted against money that had the general concave-downward shape shown in Figure 3-1. With such a curve, incremental amounts of money contribute less utility as the level of money involved increases.

Much more recently, Friedman and Savage put forward the idea that every individual has a utility function that reflects his utility for money or some other commodity.[10] Starting from a basis of Bernoulli's work, they tried to construct a utility function that would reflect observed human behavior under a variety of circumstances. They noted, for example, that any such function would need to take into account two aspects of human behavior that are apparently inconsistent: namely, gambling and buying insurance. In gambling, the individual gives up a sure thing (the stake) in return for participation in a risk, whereas an individual buying insurance gives up a risk (for example, that his or her house burns down) in favor of a sure thing (the relatively minor loss represented by the premium).

It had previously been pointed out that the shape of the utility curve suggested by Bernoulli and his contemporaries did not explain gambling behavior.[11] The Bernoulli curve supposed that people had less and less utility for money as the amount increased. Some types of gamblers clearly

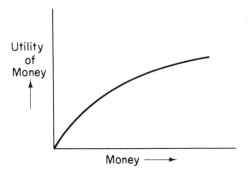

FIG. 3-1. Bernoullian utility of money.

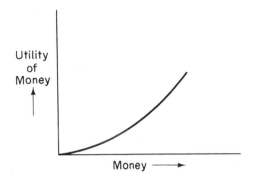

FIG. 3-2. Concave upward utility function.

have more and more utility for money as the amounts get larger, at least up to a point. This latter type of behavior can be described by a utility function of the (concave upward) type shown in Figure 3-2.

Friedman and Savage suggested further that behavior in buying insurance could be explained by a curve in the negative quadrant similar to that shown in Figure 3-3. With this curve, additional amounts of loss contribute greater amounts of disutility as the loss increases. They then combined these curves to produce a proposed general utility function of the type shown in Figure 3-4. The portion of this curve in the negative quadrant was said to explain behavior in buying insurance and the part in the upper, positive quadrant to explain gambling behavior. Note that the portions of the curve near the intersection of the two axes are close to straight lines, although the curve is not necessarily continuous in the region of the origin.

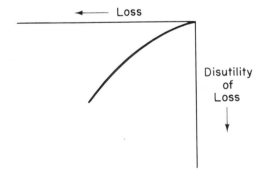

FIG. 3-3. Function representing disutility of loss.

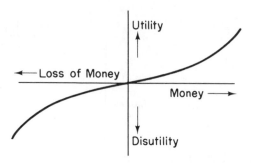

FIG. 3-4. Friedman-Savage utilitiy function.

The utility function proposed by Friedman and Savage was modified some years later by Markowitz.[12] He suggested that individuals with different amounts of wealth would not act in the same way at a particular level of money. He said, rather, that the changes of behavior implied by the changes in slope of the utility function would take place at different points of the money scale for individuals with different levels of wealth. This is the equivalent of saying that the intersection of the axes on the diagram in Figure 3-4 would be at a different point on the absolute money scale for each individual. The exact point at which this intersection is placed is determined by what Markowitz called the *customary wealth* of the individual.

Markowitz proposed further that there should be a modification of the shape of the Friedman-Savage function at each end of the curve. He said that there must surely be a point at which an individual becomes satiated

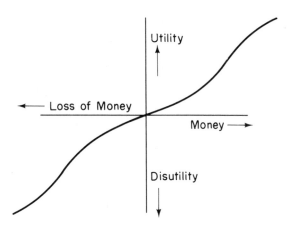

FIG. 3-5. Markowitz utility function.

with gain and that the right hand end of the curve should therefore turn downward in a manner to reflect this condition. Similarly, there is presumably a leveling off of disutility at some very large amount of loss. The left hand end of the curve should therefore reflect this disregard of further loss. These arguments lead to a curve for the utility of money of a form shown in Fig. 3-5. The intersection of the axes is at the customary wealth of the individual to which the curve refers.

MEASUREMENT OF UTILITY

Given that the utility function of an individual for money or for some other commodity is of the general form shown in Fig. 3-5, the question now arises of whether that individual's utility for various amounts of the commodity involved can be measured in a manner suitable to the construction of such a curve. In particular, it is necessary to know the units in which utility is to be measured and also the type of scale on which these units are to be placed.

Scales of Measurement

There is a hierarchy of scales that can be used in measurement. Individual scales are distinguished from one another by the extent of the restrictions that they place on the process of measurement. There are three types of scale that are in common use today. Listed in increasing order in the restrictive conditions they impose, these types of scale are:

1. *The ordinal scale* in which entities are shown ranked in order of preference in relation to some expressed objective or condition.
2. *The interval scale* in which entities are placed according to their distance from some arbitrary origin.
3. *The ratio scale* in which entities are placed according to their distance from some nonarbitrary origin.

The ordinal scale is used when it is possible or desirable to show items only in rank order. For example, we may say "I prefer that car to this one." No strength of preference is indicated by this statement nor is there any indication of a numerical difference between the two alternatives. Some idea of distance between the alternatives is given if the statement is "I prefer that car to this one by a wide margin," but there are still no numbers included in this statement using an ordinal scale of measurement.

The interval scale, on the other hand, is one in which numbers are used to express distances between different items. For example, temperature is usually measured on an interval scale. A temperature of 80°F is known to be 20° hotter than a temperature of 60°F. Note that we do not say that 80°F is twice as hot as 40°F. Statements of that nature can be made only of items measured on a ratio scale. There is no unique zero on an interval scale. The zero on the Fahrenheit scale is chosen at 32 degrees below the freezing point of water, whereas that on the Celsius scale is at that freezing point. If two interval scales are used to measure the same thing (for example, the Fahrenheit and Celsius scales) there is a relationship of the form $y = ax + b$ (called a linear transformation) that allows conversion between the two scales. To convert from Celsius to Fahrenheit, y in Fahrenheit equals 9/5 times the Celsius reading plus 32°.

By comparison, a ratio scale is one in which there is very little arbitrariness in the measurements. There is an absolute zero on a ratio scale. Items like the length or weight of an item are measured on a ratio scale because they can take an absolute value of zero. If two different ratio scales are used to measure the weight or length of an item (pounds or kilograms; inches or centimeters) there is a direct multiplication factor between the units on the two scales. Conversion between the two scales is governed by a relation of the type $y = kx$. Furthermore, a weight of 2 tons is said to be twice as heavy as one measuring one ton in weight.

A comparison between the three scales of measurement is shown in Table 3-2. In practice, an ordinal scale is used to express preferences where no quantitative measurement has been or can be made. An interval scale is used where no absolute zero can be specified but where numerical distances between items are important. Ratio scales are used where an absolute zero is possible (for example, zero money) and where the choice in measurement is limited to the selection of a unit, such as dollars or pounds sterling. An important property of the interval and ratio scales (compared with the ordinal scale) is that averages over a number of measurements can be made using these two scales.

The Von Neumann-Morgenstern Measurement of Utility

In their classic treatment of the theory of games, Von Neumann and Morgenstern proposed a method of measuring utility on an interval scale which they called the standard gamble.[13] This method can be explained in the following terms.

Let us suppose that a decision maker has three alternatives, A, B, and C and that he or she prefers A to B and B to C. We can assume for the moment that transitivity is preserved and that as a result of these preferences, A is preferred to C. Having expressed these preferences on an ordinal scale, we wish to investigate whether a more quantitative expression of the decision maker's opinions of the three alternatives can be obtained. The

TABLE 3-3. Scales of Measurement

Type of Scale	Degree of Arbitrariness	Type of Transformation Between Units in Two Scales of this Type	Items that Are Unchanged when Transformation Applied	Example
Ordinal	high	Positive monotonic; that is, the order of preferences on one scale remains the same on another scale of the same type.	Rank order of items measured	I prefer that car to this
Interval	medium	Positive linear of the form $y = ax + b$	1. rank order 2. ratio of *distances* between items on scale	Temperature in °F and °C
Ratio	low	Multiplication by a positive constant	1. rank order 2. ratio of *distances* between items on scale 3. ratio of *measured values* of items	1. *Weight, height* 2. Temperature in °K

method of Von Neumann and Morgenstern suggests that we set up the following question and investigate the decision maker's reaction to it.

The decision maker is to be asked which of the following alternatives he or she prefers:

B for sure	OR	a risk situation involving: A with probability p and C with probability $(1-p)$

Remembering that the decision maker prefers A to B and B to C and that we have assumed as a consequence that A is preferred to C (i.e., A>B, B>C, A>C), the above question is the equivalent of asking whether the decision maker would choose the intermediately preferred option for sure over a gamble giving a chance p of the *most* preferred option and the complementary chance $(1-p)$ of the *least* preferred option. The method of measuring utility consists of investigating the decision maker's behavior as p is varied from 0 to 1.

When $p=1$, the question posed is the equivalent of asking the decision maker to choose between B for sure and A with probability 1, that is, for sure. The individual concerned must, according to the assumed preferences, choose A in this case, which is the right hand side of the above alternatives. If $p=0$, the choice is between B for sure and C with probability 1 and the decision maker must choose B, the left hand side. Note that as p has been varied from 1 to 0, the decision maker has changed the choice from the right hand to the left hand alternative. It can be argued, therefore, that there must be a value of p between 1 and 0 at which the decision maker is indifferent between the two sides. This value is denoted by p^*.

Suppose now that we set up an interval scale with the zero arbitrarily set at the utility for the least preferred option C and the value 1 set as the utility for the most preferred option A. Von Neumann and Morgenstern proved that the utility for the intermediate alternative B could be represented on this interval scale by the value of the probability p^*.

If there are initially more than three alternatives, the procedure can be repeated in groups of three, with the most and least preferred alternatives always members of each group. In each case, the indifference probability is obtained for a choice between an intermediately preferred alternative and a gamble between the most and least preferred. In the case of five alternatives, say, A, B, C, D, and E, the interval scale might look like that in Figure 3-6. Note that whereas this scale has a zero, it is an *arbitrarily set* zero. Any scale derived from that shown by a linear transformation of the type $y=ax+b$ would be equally representative of the measured utility.

The Von Neumann-Morgenstern method of measuring utility is based on several assumptions, some of which are technical but some of which relate to the behavior of individuals engaged in decision making. The

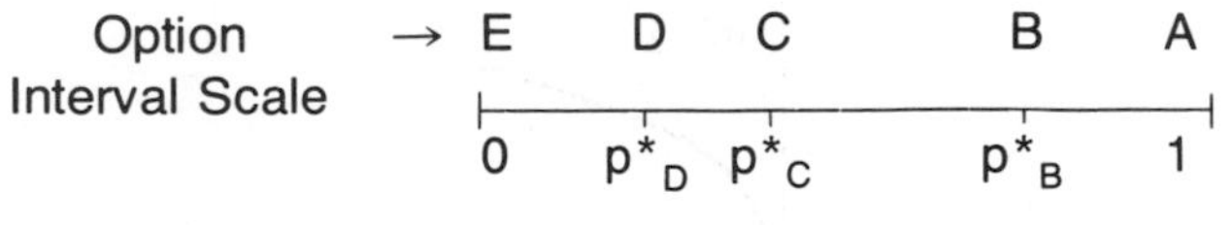

Option   →   E   D   C   B   A

Interval Scale

0   p^*_D p^*_C p^*_B 1

FIG. 3-6.   Interval scale utility for five alternatives.

most important of the assumptions relating to managerial behavior are as follows:

- The decision maker involved is assumed to have preferences for the various alternatives; with regard to any two alternatives, he or she must be able to express a preference for one or the other or indifference between them.
- Transitivity must be preserved; that is, if A is preferred to B and B to C, then A must be preferred to C rather than C to A.
- If the individual involved prefers A to B, then he or she must prefer a certainty of obtaining A to a gamble that provides only a probability of obtaining A and the complementary probability of obtaining the less preferred alternative.

The applicability of these assumptions in everyday managerial decision making and the effect on the measurement of utility if they are not met are discussed in a later section of this chapter in which the whole concept of utility is evaluated.

Experimental Measurement of Utility

The results of an experimental study of the utility functions of a group of corporate executives engaged in decision making on behalf of their firm has been reported by Swalm.[14] The first step in this study was to establish a planning horizon for each executive in terms of the amounts of money that he or she was customarily involved with in decision making. The planning horizon was set for each individual as twice the amount of money that he might recommend be spent in any one year. Each individual was then questioned using the standard gamble procedure, and the utility for gain or loss was determined on an arbitrary scale. The same scale was used for all individuals taking part in the study. The results of the study showed widely different attitudes to gain and loss on the part of the individuals involved. Typical utility functions found in the study are illustrated in Fig. 3-7.

The utility functions of the executives found in the study illustrate man-

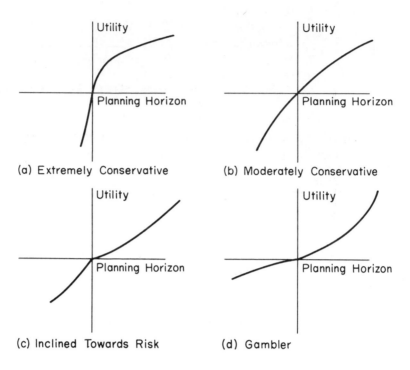

FIG. 3-7. Utility function of executives determined in an experimental study.

agerial behavior that ranges from extremely conservative to that of a gambler. A majority of the functions contained the sharp drop in the negative quadrant (as in Fig. 3-7 (a)) which denotes conservatism in situations involving loss to the corporation. The proportion of individuals showing inclination towards risk (as in Fig. 3-7 (c) and (d)) was small. This attitude no doubt inhibits the selection of alternatives in which the possibility of gain justifies the assumption of some risk of loss. They indicate perhaps that in organizational decision making the penalty for obtaining a bad outcome is considered by some managers to be much greater than the reward for choosing an alternative that works out well.

A similar set of experiments to determine utility functions in a practical situation has been reported by Spetzler.[15] In these experiments, thirty-six executives from the same company were interviewed and utility functions were obtained using a variation of the standard gamble method. The subject matter in each of the interviews was investment decisions in which the company was or could be involved. Each executive was asked to express his preferences between alternative investment situations that involved some degree of risk. This set of experiments is interesting in that the participants were asked to express opinions on the alternative investments from the point of view of the company they represented. The utillity functions obtained represented therefore the impressions of the individuals involved of what might be called a corporate utility function. A set of experiments with similar objectives has been reported by Cramer and Smith.[16]

EVALUATION OF THE CONCEPT OF UTILITY

The concept of utility is one that seems acceptable at first sight to those who have been involved in the study of decision making. It appears reasonable that if alternatives can be placed in an order of preference, then the relationship between these preferences should be capable of being expressed in numeric form. The Von Neumann-Morgenstern treatment, which allows utility to be represented on an interval scale, is similarly acceptable at first sight. The major reservations with regard to the concept center on the manner in which utility can be measured and the way in which the measured utility can be used in practical decision situations.

The two assumptions involved in the standard gamble procedure that have attracted the most comment are those of transitivity and attitude to gambling in the individuals involved. Transitivity is essentially a mathematical concept. Most individuals follow it when dealing with preferences with respect to a single objective. It appears to represent logical behavior. It seems to be normal and consistent that if an individual prefers A to B and B to C with a particular objective in mind that he or she will prefer A to C with respect to that objective. However, most of those involved in managerial decision making seldom have only one objective to consider. A manager is likely to say, "On the one hand, I prefer A to B and B to C but under some circumstances I prefer C to A". Such a statement does not obey the strict mathematical condition of transitivity. It may however represent practical conditions better than a purely transitive statement with respect to one objective. Nevertheless, if preferences do not obey the transitivity condition, the standard gamble procedure is placed in jeopardy.

The standard gamble procedure also requires the individual involved to choose between a sure thing and a gamble in establishing the interval-scale utility. This procedure could be disrupted if the individual has an aversion to or a liking for gambling that would influence the choice. The establishment of interval scale utility requires that the choice be made entirely on the basis of preferences between the alternatives available to the decision maker. Any influence on this choice introduced by the behavioral characteristics of the individual involved would cause errors in the interval scale measurement.

The concept of the "customary wealth" of an individual or of an organization which is incorporated into the Markowitz utility function is far from clear. Whereas this concept is similarly intuitively acceptable, there may be difficulty in defining the customary wealth applicable to an individual or organization with sufficient accuracy to permit the determination of a utility function. There are similar reservations with regard to the establishment of utility for alternatives that involve considerations other than gain or loss of a commodity such as money. Situations involving objectives that are concerned with matters for which money is not an appropriate proxy measure (such as health, welfare, public esteem, and social responsibility) may not be amenable to representation by a numeric quantity such as is derived by the interval scale measurement.

Some of these concerns have been investigated experimentally in the laboratory, notably by Mosteller and Nogee.[17] In these experiments, subjects were offered a series of gambles involving real money. Utility curves were constructed on the basis of responses and an attempt was made to determine whether future behavior in similar situations could be predicted from the experimentally determined utility functions. The predictions did not match the behavior of the subjects exactly. Nevertheless, the experimentors found that the higher the expected utility of a gamble, the greater was the probability that a subject would choose it. However, laboratory experiments involving persons with less immediate responsibility than executives have and sums of money far smaller than are involved in real life are probably not a satisfactory representation of the conditions under which managers must make practical decisions.[18]

Even given that a utility curve can be constructed that represents the behavior of an individual at a given time, there is reason to question whether such a curve can be used to predict the future behavior of that individual. Interval scale measurements of utility are at best *descriptive*, in that they describe the preferences and behavior of an individual at some time in the past. There is no immediately-acceptable reason why such descriptive measurements of past behavior should be used in a *prescriptive* fashion to predict future behavior. Conditions may have changed since the measurements were made and the individual's preferences may have changed along with them. The individual's view of his or her personal life and prospects may have altered considerably since the utility measurements were taken. His impression of the position of the company for which it is proposed that a utility function is being used in decision making may have changed since the function was determined. Nevertheless, repeated adherence to the same utility function over a long period of time might be regarded as evidence that future behavior will follow the same pattern. There is, however, always the chance that some event or change in conditions will bring about a change in decision making behavior.

A further serious reservation to interval scale utility results from the nature of the scale on which it is measured. The basic characteristic of the interval scale is that the zero point is chosen arbitrarily and the units on the scale can also be changed at will. In practice, therefore, the utility of one person can be measured on a scale of, say, 20 to 200 and that of another person can be measured on a scale of say 0 to 100. Furthermore, the scales of each person can be multiplied by an arbitrary factor without loss of applicability. The difference of scales matters little until an interpersonal comparison of utilities is made. However, if attempts are made to compare the utilities of different individuals for alternatives, serious difficulties arise unless a relationship between their two utility scales can be established.

Additions of individual utilities is sometimes proposed as a means of constructing a "social welfare function" for use in group decision making. Functions of this nature have been used in the assessment of the desirability of alternative social programs with respect to populations that contain segments with different views, needs, and preferences. The validity of a social welfare function obtained by adding individual utilities is in serious question amongst authorities in decision making at the present time. Apart from the difficulties inherent in the measurement of utility, questions have been raised about the nature of the function that is used. The manner in which the function is constructed clearly implies a weighting of the preferences of the individuals whose utilities contribute to it, even if all utilities are originally measured on the same scale. The whole subject of joint decisions by individuals with different preferences is raised again in Chapters 6, 7, and 8.

SITUATIONS IN WHICH NO QUANTITATIVE MEASURES OF BENEFITS AND DISBENEFITS ARE POSSIBLE

Enough has been said in this chapter to throw doubts on the feasibility in many situations of establishing quantitative measures of benefits and disbenefits that are truly representative of progress toward achievement of objectives. Situations in which all the benefits and disbenefits of all the participants can be represented by well understood quantitative measures are limited in number. There are considerable concerns and constraints with respect to the use of proxy measures. The concept of utility, while intuitively attractive, is surrounded by reservations, primarily with how it can be measured and the applicability of utility to situations involving more than the gain or loss of a simple commodity. Notwithstanding these concerns about the availability of appropriate quantitative measures of benefits and disbenefits, the bulk of the recently developed theory of decisions is based on the assumption that such quantitative measures can be determined. A large proportion of recent articles in the technical literature start with a sentence like, "Let us assume that the utilities of the decision maker for the alternatives take the following form. . . ." The question arises as to how the practical decision maker should approach the comparison of alternatives in these circumstances.

First and foremost, most authorities agree that the decision maker should earnestly seek appropriate quantitative measures of benefits and disbenefits and adopt them whenever this course of action is acceptable and feasible and necessary to the choice between alternatives. Having adopted these measures with a clear conscience, the decision maker has available a number of powerful methods and techniques involving quantitative measures to assist in the decision making process. Second, the decision maker should avoid the temptation of adopting quantitative measures merely for the sake of simplifying the decision process or of using a particular methodology. The penalties for yielding to this temptation may be severe in terms of wrong conclusions and partial rather than complete appreciation of a decision situation. Third, the decision maker should take heart in the fact that most individuals are able at least to express preferences between alternatives. Furthermore, there are methods and techniques available to assist the decision making process that can be used when only the preferences of the participants are available. These methods and techniques are described in later sections of the text, primarily in Chapters 5 and 8.

SUMMARY

The purpose of the establishment of quantitative measures of benefits and disbenefits is to allow comparison of the effectiveness of alternative courses of action in a decision situation in numeric terms. Many benefits and disbenefits can be expressed in terms of well understood factors such as profit and cost, which can be measured in dollars. It may be much more difficult to find quantitative measures in which to assess benefits and disbenefits in other circumstances.

Two particular types of measurement arise in the search for quantitative measures: those of efficiency and effectiveness. Efficiency usually relates to the economic use of resources. Effectiveness is concerned with the degree of achievement of objectives. Care should be taken to choose measures that relate to the objectives of the participants in the decision situation under consideration. Measures of efficiency may not be appropriate to assess effectiveness of achieving objectives in many situations.

Adoption of inappropriate quantitative measures of benefits and disbenefits can distort the results of analysis on which decisions are based. In circumstances in which readily appreciable quantitative measures are not available, it may be possible to adopt proxy measures of benefits and dis-benefits. A proxy measure is a measure of a factor that is not exactly the benefit or disbenefit under consideration, but which is closely enough related to it to provide a realistic indication of the consequences of a course of action. It is important in using proxy measures that no significant aspect of the benefits and disbenefits in a situation be left unrepresented. It is necessary, also, to ensure that the choice of proxy measures does not build bias into the analysis.

The natural desire for a quantitative basis for comparison between alternatives has led to the development of the concept of utility. Techniques have been put forward by which the utilities of an individual for a range of amounts of a commodity can be measured. A number of experiments have been carried out in which the utility functions of individuals have been determined. Although the concept of utility seems intuitively acceptable at first sight, there are many reservations that throw doubt on its usefulness in practical decision making. The most forceful of these reservations concerns the manner in which utility can be measured. Even given that utility can be measured, these measurements are at best descriptive of past behavior. The use of utility to predict future decision making behavior is subject to serious question. There are also major reservations about the combination of the utilities of a number of individuals into a function on which group decisions can be based.

In these circumstances, the individual decision maker is advised to adopt quantitative measures of benefits and disbenefits whenever these measures truly represent progress towards achievement of objectives. It is necessary to resist the temptation to use quantitative measures purely to simplify analysis or in order to use a particular analytical technique. If no appropriate quantitative measures can be found, the decision maker should revert to the establishment of preferences between alternatives. Adequate analytical techniques using only such preferences are available to aid in the decision making process.

PRACTICAL DECISION SITUATIONS

3.1 The Newtown Transportation Authority

The Newtown Transportation Authority is considering the possibility of constructing an addition to its rapid-transit system. The addition would consist of a rail line linking the airport to existing rail and bus routes. Several alternative routes exist for this rail link. A number of user groups and representatives of the community have expressed views about the desirability of the new rail link and about the alternative routes available. You have been hired as a consultant to suggest methods of assessing the benefits and disbenefits of the alternatives in a manner appropriate to the objectives of all of the participants in the decision situation.

3.2 The Modern Manufacturing Company

The Modern Manufacturing Company has four major objectives that appear in its statement to shareholders. These objectives can be summarized as follows:

1. To provide shareholders with a return on their investment appropriate to conditions existing now and in the future.
2. To conduct business in a manner that demonstrates social responsibility of the company toward the communities in which it operates.
3. To continually seek opportunities to diversify the operations of the company in a manner that will keep the company abreast of changes in its operating environment.
4. To provide a climate within the company conducive to good relations with its employees at all levels.

The company needs to devise measures of progress toward the achievement of these objectives. What quantitative measures, including proxy measures, do you think would be appropriate?

3.3 The Interstate Power Authority

The Interstate Power Authority has plans to build a large new power station at a site near a small town on the U.S.-Canadian border. The site is ideally located with respect to markets for the power that will be generated and with regard to the services the site will need. A meeting is to be held in the area at which the Authority hopes to convince members of the local community of the benefits that will accrue from the construction of the station. Members of the community are likely to question the basis for assessing these benefits. What steps would you take on behalf of the Authority to prepare for the meeting?

3.4 The Newstate Manufacturing Company

The Newstate Manufacturing Company must decide which of a number of sites located close to a major population center is most appropriate for a new industrial plant. What might be the measures in both direct and proxy categories that could be used in making a comparison between the alternative sites? Which of these measures might be appropriate to the objectives of the company in this situation and which might refer to the objectives of the community?

DISCUSSION TOPICS

1. Why is money so often selected as a medium for measuring the benefits and disbenefits of alternative courses of action? Is there any other commodity that has similar appeal, and if so, why?

2. Can you think of any practical situations in which maximum efficiency does not coincide with maximum effectiveness?

3. Can you describe any practical situations in which quantitative measures of benefits or disbenefits were used ill-advisedly in decision making?

4. What are the advantages and possible disadvantages of using proxy measures? How can the use of an inappropriate proxy measure distort the results of an analysis upon which decisions are to be based?

5. Do you think it is useful to construct a utility curve in the form proposed by Friedman-Savage or Markowitz? To what uses can such a curve be put?

6. What reservations do you have about the measurement of utility by the standard gamble technique? Would these reservations cause you to reject the concept of utility altogether?

7. What is the relationship between measurements of the utility of one person to those concerning another person? Can comparisons be made between individuals on the basis of such measurements?

8. How can a utility function representing the preferences of a group of two or more persons be constructed from their individual utility functions? Are there any reasons why such a joint utility function cannot be useful in making a joint decision?

9. Use the standard gamble technique to establish a utility function describing your own approach to monetary gain and loss. Try to do the same for the part of your company or organization for which you have decision making responsibility. Note any differences.

10. Do managers in modern corporations operate in a manner that would allow the Von Neumann-Morgenstern method of measurement of interval scale utility to be made? If not, what do you consider to be the major characteristics of managers that would cause a breakdown in the analysis?

REFERENCES

1. Hatry, Harry P., "Measuring the Effectiveness of Non-Defense Public Programs," *Operations Research*, Vol 18, No 5, Sept/Oct 1970, pp 772–784.

2. Dorfman, R. (ed), *Measuring Benefits of Government Investments*, The Brookings Institution, 1965.

3. Prest, A. R. and Turvey, R., "Cost-Benefit Analysis: A Survey," *The Economic Journal*, No 300, Vol LXXV, December 1965, pp 683–735.

4. *Commission on the Third London Airport*, Report, HMSO 1971; Papers and Proceedings, Vol 7, HMSO 1970.

5. Barker, P. and Button, K., *Case Studies in Economic Analysis 2*, Henemann Educational Books, 1975: this book contains a number of other references to the work of the Roskill Commission.

6. Hatry, H. P., *op cit*, pp 779–780.

7. Bishop, J. and Cicchetti, C., "Some Institutional and Conceptual Thoughts on the Measurement of Indirect and Intangible Benefits and Costs" in Peskin, H. M. and Seskin, E. P. (eds), *Cost Benefit Analysis and Water Pollution Policy*, The Urban Institute, Washington, D. C., 1975, pp 105–126.

8. Gorham, W., "Improvement of the Allocation of Public Funds" in Paelinck, J. H. P. (ed) *Programming for Europe's Collective Needs*, North Holland, 1970, pp 136–168.

9. For an historical account of this work, see L. J. Savage, *The Foundations of Statistics*, Wiley, 1954, pp 91–104, reprinted in Ward Edwards and Amos Tversky (eds) *Decision Making*, Penguin Books, 1967, pp 96–110.

10. Friedman, M. and Savage, L. J., "The Utility Analysis of Choices Involving Risk," *Journal of Political Economy*, Vol 56, 1948, pp 279–304.

11. Vickrey, W., "Measuring Marginal Utility by Reactions to Risk," *Econometrica*, Vol 13, 1945, pp 319–333.

12. Markowitz, H. "The Utility of Wealth" in *Mathematical Models of Human Behavior*, Dunlap, 1955, pp 54–62.

13. Von Neumann, J. and Morgenstern, O., *Theory of Games and Economic Behavior*, 3rd Ed., Princeton University Press, 1953.

14. Swalm, R. O, "Utility Theory-Insights into Risk Taking," *Harvard Business Review*, Nov/Dec 1966.

15. Spetzler, C. S. "The Development of a Corporate Risk Policy for Capital Investment Decisions," *IEEE Transactions on Systems Science and Cybernetics*, Vol SSC-4, No 3, September 1968.

16. Cramer, R. H. and Smith, B. E., "Decision Models for Selection of Research Projects," *The Engineering Economist*, Vol 9, No 2, Winter, 1964.

17. Mosteller, F. and Nogee, P., "An Experimental Measurement of Utility," *Journal of Political Economy*, Vol 59, No 5, 1951, pp 371–404: reprinted in W. Edwards and A. Tversky (eds), *Decision Making*, Penguin Books, 1967, pp 124–169.

18. Marchak, J., "Actual and Consistent Decision Behavior," *Behavioral Science*, April 1964, p 104.

 *Chapter Four*

Methods for Dealing With Uncertainty

INTRODUCTION

Uncertainty is a factor in a very large proportion of decision situations faced by managers in modern organizations. It arises from an absence of complete information about the particular situation under consideration. It results in lack of confidence on the part of the decision maker that

1. a formulation of the situation based on the available information contains all the factors that bear upon the decision;
2. the correct numerical values have been assigned to some or all of the parameters involved in the situation; and
3. the future state of the environment in which the courses of action selected in the decision making process must be implemented will be as predicted at the time of the decision.

The effect of these uncertainties is that the outcome of the decision situation actually experienced may be different from that which is estimated during the decision process itself.

The effects of uncertainty and methods for dealing with it are considered in stages in this chapter. As a first step, the effects of variation of numeric values used in models of the decision process is discussed. The treatment is then broadened to cover situations in which there is uncertainty about the formulation of the decision problem and about the outcome resulting from selection of a particular course of action. Decision making under conditions of uncertainty is seen as a process in which the attitudes and behavior of the individuals involved have a considerable effect on the course of action chosen. The discussion continues with the introduction of probability as a means of quantifying uncertainty. The use of decision trees and the advantages and disadvantages of this methodology are covered in detail. The effects of human behavior in decision situations involving uncertainty and the attitudes and methodology that individuals adopt intuitively when faced with uncertainty in a decision situation are emphasized in this chapter. The decision situations covered are those in Category 3 of Table 1-1.

A FIRST INTRODUCTION OF UNCERTAINTY INTO DECISION ANALYSIS

A first step in the introduction of uncertainty into the decision making process is known as *sensitivity analysis*.[1, 2] This type of analysis investigates the effect of deviations from the values assigned to the parameters in a model of the decision situation. In the simplest cases, this investigation is done one parameter at a time. For example, in the product mix situation analyzed in Chapter 2, the profit contributed per unit produced by Process 2 is $5. The optimal product mix was found to contain no units produced by Process 2 and the total profit from the optimal product mix was $695/7. Using the techniques of sensitivity analysis it is possible to calculate that if the profit contributed by a unit produced by Process 2 increased by 3/7 of a dollar, the original solution would not remain optimal. In these circumstances, a different mix of products would yield more profit. In similar fashion, it can be determined that the original solution would not remain optimal if the contribution to profit of a unit from Process 4 were greater than $12½.

A similar type of analysis can be used to investigate the effects of changing the availability of any one of the materials used in the production process. For example, it can be shown that the original optimal solution to the product mix problem ceases to be feasible if the amount of material B that is available is less than 73⅓ units rather than the 120 units originally assumed in the analysis. In similar fashion, it can be determined that a new and improved solution to the decision situation can be found if a new production process becomes available with a unit profit contribution that is more than $14.

This type of analysis provides useful information about the sensitivity of the choice of a course of action to variations in the parameters that describe a decision situation. It allows a check to be made on whether the original choice would be altered if the values assigned to these parameters in the original analysis were changed. If the original choice remains unaffected in the face of significant changes in these parameters, there is reason to believe that the selection will apply over a wide range of conditions. On the other hand, if small variations in the parameters involved cause major changes in the apparently desirable courses of action, must less confidence can be placed in the choice of any one of them if there is some uncertainty in the decision situation under consideration.

Sensitivity analysis is much more complex if two or more parameters are subject to variation at the same time. In these circumstances, the analysis involves investigation of the effects of groups of simultaneous deviations from the values assumed in the original treatment. The amount of calculation required in such an investigation may be very great. If many parameters are to be varied in these calculations, the simple technique of sensitivity analysis may be less practicable than other methods of treating uncertainty in a decision situation.

THE USE OF PROBABILISTIC MODELS

One such alternative method is the construction of a probabilistic model of the decision situation. In such models, each parameter is represented not only by a single value as in the case without uncertainty, but by a probability distribution representing all values that the parameter may take and their probabilities of occurrence. The solution procedures for such models take into account all possible combinations of values of the parameters involved by means of analytical manipulation of the probability distributions.[3] These combinations may be thought of as an infinite set of alternatives on a continuous scale. One of the most successful and useful applications of probabilistic models in practical situations is to the investigation of queues.

Queues are a common experience in modern life. Cars line up at a toll booth on a highway or before proceeding over a bridge. People queue at the windows of a bank and at the check-out counters of a supermarket. Incoming calls sometimes have to wait to be connected to an airline reservation clerk. Soft drink bottles are lined up to be capped in a production facility. Parcels wait to be sorted in a post office. All of these situations have a number of characteristics in common. They all concern a population of people or things that require a service. They can obtain this service in a channel that can normally serve one arrival at a time. In many cases, such as at a bank or in a telephone exchange, there are a number of parallel channels available to service the arrivals. The general characteristics of a single channel queueing system are illustrated in Fig. 4-1. A multichannel system can be envisaged from this diagram by allowing arrivals to select any one of the service channels on entering the system.

Generally speaking, arrivals at the service channel desire that the re-

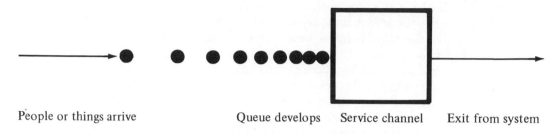

People or things arrive   Queue develops   Service channel   Exit from system

FIG. 4-1.   General characteristics of a single-channel queueing system.

quired service start immediately. However, the service takes a certain time to perform. If a previous arrival is in the middle of this service time, a new arrival must wait in a queue for service, or in a multichannel system switch to another channel. The time spent in the queue is called the queueing time and the sum of the queueing time and the service time is called the waiting time. Analytical models are available that relate the queueing and waiting time to the characteristics of the queueing system. These models have as input the following factors:

1. *The arrival pattern* of units entering the queueing system. This pattern is usually expressed in terms of the probability distribution of arrival times of the units. In most cases, units do not arrive at uniform intervals. A common experience is that arrivals occur at random times but at a certain average rate (that is, the number of units arriving until a specific time has a Poisson distribution). Arrival patterns often vary with time of day or some other factor.

2. *The number of channels.*

3. *The queue discipline,* which determines the method by which the next unit is selected for service from those waiting in the queue. A common queue discipline is first-in-first-out, denoted by FIFO. The FIFO discipline is usually enforced in queues involving people, such as in a bank or at a ticket window. However, priorities may exist which generate other queue disciplines.

4. *The service mechanism,* which defines when service is available in a channel, how many units can be served at a time, how long service takes, and any possible variations in the service time to meet the needs of the arrivals.

Formulae linking these factors with some characteristics of the queue that develops in a system are given in Exhibit 4-1. It should be noted that these formulae apply only to the conditions stated in the exhibit. These conditions are typical of those found in many practical situations.

EXHIBIT 4-1. Analysis of a Single Channel Queueing System with Random Arrivals and Arbitrary Service Times[4]

Terminology

L = expected line length = the expected number of units in the queueing system
L_q = expected queue length = expected number of units awaiting service
= expected line length − number of units being served
W = expected waiting time in system (includes service time)
W_q = expected waiting time in the queue (excludes service time)
λ = mean arrival rate
μ = mean service rate
ρ = λ/μ = expected fraction of the time the serving channel is busy

Assumptions

1. arrivals at random times with average rate λ
2. service times for respective units are independent with some common probability distribution with mean $1/\mu$ and variance σ^2
3. $\rho = \lambda/\mu < 1$
4. queue discipline—FIFO

Formulae

Probability that no units are in the queueing system $P_0 = 1 - \rho$
Expected queue length
$$L_q = \frac{\lambda^2\sigma^2 + \rho^2}{2(1 - \rho)}$$
Expected line length $L = \rho + L_q$
Expected waiting time in the queue $W_q = L_q/\lambda$
Expected waiting time in the system $W = W_q + 1/\mu$
Notes 1. if the service time for each unit is constant $\sigma^2 = 0$
2. if the service times are exponentially distributed $\sigma^2 = 1/\mu^2$

However, different formulae are necessary if any of these conditions are changed.

Consider, for example, a large automobile repair shop which has a single check-out point for spare parts taken from a store. Mechanics requiring spare parts arrive at the check-out point during working hours at a constant mean rate of 15 per hour. A manual system is used for checking out the parts and it takes an average of 3.5 minutes to serve each arrival at the checkout point on a first-in–first-out basis. The service time is variable with variance equal to 1. Management has been investigating a computerized check out system that would reduce the average service time to 2.5 minutes and the variance to 0.75. A decision between the computerized and the existing system depends on the extent to which the new system would reduce the time lost by mechanics waiting for check out from the spare parts store.

Applying the formula from Exhibit 4-1 for L_q, the expected queue length, it can be seen that the expected number of mechanics awaiting service can be reduced from 3.31 to 0.57 by installing the computerized system. Furthermore, the expected waiting time for each mechanic can be reduced from 16.75 minutes with the present system to 4.77 minutes with the computerized system. A reduction in mean service time of 1 minute therefore reduces the time each mechanic spends on checking out by almost 12 minutes.

Results obtained from analysis of this sort are dependent on the conditions assumed to be present in the queueing system. They can vary substantially with changes in these assumptions. It is important, therefore, to ensure that mathematical formulae used in this type of analysis are appropriate to the conditions observed in the practical decision situations. Over-zealous application of convenient mathematical formulae is as undesirable in the consideration of queueing situations as it is in all of the other situations considered in this text.

Some probabilistic models are very complex and they may be very difficult to apply in practical decision situations. For example, it is quite rare that a probabilistic version of the linear programming model can be found to apply completely to a practical problem involving uncertainty. On the other hand, probabilistic models in dynamic programming are not significantly more difficult to solve than their deterministic counterparts.[5] In many cases where such models are applied, however, the amount of computation required to produce an acceptable solution may be very great.

In all applications of probabilistic models, some difficulty may be experienced in obtaining sufficient data on the relevant parameters to allow proper determination of the type of probability distribution that should be used to represent the existing uncertainty. In such circumstances, there may be a temptation to use easily manipulated probability distributions rather than observed data, in order to reduce the amount of analytical and computational work involved. Needless to say, this temptation should be resisted if there is any doubt that these probability distributions are appropriate to the problem at hand.

SIMULATION

In well defined situations where the data collected can be judged to fit well known probability distributions, the analytical techniques associated with probabilistic models can be applied with some degree of confidence. Unfortunately, the data collected cannot be said to fit such distributions in many practical decision situations. In such cases, the best recourse is to the technique of *simulation.*

The method of simulation has been covered extensively in the literature.[6, 7] It consists of the formulation of a detailed description of the operation or system under study, using practically observed relationships and possibly some mathematical models. This detailed description contains details of the relationships between all the variables and factors that are pertinent to the decision process at hand. The model that is formulated in this manner may refer to a single time point or it may cover a number of time periods appropriate to a sequential decision process. All data available on the variables and factors involved are stored in the simulation model, in the form in which they can be best represented.

Once the simulation model is constructed, a "run" of the decision process can be undertaken using the model to represent the practical decision situation. In this run, a value for each variable is sampled from the available data at random. These values are combined to arrive at a value of the objective function that has been selected as the measure of effectiveness for comparing alternatives in the situation under study. This single value of the objective function represents only one sample from a probabilistic distribution of that parameter. This distribution is then investigated by a series of repeated runs of the simulation model.

Consider, for example, the situation in which a company's customers call a central number to make reservations or to order from a catalog. The variables that are under the company's control are the number of inward telephone lines, the number of agents available to answer them, the time required to satisfy the customer's request, and the order in which incoming calls are handled. The variables not under the company's control include the rate at which calls are made by customers and their attitude to delays in attending to their requirements. The company needs to know the number of agents required at various times of the day in order to minimize the number of calls delayed or lost by virtue of delay, and in order to retain customer good will.

A decision situation of this nature is a candidate for treatment by the type of queueing model described earlier in this chapter. However, it may be that the distributions of the variables involved in the situation cannot be determined in detail or that they do not follow well known mathematical forms. In these circumstances, a simulation model of the telephone answering system can be written in which a history of a number of calls is traced. Data observed in actual operations can be used to represent both the arrival of calls and the time taken to service a call once it is received. In each of the runs of the simulation model, the actual arrival time of the call and the actual service time used can be sampled from the observed practical data. Since the simulation is designed to represent actual operations, measurements of system performance such as the average delay experienced by callers can be obtained. In addition, the simulation allows the effects of changes in the system being studied (such as an increase in the number of agents answering calls) to be investigated.

Large scale simulations are usually computer supported because they involve a considerable amount of manipulation of data. These simulations may be costly, especially if a large number of runs are necessary to produce the required degree of precision in estimating the distribution of the performance variables being studied. However, simulation may be the only method available in practical circumstances, if the data referring to the parameters involved cannot be fitted to easily manipulated probability distributions or if analytical methods cannot be devised to represent the decision process under study.

OUTPUT OF STUDIES INVOLVING UNCERTAINTY

The output of a study in which uncertainty is involved is not a single estimate of benefit or cost. It takes the form instead of a probability distribution of such a parameter. A typical form in which this output is expressed is shown in Fig. 4-2. This diagram indicates that there are a number of different possible values of the output parameter (shown on the horizontal axis) and that for each of these values there is a probability of occurrence (shown on the vertical axis). The most likely value of the output parameter is shown at the peak of the curve. However, there is a considerable spread of possible values of this parameter resulting from the uncertainty in the decision situations. The only statement that can be made as a result of output as shown in Fig. 4-2 concerns the most likely

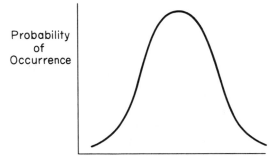

Output Parameter or Value of Objective Function
(expressed for example in money or time)

FIG. 4-2.   Output of a study involving uncertainty.

result of a course of action and the spread of results that is possible about that most likely result.

Suppose, for example, that a company is contemplating a sizeable capital investment and that two possible projects A and B are being studied.[8] After considerable analysis, the probability of each of a range of percentage returns on investment have been determined for each project in the form of Fig. 4-2. These percentage returns have been converted into the form shown in Fig. 4-3 in order to facilitate comparison between the results expected from the two projects. The curves shown in Fig. 4-3 represent the probabilities that a particular rate of return will be achieved or exceeded for each of the projects.

It can be seen from Fig. 4-3 that the average rate of return of the two projects is about the same. However, the spread of rate of return with Project B is considerably higher than with Project A. Choice of Project B would involve a much higher risk of a lower rate of return but at the same time a much greater chance of a higher rate of return than Project A. Selection of Project B would indicate a willingness on the part of the individual making the choice to risk a bad outcome in order to have the chance of a very good outcome. Choice of Project A would indicate a much more conservative approach to decision making.

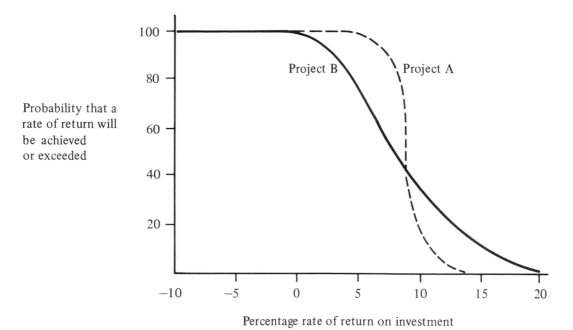

FIG. 4-3.   Comparison of results of evaluation of two projects.

INDIVIDUAL BEHAVIOR IN DECISION MAKING IN THE PRESENCE OF UNCERTAINTY

Decision making behavior of individuals in the presence of uncertainty is influenced by their attitude to risk. A conservative individual who is very averse to risk would probably concentrate on the possible adverse outcomes in the choice between alternatives. An individual with a more entrepreneurial attitude would no doubt stress the possible beneficial outcomes in a decision situation.

Consider, for example, an individual who is the owner of a manufacturing plant that serves an expanding market. This individual is faced with a decision regarding the expansion of the capacity of the plant. The alternatives are to build a large extension, to build a small extension, or to remain with the existing facilities. The choice between these alternatives is mostly influenced by the possible future size of the market for the product manufactured at the plant. Let us suppose for simplicity at this stage that the possible states of the future market for the product can be characterized by the descriptions low, medium, or high. Let us assume, further, that it is possible to assess the profit that would accrue for each alternative for each of the three future market conditions. These profits are shown in Table 4-1 in terms relative to the alternative of staying with the present plant.

The alternative of staying with the present plant provides no change in net profit in each possible future market condition. Building the large extension gives a high profit if the market is high, but a large loss if the market is low. The alternative of building the small extension allows the best profitability increase in a medium future market, but also positive contributions to profit in both of the other conditions.

The owner could argue in the following manner. The minimum profit situation for each of the available alternatives is as shown in Table 4-2. The alternative of building a small extension results in a maximum amongst these minimum profits. It is the alternative which is the most advantageous to the decision maker under the worst conditions.

TABLE 4-1. The Plant Expansion Situation

	Possible Future States of the Market		
	Low	Medium	High
Available Alternatives			
1. Stay with present plant	0	0	0
2. Build small extension	50	300	200
3. Build large extension	−500	100	600

TABLE 4-2.   Minimum Profits for Each Alternative in the Plant Expansion Situation

Available Alternatives	Minimum Profits
1. Stay with present plant	0
2. Build small extension	50
3. Build large extension	−500

Maximin and Minimax

Decision making behavior in which an individual consciously or unconsciously determines the minimum benefit for each of the alternatives and then selects the alternative that gives the maximum of these minima is called *maximin*. Note that if the decision maker is endeavoring to minimize cost, the approach would require minimization of the maximum cost. This principle is called *minimax*. Conceptually, maximin and minimax are the same thing, one referring to benefits and the other to costs.

Maximin and minimax are principles of conservatism. They were originally described as criteria of pessimism, by which the worst that can happen with each alternative is investigated and the alternative for which the worst outcome is most advantageous to the decision maker is selected.[9] In the example shown in Table 4-1, maximin avoids the possibility of a loss of 500 by giving up the possibilitiy of a gain of 600. Application of the maximin principle in this case allows at least a gain of 50 and possibly a gain of 200 or 300. It represents play-safe behavior which recommends itself to individuals who are risk-averse.

It is interesting to note that maximin and minimax can be applied equally well to situations in which the outcomes cannot be expressed in quantitative terms. Consider, for example, the simple problem of whether to carry a raincoat on leaving the house early in the morning when there is a threat of rain later in the day. This problem can be summarized as in Table 4-3. In this situation, the worst that can happen if the first alternative is selected is that the decision maker may have carried the raincoat unnecessarily. Under the second alternative the worst outcome is that he gets wet. Assuming that the decision maker has a greater preference for remaining dry than for getting wet, use of the minimax aproach would result in selection of the alternative of carrying the raincoat.

Maximax

The opposite to behavior leading to maximin or minimax selection of alternatives is that of the risk taking or entrepreneurial individual. Hur-

TABLE 4-3. The Raincoat Problem

	Future States of the World	
	Rain	*No Rain*
Available Alternatives		
1. Carry raincoat	Dry and satisfied at judgment	Dry, but has carried raincoat unnecessarily
2. Do not carry raincoat	Wet	Dry without having carried raincoat

wicz has suggested that if a decision maker feels lucky or has a conviction that the outcome of a decision situation will be favorable, the alternative should be selected that provides the maximum benefit.[10] This type of decision making behavior can be formalized by writing down the maximum benefit for each available alternative and then choosing the alternative that provides the maximum of these maximum benefits. This optimistic approach to decision making has naturally been called *maximax*. In the plant expansion situation in Table 4-1, the maximax alternative is to build the large extension.

Hurwicz went further to sugggest that positions between the extremes of optimism and pessimism could be represented by a coefficient of optimism, which takes the value 0 with maximin or minimax behvaior and 1 with a maximax approach. This degree of precision in the quantification of human behavior does not seem to be applicable in practice. Managers are not observed saying to themselves, "I feel 60 per cent optimistic today". Nevertheless, its mention may be useful, if only to point out that a range of behavior is possible between the positions that lead to the maximin/minimax and maximax criteria for selection of alternatives in practical decision situations.

Regret

Another type of decision making behavior is closely linked to the concept of opportunity costs, which is well known to economists. A number of authors have suggested that decision makers are influenced in their choice between alternatives by the difference between the benefits associated with any particular alternative and the maximum benefit that could be expected by the "correct" choice for a particular future state of the world. This type of behavior can be represented by constructing a table showing a quantity called "regret" for each of the alternatives available to the decision maker.[11] Regret represents the loss that a decision maker suffers because the exact future state of the world was not known at the time

TABLE 4-4.   Regret in the Plant Expansion Problem

	Future States of the Market		
	Low	Medium	High
Available Alternatives			
1. Stay with present plant	50	300	600
2. Build small extension	0	0	400
3. Build large extension	550	200	0

of selection of an alternative. It can be regarded as the cost of lost opportunities. The regret for each of the alternatives in each of the future states of the market in the plant expansion situation is shown in Table 4-4. The figures for regret are obtained in the following manner. If the market turns out to be low, the decision maker would have done best by selecting the alternative of building a small extension. This is the position of zero regret. If the alternative of staying with the present plant had been selected, the regret is the 50 units of benefit that might have been obtained by building the small extension. The other regret figures in Table 4-4 can be obtained from the outcomes shown in Table 4-1 in the same way.

The idea of regret can be combined with that of minimax to obtain a description of decision making behavior that is called *minimax regret.* Note that the term minimax is used here because we are seeking to minimize the maximum loss of opportunity. In the particular example chosen, the choice on the basis of minimax regret is to build the small extension, since the minimum maximum regret that would be experienced in that case is 400 units.

Uncertainty Avoidance

Studies of decision making in modern organizations indicate that individuals and organizations often adopt strategies designed to assist them in avoiding uncertainty.[12] These strategies sometimes stress the solution of short term problems rather than the development of long term plans. In this way, the difficulties of anticipation of future events and future conditions in the environment in which they must operate are minimized. Individuals and organizations may try to negotiate and control the environment in which the outcome of their selection between alternatives will be experienced. Courses of action are often selected on the basis of the degree of control that the individual or organization is thought to have over the implementation. Individuals sometimes seek to marshal human and financial resources in such a way as to ensure a favorable outcome once they have committed themselves to a course of action.[13] In other circumstances, they may align themselves with a decision once it is made even if they had not previously agreed with the course of action selected in order to avoid the appearance of disagreement and dissonance.[14]

Bounded Rationality

A somewhat different description of the manner in which individuals make decisions has been put forward by Simon and March.[15, 16] They contend that two types of decision makers can be observed in practical situations. The first of these types, called "economic man," selects the best alternative from those available to him after a process of analysis that allows a choice to be made on the basis of maximization of benefits. On the other hand, his colleague called "administrative man," is content with a less complete process of analysis, primarily because he is aware of the uncertainty that is a pervasive characteristic of most decision situations. The "administrative man" makes his choice on the basis of a simple appreciation of the situation that takes into account only those factors regarded as most relevant and crucial. Instead of trying to consider all alternatives, "administrative man" operates in accordance with a principle of bounded rationality and seeks a course of action regarded as satisfactory or good enough. Simon referred to this sort of decision making behavior as "satisficing."

The distinction between "economic" and "administrative" man illustrates the difference between the two main approaches to the study of decision making over the past thirty years. The individual who is devoted to a mathematical and quantitative approach to decision making believes that any decision situation can eventually be modeled and an optimum solution found. The person who is less inclined to such an approach believes that in many situations no strictly optimal solution is possible. In such circumstances, the manner in which a decision situation is resolved depends upon the actions of the individuals involved and upon their behavior in the situation as they perceive it. Clearly, there is much to say on behalf of each point of view. The recommended approach in most practical situations is to undertake as much quantitative analysis as is feasible, while at the same time viewing the choice between alternatives from as many aspects as possible. The ultimate selection of a course of action can then be made using the experience, judgment, and intuition of the decision maker in the light of as much analytical comparison as is possible under the circumstances.

THE USE OF SUBJECTIVE PROBABILITY ESTIMATES

Many of us use probability as a quantitative expression of uncertainty. We will say, for example, that we think the possibility of rain tomorrow is

40 per cent. This estimate means nothing in itself. It does not mean that if it rains tomorrow we will get 40 per cent wet. It also probably does not mean that we have studied all past circumstances similar to those of today and that in all these situations it rained on 40 per cent of the following days. An expression of probability of this nature represents instead a degree of belief about an event. It is subjective and personalistic in that it is derived from judgment based on a set of information that is personal, at least in part. Note that a probability statement of this sort is not necessarily made only about a future event of which the outcome is uncertain. It can be made about a past event, the result of which is unknown, in exactly the same way. For example, when asked about the result of a hockey game that was played in 1970 between the Montreal Candians and the Chicago Black Hawks I might say I did not know the result for sure. I would estimate, however, that there is an 80 per cent chance that the Canadians won the game. This opinion would be based on the information available to me about the general performance of the two teams at that time.

Subjective probability is different from the type of probability often taught in introductory courses on the subject.[17] The other sort of probability (which may be called objective probability) is based on the frequency of occurrence of an event in a series of past observations. Suppose, for example, that a coin is tossed a very large number of times and that the number of heads in the trials is equal to the number of tails. The objective probability of a head in any toss with that coin is then said to be one half, based on the frequency of occurrence in the trials. In contrast, subjective probability estimates are usually made about a single occurrence of an event. Suppose, for example, that one is in the habit of catching the 5:40 p.m. plane from a certain city. It is possible to express a subjective probability based on past experience that the plane will be on time tomorrow. This estimate may, however, be different for different persons, because it is based on personal judgment and on personal information sets. Furthermore, the probability estimate may change if new information is received. For example, if a weather bulletin mentions the possibility of fog in the region tomorrow, every person's estimate of whether the plane will be on time tomorrow may be subject to change. The amount of change will depend on each individual's evaluation of the new information, once again based on experience of past events.

A number of empirical studies have been undertaken to investigate the nature of subjective probability estimates in situations where the "true" (or frequency-school) probability is known, such as in the toss of a coin.[18] The general conclusion of these studies is that individuals are not consistent in their formulation of subjective probabilities. For example, mathematical probability theory requires that the sum of the probabilities of members of a set of mutually exclusive and exhaustive events (such as a plane early, late, or on time) must be equal to 1. Experiments have shown that this is not always so when individuals estimate subjective probabilities. Sometimes individuals may say at one time, for example, that the probability of the plane's being on time tomorrow is 0.8 and then later when attention is distracted from the earlier estimate say that the probability of its being late tomorrow is 0.4. Again, in experiments with groups of individuals, the average subjective probabilities for the lower probability events have been shown to be larger than the objective probabilities, whereas the average subjective probabilities for higher probability events are smaller than the corresponding objective probabilities.

Two other considerations that may affect subjective probabilities are individual perceptions of skill and luck. Each of us has a perception of these factors based on our own experiences and on observation of those of others. These perceptions are highly subjective, and may not be based on all the available information. For example, we may refer to a successful man as lucky in order to explain a success that might have been ours in different circumstances. All of these factors may be present in a situation confronting an individual decision maker. Considerable care must be taken, therefore, in the conversion of opinions to subjective probabilities. If this can be done with confidence, however, it provides a means by which decision situations in which there is considerable uncertainty can be treated in a somewhat more quantitative fashion.

Returning to the Plant Expansion situation treated earlier in this chapter, suppose that the decision maker estimates that the probabilities of a low, medium, and high future market are 1/4, 1/4, and 1/2 respectively. It is now possible to calculate the expected value of the outcome for each alternative by multiplying the outcome for each of the future states of the market by the subjective probability of that state actually occurring. For example, the expected value of the outcome of building a small extension is $1/4 \times 50 + 1/4 \times 300 + 1/2 \times 200 = 187.5$, as shown in Table 4-5. Some authors suggest that a decision can be made in these circumstances on the basis of the maximum expected value of the outcomes of the alternatives. In the above case, the choice according to this criterion would be to build

TABLE 4-5. The Plant Expansion Problem—Calculation of Expected Values

	Future States of the Market			
	Low	Medium	High	
Subjective probabilities	¼	¼	½	Expected Outcomes
Available Alternatives				
Stay with present plant	0	0	0	0
Build small extension	50	300	200	187.5
Build large extension	−500	100	600	200

the large extension. There are, however, serious reservations with respect to the use of the maximum expected value criterion in many types of decision situations. These reservations and the counter arguments to them are discussed in the next section.

ACCEPTABILITY OF THE CRITERION OF MAXIMUM EXPECTED VALUE

The main argument advanced against unrestricted use of maximum expected value as a criterion in decision making is that it is appropriate only to decision situations that are encountered many times in essentially the same form. In a single encounter, the outcome actually experienced may be very different from the expected value for the alternative selected. Suppose, for example, that two individuals agree to play a game in which one of them tosses a fair coin. If the result is a head, it is agreed that the individual tossing the coin pays the other $200. If the outcome is a tail, the individual tossing the coin receives $100 from the other player. Since the coin is fair the probabilities of the two outcomes are each one half. The expected value of the game to the second individual is thus $1/2 \times \$200 + 1/2 (-100) = \$50$. On the basis of maximization of expected value, the second individual must decide to play, since the expected value of playing is $50 compared to zero value of not taking part in the game.

In a single play of the game, however, neither player gives or receives the expected value. The second individual receives $200 or gives $100 depending on the result of the toss of the coin. If that individual is averse to the loss of $100, he might prefer not to take part in a single play of the game, even though the expected value of the game is seen as positive. In the same way, the manager involved in the plant expansion situation might prefer to build the small extension rather than the large one, even though the expected value of the outcome for the large extension is greater. In making a decision of that sort, the individual concerned would demonstrate an aversion to the loss that would be incurred if the future market turned out to be low. In the coin tossing game, the second individual would be well advised to take part if he were assured of a large number of repeats of the play under the same circumstances. In the plant expansion situation, however, it is unlikely that the manager involved would experience a second situation with exactly the same characteristics. He almost certainly would not be in a position to make a second decision if his first encounter with the situation resulted in a sizeable loss.

A number of authors have pointed out that many persons consistently choose an alternative with a lower expected value in practical situations.[19] For example, people continually pay for tickets in lotteries where the chance of winning a prize is very low and the expected value of the alternative of entering the lottery is less than that of not participating. The probable reason for this behvior is that the loss represented by the cost of the lottery ticket is regarded as small. The decision to enter a lottery is also probably made on the basis of entertainment value rather than the expected value of the outcome in monetary terms. In similar fashion, people buy insurance to guard them against a crippling loss even though the expected value of this course of action is lower than that of not buying insurance. They buy this insurance because they do not expect the event against which they insure (such as a house burning down) to take place many times and they are not prepared to experience the large loss that would result. It is significant that many persons are prepared to assume the burden of insurance against small losses (as in the deductible clause of automobile insurance) rather than select the course of buying insurance that has a lower expected value.

Proponents of the criterion of maximum expected value maintain that the argument with regard to the inapplicability of the criterion in a single resolution of a decision situation loses its force if the outcome is considered in terms of the utility of the decision maker for the outcome, rather than monetary value. If the disutility for loss of the decision maker is very great in the coin tossing situation (they point out), the expected utility of playing the game to that individual becomes negative. Application of the criterion of maximum expected value then leads the decision maker to the option of refusing the play. Suppose, as illustration, that the utility of the decision maker for a \$200 gain is +200 units and the disutility for a \$100 loss is −1000 units. The expected value of the game to that decision maker is then $1/2 \times 200 + 1/2 (-1000) = -400$ units. Under these circumstances, the option of not playing, which is zero, has the maximum expected utility. However, the validity of this position depends upon the ability to measure the utility of individuals for outcomes with some degree of accuracy. The possibility of making such measurements has been questioned in Chapter 3.

The choice to use or not to use the criterion of maximum expected value is left to the reader. Clearly it is applicable in repeated encounters with the same decision situation. In a situation which is likely to be encountered once, however, the position taken here is that the results of the use of criterion of maximization of expected value should be considered along with those of other criteria such as maximin and minimax regret. The ultimate choice between alternatives can then be left to the individual who can review the results of application of a number of criteria before making a selection on the basis of personal judgment, experience, and intuition.

An Interesting Historical Diversion

In an article written in the early eighteenth century (and recently translated[20]) the Swiss mathematician and philosopher Daniel Bernoulli discusses a number of situations in which the principle of maximizing expected monetary value does not seem to be appropriate. The most famous of these situations is known as the St. Petersburg Paradox. This paradox concerns a hypothetical game in which one player proposes to toss a "fair" coin as many times as necessary to get a head. As soon as a toss results in a head, the process stops. The first player agrees, as part of the game, to give a second player $1 if the head appears on the first toss, $2 if this occurs at the second toss, $4 at the third, and so on. This arrangement can be stated generally as an agreement to pay 2^{n-1} if a head appears at the nth toss. The point of the game is to ask the second player how much he is willing to pay to take part in the game.

The second player can argue as follows. The probability of a head at the first toss of the fair coin is 1/2. This probability holds for each toss of the coin. Assuming that the coin tossings are independent events, the chance of a head occurring at the *second toss* is $1/2 \times 1/2 = 1/4$. In general form, the chance of a head occurring at the nth toss is $(1/2)^n$. The various future states of the world can then be regarded as a head appearing at each of the tosses from the first to the nth, where n can be assumed to become as large as necessary to obtain a head. The second player has two options: to play or not to play. The expected value of not playing is zero. The expected value of taking part in the game to the second player at each toss of the coin can be written in general form (for the nth toss) as the product of the payment expected ($\$2^{n-1}$) and the probability of a head occurring ($(1/2)^n$). This product can be seen to be equal to 1/2 for each toss of the coin. The sum of the outcomes to the second player is therefore equal to 1/2 summed over all tosses of the coin for $n = 1$ to $n =$ infinity. This sum is of course infinity. The paradox is, therefore, that the expected value to the second player of taking part in the game is infinite. If the second player makes a decision on the basis of maximizing the expected value, the choice must be to play. That player should, in addition, be willing to pay any price for the privilege of playing. However, to pay a very high price would clearly be a bad decision if there is only one play of the game.

In discussing this paradox, Bernoulli suggested that the criterion used should be maximization of the expected utility of money. He argued that the increase in utility linked with an increase in an amount of money should be less as the amount of money grows larger. The utilities of the larger amounts of money payable when no head appears in the earlier tosses of the coin are then proportionately much less. Under these conditions, the expected utility for the second player approaches a finite value as the number of tosses increases. The amount of money he should be willing to pay should therefore be limited in similar fashion. This resolves the dilemma of an infinite expected value. However, it does not seem to resolve all the aspects of the paradox.

The introduction of subjective probability throws a new light on the St.

Petersburg paradox. Bernoulli's explanation goes part way in that it points out that the value of playing the game to the second player is finite if a utility function such as he proposed is used. A further explanation of the paradox can be seen in terms of this player's subjective estimates of the probabilities of no head occurring in each of the tosses. The experience and information available to most people would suggest that the chance of no head appearing until say, the sixth or eighth toss, is so small as to be essentially zero. Despite the very large payoffs associated with these rare events, the average player may therefore be expected to neglect them altogether. Such a player would then base the payment offered for taking part in the game on the subjective expected utility of the alternative of playing, taking into account the payoffs and probabilities in the first few throws only. This behavior would result in a considerably reduced estimate of the value to the second player of taking part in the game.

DECISION TREES

Some types of decision situations in which uncertainty about future conditions is a major factor can be illustrated by the use of decision trees.[21, 22, 23] A decision tree is a diagram in which the alternatives available to the decision maker are shown as possible paths in a tree-like structure. The occurrence of future conditions is denoted by a branching of the tree at some time after the decision has been made.

Suppose, for example, that a company is planning to drill for oil at a particular site. If the drilling encounters normal conditions, the gain from the operation will be 24 units of profit. However, if the drilling encounters difficult conditions, there will be a loss on the operation of 20 units. It is not known whether the drilling will be normal or difficult at the site until it is too late to prevent a loss. The company expects to undertake a large number of drilling operations of essentially the same type in the course of the next 12 months. This description of a decision situation often encountered in the oil industry has been simplified for the sake of clarity in discussing the methodology of decision trees. The alternatives available to the oil company in this description of the situation are to commit resources to a drilling operation in the area concerned or not to drill in the area at all. These alternatives and the outcomes for the company under normal and difficult drilling conditions are shown in Table 4-6.

This decision situation can be illustrated in a decision tree diagram as illustrated in Fig. 4-4. The decision maker is placed to the left of the first branch in the tree in this diagram. He or she is engaged in considering the question "Should we commit to a drilling operation or should we not drill at all?" This question is considered by examining the two possibilities:

TABLE 4-6.   The Oil Drilling Situation

	State of Drilling	
	Normal	*Difficult*
Available Alternatives		
Do not drill at all	0	0
Commit to drilling program	24	−20

"What if we do not drill" and "What if we drill" represented by the two branches of the tree emanating from the initial decision node. The two possible states of the drilling are denoted by the branches at the right of the diagram. Which of these branches is applicable at the site in question becomes known only at some future time after drilling starts. Note that the decision maker never crosses the initial decision node in the deliberations prior to making a decision. The question at issue is entirely an examination of what if he or she went that or this way.

There is very little difference at this stage between the information provided by Fig. 4-4 and that given in Table 4-6. The only addition in Fig. 4-4 is an indication of the passage of time. The decision maker can see the outcomes given in the table at the tips of the tree in the figure and he may choose an alternative on this information alone. Minimax behavior on the part of the decision maker would lead to the decision not to drill. Maximax behavior would result in starting a drilling operation, as would the application of the minimax regret criterion.

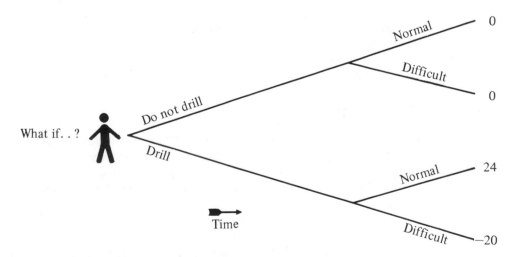

FIG. 4-4.   Initial decision tree for the oil drilling situation.

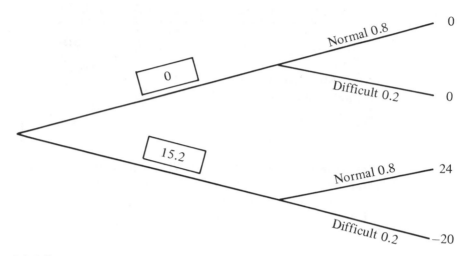

FIG. 4-5. Oil drilling situation: introduction of subjective probabilities.

Let us suppose further that it is possible to arrive at subjective estimates of the probability that the drilling will be normal or difficult. Suppose, for example, that these subjective estimates are that the probability that the drilling is normal is 0.8 and the probability that the drilling is difficult is 0.2. These probabilities can be introduced on to the branches of the decision tree as in Fig. 4-5. Expected values of the outcomes of the alternatives "Do Not Drill" and "Drill" can be calculated and shown in the boxes on the appropriate branches. A decision maker applying the criterion of maximization of expected value would choose the alternative "Drill" because the expected value of the course of action is 15.2 compared with zero for "Do Not Drill." Application of that criterion would be justified in this case because the overall decision situation refers to drilling at a large number of sites under exactly the same conditions at each site.

The Value of Perfect Information

In circumstances like the oil drilling situation, it is often helpful to know whether the cost of an information gathering activity (such as measurements at the site to throw light on drilling conditions) would be justified in the light of the return from the overall venture. Similar considerations arise when considering a possible program of market research connected with the launching of a new product. The problem can be approached by first considering the value of *perfect information.*

Suppose that the decision maker in the oil drilling situation has temporarily postponed the decision and is about to embark on a program of experiments designed to provide information on the possibility of normal or

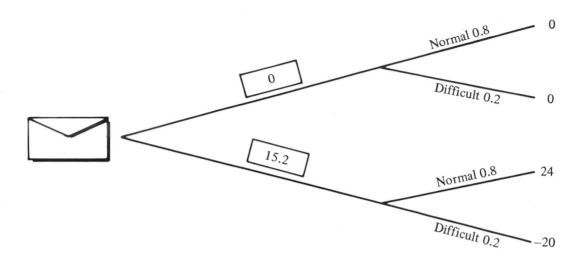

FIG. 4-6. Oil drilling situation: the effect of information.

difficult drilling conditions at the site under consideration. At this moment, a consultant telephones to say that he has heard of the problem facing the decision maker. It turns out that the consultant has been studying drilling conditions at sites with similar characteristics for some time. As a result, he has what he considers to be perfect information about the drilling conditions the oil company is likely to encounter. He is prepared to offer this information to the company at a price.

The question now before the decision maker is what price to offer for the consultant's information. Suppose that this information is contained in a sealed envelope shown to the left of the first decision node in Fig. 4-6. The decision maker can now reason in this way.

"The consultant states that the envelope contains perfect information about the drilling conditions at the site under consideration. If I open the envelope and find the word 'normal', I should decide to start the drilling operation and the company will make 24 units of profit. However, if the envelope contains the word 'difficult', I should decide not to drill at that site. The outcome under these circumstances is that the company makes zero profit in the operation. My problem is that I cannot open the envelope without first paying for it. However, I believe that there is an 80% chance that the drilling conditions at the site are normal. Therefore, to be consistent, I must believe that there is an 80% chance that the envelope contains the word 'normal' and a 20% chance that the envelope contains the word 'difficult'. The expected value of the decision situation in which the envelope is purchased is therefore $0.8 \times 24 + 0.2 \times 0 = 19.2$ units of profit. The expected value of the situation prior to the introduction of the envelope is 15.2 units. The increase in expected value due to the introduction of the envelope is therefore 4.0 units of profit. This figure must then represent the expected value of the perfect information in the envelope."

This result can be reached in another way. The decision maker could reason thus:

"If I open the envelope and see the word 'normal', I would be smart to start the drilling operation and take the 24 units of profit. However, if I see the word 'difficult', I should not drill. By having the envelope, I avoid the problem of encountering difficult conditions once I am committed to a drilling operation and losing 20 units as in the lower branch of the tree. I believe there is a 20% chance that the envelope contains the word 'difficult'. The expected value of the loss that I shall avoid by buying the envelope is therefore 0.20×20 or 4 units. This figure then represents the value of the perfect information contained in the envelope."

It is unlikely that a decision maker in a practical situation will be presented with perfect information. Any practical process of information gathering normally results in less than perfect information being obtained. However, if the value of perfect information can be determined, that of imperfect information must necessarily be less. The value of perfect information therefore represents an upper limit on the amount that it would be advisable to commit to a practical program of information gathering.

The Effect of Changing the Available Alternatives

The expected value of perfect information may change if the available alternatives considered in the decision situation change. Suppose in the oil drilling situation that the company can use new drilling equipment that is less efficient than the conventional type under normal conditions but more efficient under difficult conditions. The amounts of profit when this new equipment is used are 8 units under normal conditions and 2 units under difficult conditions. The addition of this alternative is shown in Fig. 4-7 by a new branch of the tree. Under these changed circumstances, the decision maker can argue in this way.

"If I open the envelope and see the word 'normal' I will undertake the drilling operation using conventional equipment. If I see the word 'difficult', however, I should still undertake the drilling but use the new equipment. Calculating as before, the expected value of the outcome having opened the envelope is $0.8 \times 24 + 0.2 \times 2 = 19.6$. The expected value of the operation without the envelope is 15.2. The expected value of perfect information with the new alternative is therefore 4.4 units, a change from the value of 4.0 which was calculated before that alternative was considered."

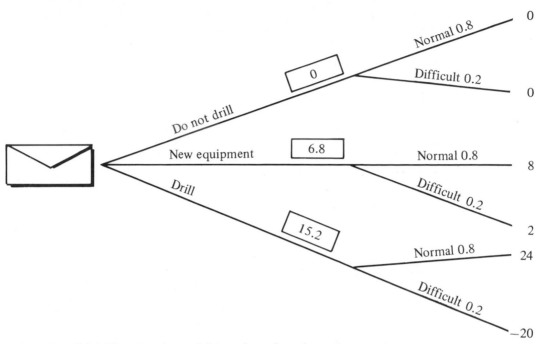

FIG. 4-7. Oil drilling situation: addition of another alternative.

This example shows that the expected value of perfect information may change with the available alternatives considered. It is wise therefore to ensure that all available alternatives have been considered before making decisions regarding the commitment of resources to information gathering.

The Value of Partial Information

In many practical decision situations, it may be desirable to undertake a program of information gathering before a final choice between alternatives is made. Calculation of the expected value of perfect information provides an upper limit to the amount that should be expended on such a program. A further method exists by which the value of a series of experiments or measurements designed to provide only partial information can be assessed.

In order to illustrate this method, let us assume that the oil company has in mind a program of measurements at the drilling site designed to provide some information on whether the drilling is likely to be normal or difficult. These measurements can be made before starting to drill and before large amounts of money are committed to drilling at a particular site. The company can choose between ten possible tests. One of these tests can be conducted at the site at a cost of 2 units of profit. This information gathering activity with respect to a drilling operation is not unlike a program of market research which can be conducted in any number of population centers from one to ten.

Let us assume that the decision maker wishes to assess the value of carrying out one test at the drilling site. This test will be carried out on contract by a firm that has considerable experience with the techniques involved. The result of the test gives an indication of whether the drilling at the site is likely to be normal or difficult. However, the test is not infallible. Past experience has shown that on average the test will show "normal" at a site at which the drilling is later found to be normal on an average of nine out of ten occasions. In addition, on average, the test will indicate "difficult" six times out of ten, if the drilling later turns out to be difficult. The problem confronting the decision maker is whether it is worthwhile to commit 2 units of resources to an on-site test that will admittedly provide only partial information on the major factor that affects future profits. The decision maker can argue in the following way in these circumstances.

> "If the test indicates normal drilling at the site, there is a very good chance that the actual drilling will be normal. Under these conditions, therefore, my subjective probability estimate of normal drilling conditions should be increased from the figure of 0.8 (which was my opinion prior to the test) to say, 0.9. The probability of difficult drilling should also be changed correspondingly from 0.2 to 0.1 in these circumstances. If, on the other hand, the test indicates difficult drilling, my subjective probability estimate of future normal drilling conditions should be lowered substantially from the earlier figure of 0.8, maybe to 0.4. The corresponding estimate of difficult drilling conditions should then be raised from 0.2 to 0.6.

These new subjective probability estimates can be entered on an expanded version of the decision tree as shown in Fig. 4-8. In this diagram, the top portion is exactly as shown in Fig. 4-7. The lower two parts of the diagram incorporate the new probability estimates. Note that the outcomes at the tips of the tree do not change. It is only the expected values shown in the rectangular boxes that are affected by the changes of subjective probabilities. Note also that the expected value of drilling with conventional equipment increases from 15.2 units to 19.6 units if the measurements indicate that the drilling conditions are likely to be normal. The same expected value decreases from 15.2 units to −2.4 units if the measurements suggest difficult drilling conditions. The expected value of the most profitable course of action for each of the possible indications of the measurement program is shown in the lower part of the diagram in Fig. 4-8. This expected value is 19.6 units if the indication of the measurement

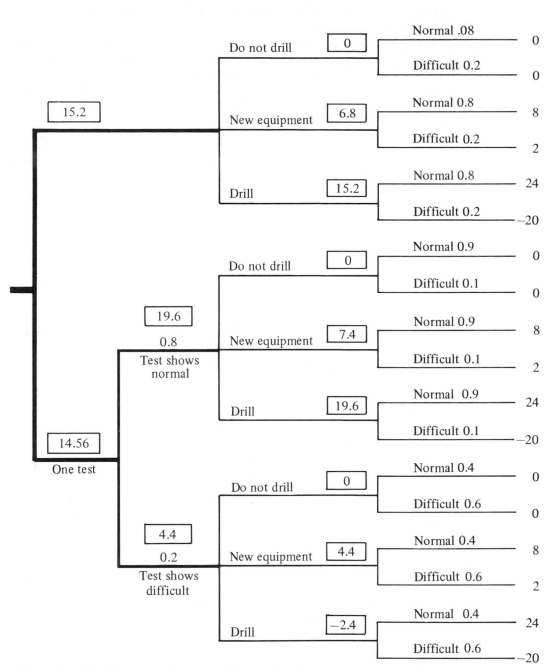

FIG. 4-8. Oil drilling situation: use of the results of a program of measurements.

program is that the drilling will be normal and 4.4 units if the indication is of difficult conditions.

One further step is required to assess the value of the program of measurements. We need to know the probability that the measurements will indicate normal drilling conditions when the conditions actually are normal and also the probability that the measurements will indicate difficult conditions when the conditions actually are difficult. These two probabilities can be calculated as follows:

probability of a normal indication = probability of a normal indication, given that future conditions are indeed normal + probability of a normal indication, given that future conditions are difficult.

and similarly for the probability of a difficult indication in the tests. Using the decision maker's original subjective probabilities and the past experience with test results, this leads to the following equation:

probability of a normal indication =
$(0.9 \times 0.8) + (0.4 \times 0.2) = 0.8$

probability of a difficult indication =
$(0.1 \times 0.8) + (0.6 \times 0.2) = 0.2$

Note that these values are the same as the decision maker's original subjective probability estimates, but that this is only by coincidence. The expected value for the option of gathering information is, therefore, from the lower part of Fig. 4-8):

$$(0.8 \times 19.6) + (0.2 \times 4.4) = 16.56$$

The net expected value, taking into account the 2-unit cost of the tests, is therefore $16.56 - 2 = 14.56$. This is shown at the appropriate place in Figure 4-8 and can be compared with the 15.2 unit figure at the top of the diagram for conditions when no tests are carried out. The decision maker could argue on the basis of the above calculations that the program of tests costing 2 units of profit is not worthwhile. This argument would be based on the lower expected value obtained when the tests are done (14.56 units) compared with that obtained with no program of tests (15.2 units).

Bayesian Probability Revision

The results of the analysis just described are very dependent on the subjective probability estimates of those involved and in particular upon the changes in these estimates after the test results are known. For example, it was assumed, apparently somewhat arbitrarily, that the subjective probability estimate of normal drilling conditions would change from 0.8 to 0.9 if the test indicated that such conditions were likely to be found. The changed subjective probability estimates shown in the lower two-thirds of Fig. 4-8 are not, however, completely arbitrary. They are derived from a formula in probability called Bayes' Theorem, which is explained in Exhibit 4-2. Bayes' Theorem links a subjective probability estimate before test results are received (the *prior* probability) with those that might be expected after the results are received (the *posterior* probability) in the light of previous experience in similar test programs (called the *likelihood*). The manner in which the posterior probabilities of normal conditions of 0.9 and 0.1 are derived from the prior probabilities of 0.8 and 0.2 is explained in detail in Exhibit 4-2.

The application of Bayes' Theorem to changes in a person's subjective probabilities may seem to be a somewhat arbitrary application of a theoretical formula. It is open to question whether individuals do in fact adjust their probability estimates in the manner which the formula suggests. Some experiments have been conducted to investigate the difference between posterior probabilities stated by individuals after receiving information and the figures that would be suggested by Bayes' Theorem.[24] These experiments show that in the majority of cases the impact on subjective probability estimates is likely to be less than is suggested by the formula. This smaller amount of change has been called the *conservatism effect*. Notwithstanding some apparent overestimation of changes in subjective probabilities, Bayesian probability revision may, however, be useful as a guide to the likely effect on these probabilities of the results of experiments.

Advantages of the Decision Tree Method

The decision tree method just described may seem to be more detailed in its quantitative aspects than can be justified in many practical decision situations. Even if quantitative estimates of the factors involved can be obtained, it may be that they do not express all of the aspects and all of the uncertainty inherent in many situations. On the other hand, the method does provide a means of exploration of the structure of a decision situation. In addition:

- It provides a logical method of linking together such quantitative data as are available and of investigating the consequences of those values of the parameters involved.
- It serves to clarify the decision situation, even if the ultimate selection of a course of action is not made solely on the basis of the quantitative analysis.
- It provides a guide to the value of information and to the resources that should be committed to gathering of information in a decision situation.
- It may serve to make managers' preferences and perceptions more explicit during the course of discussions that arise with respect to the analytical approach.

Exhibit 4-2. Bayesian Probability Revision

In the context of the oil drilling decision situation, Bayes formula can be stated as follows:

The *posterior* probability ($p(N \mid X)$) of normal drilling conditions (N) given that some data (X) have been collected is equal to the probability taken from previous experience that such data would be found if the drilling conditions are indeed normal ($p(X \mid N)$), (the *likelihood*), times the *prior* subjective probability of normal drilling conditions $p(N)$, all divided by the sum of all possible products like $p(X \mid N) \times p(N)$.

That is:

$$p(N \mid X) = \frac{p(X \mid N) \times p(N)}{p(X \mid N) \times p(N) + p(X \mid D) \times p(D)}$$

In the problem at hand, the *prior* probabilities $p(N)$ and $p(D)$ are the decision maker's original subjective probability estimates, i.e., 0.8 and 0.2 respectively. The likelihood that $p(X \mid N)$ is the probability of the test indicating normal conditions if the drilling conditions at the site are indeed normal. From the previous experience mentioned above, this likelihood is 0.9, since only one of the tests has been found to indicate difficult conditions under such circumstances. Similarly, the likelihood $p(X \mid D)$ is 0.4.

The posterior subjective probability estimate of normal drilling conditions given that only one of the test indicates difficult conditions can then be calculated as:

$$p(N \mid X) = \frac{0.9 \times 0.8}{0.9 \times 0.8 + 0.4 \times 0.2} = 0.9$$

Similarly,

$$p(D \mid X) = \frac{0.4 \times 0.2}{0.9 \times 0.8 + 0.4 \times 0.2} = 0.1$$

Similarly if X' represents difficult drilling conditions indicated in the test,

$$p(N \mid X') = \frac{0.1 \times 0.8}{0.1 \times 0.8 + 0.6 \times 0.2} = 0.4$$

and $p(D \mid X') = 0.6$

As in the case of other methodologies, it is recommended that the decision tree method not be the only analytical approach used in the analysis of a decision situation in which there is uncertainty. Taken in conjunction with other methods of analysis, however, it may provide some new insights into a situation that can be used to advantage by a decision maker charged with the selection of a course of action from a range of possible alternatives.

SUMMARY

Uncertainty arises from a lack of complete information about a decision situation. It results in lack of certainty that the formulation of the situation by the decision maker contains all the factors that bear upon the outcome. Under these circumstances, the outcome of the situation may be different from that which is estimated during the decision process itself.

Methods of dealing with uncertainty can be considered in a number of stages. A first step in this respect is called sensitivity analysis. This type of analysis consists of an investigation of the effect of variations from the assumed conditions in the situation and from the values assigned to the factors and parameters which contribute to a model of the situation. If a choice of an alternative remains unaffected by such variations, there is reason to believe that the selection will apply over a range of conditions. If small variations in the assumed conditions cause major changes in the choice of a course of action, much less confidence can be placed in the original selection.

A somewhat more complex method of dealing with uncertainty is the construction of a probabilistic model of the situation under consideration. It may be difficult in many situations to obtain sufficient information to allow proper determination of the type of probability distributions that should be used to represent the uncertainty experienced. In these circumstances, it is possible to resort to the use of the technique of simulation. In simulating a decision situation, a model is constructed using the practically observed relationships between the factors involved as well as some mathematical models. Once the model is constructed, a series of simulated resolutions of the decision situation can be made using different values of the factors involved to take account of the uncertainty. The results of these simulated resolutions provide a range of possible outcomes that can be used as a basis for selection of a course of action in the light of the effects of the uncertainty in the situation.

The results of studies of situations involving uncertainty are likely to show a considerable spread of possible outcomes. Decision makers may be faced with a choice between a course of action that has a lower average outcome but less expected variation about that outcome and one that has a higher average outcome but higher expected variation from that average. The selection betwen alternatives in such situations is likely to depend upon the individual decision maker's attitudes to risk. A conservative individual is likely to make the selection on the basis of maximin or minimax, while a more entreprenurial person may use a criterion called maximax. Another criterion called minimax regret allows for minimization of the cost of lost opportunities. Many decision makers do not use specific criteria for choice between alternatives but pursue a policy in which the effects of uncertainty are minimized.

It is possible to arrive at a quantitative expression of uncertainty in terms of subjective probability estimates of the occurrence of events or conditions. These estimates can be used to calculate expected values of outcomes of a decision situation. It is generally agreed, however, that the use of expected values is appropriate only in cases in which a decision situation is encountered many times in essentially the same form. Many decision situations in which uncertainty is a major factor can be analyzed by means of decision trees. These diagrams serve to illustrate the conditions of the decision situation, and to make explicit the characteristics of the choices open to the decision maker.

In decision situations in which quantitative estimates can be made of likely outcomes, it is possible to calculate the value of information in the decision process. A first step towards this calculation is the estimation of the expected value of perfect information. This value puts an upper limit on the value that might be expected from a set of tasks or measurements. The value of partial information can be estimated by assessing the effect of that information on the decision maker's subjective probability estimates. These probability estimates change as information is received. In certain circumstances, the amount of the change can be calculated by use of Bayes' Theorem. These calculations may be too arbitrary for many practical decision situations. In others, however, application of the revised subjective probability may be useful in the comparison of alternatives available to the decision maker.

PRACTICAL DECISION SITUATIONS

4.1 The Newtown Hospital Clinic

The Newtown Hospital runs a clinic for outpatients. A doctor is assigned to the clinic from 9:00 a.m. until noon and it is important to this doctor that she be free to leave at noon or as soon after as possible. Patients are given appointments of 15 minutes or 30 minutes duration according to the nature of the case. Past experience is that the expected duration of 15 minute appointments is 20 minutes, but that 30 minute appointments can be expected to be completed in that time. Patients are mostly on time for their appointments but some are early and some are late. There is also a variation of the length of the actual appointment about the expected time. The hospital would like to know the amount of time patients can be expected to wait for their appointments and the chance that the doctor will be able to leave by noon. It has been suggested that a simulation be developed to determine the answers to these questions. What steps should be taken to develop this simulation?

4.2 The Television Service Company

A large television service company requires its employees to check supplies out of a central store. An average of 25 employees draw supplies in each hour of normal operation. A full time clerk is required to check out the supplies. Each requisition takes an average of 2 minutes to service, so that a maximum of 30 requests per hour can be accommodated. Arrivals of employees at the store requesting supplies are random. The service times are exponentially distributed; that is the variance σ^2 is equal to $1/\mu^2$.

Management feels that a lot of time is wasted by having employees wait in line for supplies. Furthermore, employees requesting supplies are paid an average of $14 per hour while the supply clerk is paid only $10 per hour. Should a second clerk be hired? If so what would be the saving that could be achieved?

4.3 The Uncertain Investor

An investor is faced with uncertainty with regard to the future state of the economy. He has the choice of investing in common stocks, long term bonds, oil drilling funds, or real estate. The gains or losses to his capital amount in a given period under future conditions of depression, recession, and prosperity are shown in the following table:

Investment Alternatives	Depression	Recession	Prosperity
Stocks	−20	−12	18
Bonds	5	5	5
Drilling funds	−36	0	54
Real Estate	2	8	16

The investor wishes to invest in one alternative only in the period under consideration. Which alternative should be chosen under the maximin, maximax, and minimax regret criterion? Suppose that the probabilities of depression, recession, and prosperity are estimated as 0.2, 0.5, and 0.3 respectively. Which alternative would maximize the expected value of gains? Are the choices recommended sensitive to changes in the gains and losses shown in the above table?

4.4 The Premier Manufacturing Company

The Premier Manufacturing Company is planning to introduce a new product. It suspects that its main competitor may have a competing product on the market within a month of the introduction. The wholesale price that Premier will charge retailers for the product must be set before it knows whether a competing product will be introduced. Traditional pricing practice in the industry suggests three prices that both Premier and its competitors could use. These prices are $1.98, $2.58, and $3.18.

Premier estimates that there is a 70% chance that its competitor will enter the market. The profitability of the product to Premier depends upon the competitor's price as shown in the following table:

Premier's Price	Competitor's Price			Profit If No Competition
	$1.98	$2.58	$3.18	
$1.98	60	80	90	100
$2.58	42	84	90	140
$3.18	20	60	106	180

Premier has also estimated the probability that the competitor will set a particular price given that Premier first sets that price as follows:

Premier's Price	Probability That Competitor's Price Will Be		
	$1.98	$2.58	$3.18
$1.98	0.80	0.15	0.05
$2.58	0.20	0.70	0.10
$3.18	0.05	0.35	0.60

Draw a decision tree to illustrate Premier's decision situation. What price should Premier choose based on maximum expected profit?

4.5 The Neighborhood Fast-Food Franchise

An entrepreneur is planning to open a chain of fast-food outlets using the facilities of a chain that has recently gone bankrupt. He is convinced that the new chain can make a profit, but the actual profit obtained will depend on the acceptance of the food by the public. This acceptance can be classified for the purposes of this example as High, Medium, or Low. The entrepreneur must decide whether to redecorate the existing outlets, to expand the facilities at each of them, or to leave them essentially as they are. He estimates the profit to be obtained with the three alternatives will be as follows:

	Public Acceptance		
Available Courses of Action	Low	Medium	High
Leave facilities as they are	− 5	0	10
Redecorate facilities	−15	15	20
Expand facilities	−50	10	35

The entrepreneur estimates subjectively that the probabilities of Low, Medium, and High acceptance are 0.2, 0.5, and 0.3 respectively.

What course of action would a minimax, maximax, and minimax regret decision maker select? What is the maximum amount that the entrepreneur should pay for a market study to determine future public acceptance of his food?

4.6 The Textile Importer

An importer of textiles is contemplating buying a consignment of 10,000 yards of cloth from an offshore source for $5 a yard. He is sure that the cloth can be sold for $8 a yard once an import license has been obtained. There are many more opportunities available in the future with similar characteristics. However, the government may refuse to grant a license for import of the cloth. If this happens, the contract will have to be cancelled at a cost of $1 per yard of cloth. The importer estimates subjectively that the chance that a license will be granted is 50%. It is possible that an importer in another country would be willing to take over the contract if the government refuses the license. It is estimated that the probability that this importer will assume the contract given that the license is refused is 60%. In that case, the $1 per yard of cloth cancellation cost is avoided. Analyze this problem and formulate a recommendation to the broker with regard to a course of action. What is the expected value of perfect information in this case?

It may be a good idea in circumstances of this sort to delay signing the contract until the result of the license application is known. In that case, however, it is estimated that there is a 50% chance that the opportunity to buy will not be available at that time. Is the tactic of delaying the signing of the contract advantageous?

It is possible to hire a consultant who can report to the broker on whether the licensing application is likely to be approved. The consultant will provide a study stating whether conditions are favorable or unfavorable to the application. In the case in which the application is eventually approved, it is estimated that the probability of a favorable report is 90%. However, if the application is eventually rejected, it is expected that there is only a 40% chance of a favorable report. What is the maximum amount that the broker should pay the consultant for his services?

DISCUSSION TOPICS

1. What are the primary reasons that probabilistic models of decision situations are not more applicable to practical decision situations? In what types of situation are these models most applicable?

2. Simulation has been referred to as a method of analysis to be used when all else fails. Do you think that this comment is a fair representation of the simulation technique? In what circumstances do you think simulation is most effective?

3. How does an individual's attitude to risk affect the selection between alternatives in a decision situation involving uncertainty? What types of behavior have you noticed that illustrate the effect of this attitude in practical decision making?

4. How do individuals try to minimize the effect of uncertainty on the outcomes or practical decision situations? Do you think that the minimization of uncertainty is effective behavior for managers in modern organizations?

5. How is the criterion of minimax regret related to the principle of avoiding opportunity costs?

6. How does subjective probability differ from probability estimates derived from the frequency of occurrence of an event in a series of past observations?

7. In what ways are subjective probability estimates influenced by individual perceptions of skill and luck?

8. In what circumstances do you think that the choice between alternatives can be made on the basis of maximization of the expected value of outcomes?

9.   What is the usefulness of calculations of the expected value of perfect information? In the example in the text, this value increased when another alternative course of action was considered. Can the expected value of information decrease in any circumstances?

10.   In what ways do you think Bayes' formula is useful in estimating the change in subjective probability estimates when information is received concerning a decision situation?

11.   Do you think that practical managers exhibit conservatism in adjusting subjective probabilities in real-life decision situations? If so, what do you think to be the reason for this behavior?

12.   What are the advantages of decision tree analysis? In what sorts of practical decision situations do you think it can be used effectively?

REFERENCES

1.   Wagner, H., *Principles of Operations Research*, 2nd Ed., Prentice Hall, 1975, Chapter 5.

2.   Hillier, F. S. and Lieberman, G. J., *Introduction to Operations Research*, 1st Ed., Holden-Day, 1967, pp 163-166 and 490-504.

3.   Wagner, H., *op cit*, pp 651-849.

4.   Hillier, F. S. and Lieberman, G. J., op cit, p 301.

5.   Peterson, R. and Silver, E. A., *Decision Systems for Inventory Management and Production Planning*, Wiley, 1978.

6.   Wagner, H., *op cit*, Chap. 21.

7.   Hillier, F. S. and Lieberman, G. J., *op cit*, Chap. 14.

8.   See Hertz, D. B., "Risk Analysis in Capital Investment," *Harvard Business Review*, Jan/Feb 1964, for more detail on this subject.

9.   Wald, A., "Statistical Decision Functions which Minimize the Maximum Risk," *Annals of Mathematics*, Vol 46, 1945, pp 265-280.

10.   Hurwicz, L., "Optimality Criteria for Decision Making Under Ignorance," Cowles Commission Discussion Paper, Statistics No. 370, 1951: discussed in Luce, R. D. and Raiffa, H., *Games and Decisions*, Wiley, 1957, pp 282-284.

11.   Savage, L. J., "The Theory of Statistical Decision," *Journal of the American Statistical Association*," Vol 46, 1951, pp 55-67.

12.   Cyert, R. M. and March, J. G., *A Behavioral Theory of The Firm*, Prentice-Hall, 1963, pp 118-120.

13.   Argyris, C., "Management Information Systems: the Challenge to Rationality and Emotionality," *Management Science*, Vol 17, No 6, February 1971, p B279.

14.   Festinger, L., "Cognitive Dissonance," *Scientific American*, October 1972, pp 93-102.

15. Simon, H. A., *Administrative Behavior*, The Free Press, 1965, pp xxiv-xxvii.
16. March, J. G. and Simon, H. A., *Organizations*, Wiley, 1958.
17. For a review of the different concepts in probability in highly readable form see Chapter 10 of Raiffa, H., *Decision Analysis: Introductory Lectures on Choices under Uncertainty*, Addison Wesley, 1968.
18. Lee, Wayne, *Decision Theory and Human Behavior*, Wiley 1971, pp 56-65.
19. Miller, D. W. and Starr, M. K., *The Structure of Human Decisions*, Prentice-Hall, 1967, p 82.
20. Bernoulli, Daniel, "Exposition of a New Theory on the Measurement of Risk" (translated by L. Sommer), *Econometrica*, Vol 22, 1954, pp 23-26.
21. Newman, J. W., *Managerial Applications of Decision Theory*, Harper and Row, 1971.
22. Magee, J. F., "How to Use Decision Trees in Capital Investment," *Harvard Business Review*, Sept/Oct 1964.
23. Howard, R. A., Matheson, J. E., North, D. W., "The Decision to Seed Hurricanes," *Science*, Vol 76, No 4040, 16 June 1972, pp 1191-1202.
24. Lee, Wayne, *op cit*, pp 253-254.

Chapter Five

Decision Situations Involving Multiple Objectives

INTRODUCTION

The participants in many modern decision situations must attempt to satisfy more than one objective in their decision making process. The need to satisfy these objectives simultaneously is a major factor in determining their order of preference for available alternatives. Some of a participant's objectives may be in conflict with one or more of the others that must be considered in a decision situation. Courses of action that are more preferred than others in terms of satisfying one objective may be less preferred when other objectives are considered. The frustrated decision maker is often heard to say, "On the one hand I prefer this course of action, but on the other hand, I prefer that alternative." There are unfortunately very few generally applicable decision making methods that can be used to resolve this dilemma.

Discussion of the methods available to assist decision makers in multiple objective situations can be conducted conveniently in terms of the type of situation to which they can be applied. The characteristics that determine the type of multiple objective situation are as follows:

1. Whether meaningful quantitative measures of progress towards the achievement of each of the objectives can be established.

2. Whether the measures established for the objectives can be expressed in terms of the same unit (for example, dollars or hours) or whether the measures used for some of the objectives are different from those employed for others.

3. Whether relative priorities for achievement of the objectives can be expressed either in terms of numeric weighting factors or ordinal preferences.

The available techniques fall into three broad classes, defined by certain of the above characteristics. These classes and the information necessary for their use are shown in Table 5-1. The content of this chapter consists of a discussion of the techniques in each of the three classes. This discussion is undertaken from the point of view of a single decision maker wishing to place a series of alternative courses of action in order of preference in the light of the existence of a number of objectives that must be pursued simultaneously. Uncertainty is not considered explicitly in the discussion, although the possibility that the measures of achievement of each of the objectives are subject to uncertainty must be kept constantly in mind. The methods of sensitivity analysis are as applicable to the analysis described in this chapter as they are to the situations treated under any of the other headings in the text. The situations discussed in the following sections are essentially those of Category 4 of the classification of decision situations contained in Table 1-1.

WEIGHTING METHODS

Weighting methods are applicable for choice between alternatives in a multiple objective situation when the following conditions are observed:

1. Quantitative measures can be established relative to each of the objectives.
2. These measures can be expressed in the same units (such as dollars) or in units that are directly related (such as dollars and time worked at a given hourly rate).
3. Numerical weighting factors are available that express the priorities of the decision maker between objectives.

Consider, for example, a manufacturing company that is entirely profit oriented. Objectives other than profit either do not exist for this company or such other objectives as do exist have been relegated to a position of very little importance. The management of the company is aware, however, of the need to plan for profit in each of three periods which can be

TABLE 5-1.   Techniques For Use in Multiple Objective Situations and the Attendant Necessary Conditions

Type of Technique	Information Necessary before Technique Can Be Used
Weighting Methods	1. Quantitative measures of progress towards achievement of each objective exist.
	2. A direct relationship exists between the units in which these measures are expressed.
	3. Numerical weighting factors available expressing priorities between objectives.
Minimizing Deviations from Targets	1. Quantitative measures of progress towards achievement of each objective exist but not necessarily a direct relationship between the units in which these measures are expressed.
	2. Numerical weighting factors or ordinal preferences exist describing priorities between objectives.
Elimination Methods	1. Ordinal preferences between alternative courses of action against each objective (or quantitative measures of progress towards achievement) exist: ordinal preferences exist describing priorities between objectives (methods are weaker when no priorities exist).

described as the short, medium, and long terms. Naturally, any plans for activities that would lead to profits in the long term may detract from those in the short and medium terms. The profits in the three periods can be measured in terms of the same dollar units. Let us suppose that the management of the company has decided that it considers potential profits in the three periods to have a ratio of importance of 1:4:2. It might then be considered to be an acceptable procedure for the company to compare alternative plans or courses of action in terms of the expression for the total profit over all three periods $P = p_1 + 4p_2 + 2p_3$, where p_1, p_2, and p_3 are the expected profits to be obtained from a course of action in the short, medium, and long terms respectively. Courses of action having higher values of P than others can be judged to be preferable in terms of overall profitability, taking into account the multiple objectives of profits in the short, medium, and long terms and the relative priorities assigned to these multiple objectives. A similar method of choice between alternatives would be applicable if the company had objectives of making profit from three products and had established priorities between the earning of profits on these three products.

Conditions in situations such as those just described allow the formulation of a single objective function for comparison between alternatives. A multiple objective situation is converted in this way into a single objective situation. This conversion is possible because the measures of progress toward each of the objectives are expressed in the same units and numerical weightings exist to express priorities between objectives. These conditions exist in some multiple objective situations but by no means in all of them. Nevertheless, the analytical procedures that can be used when a single objective function is established are simple and unequivocal. The ease with which alternatives can be compared using this technique provides a considerable source of temptation to the analyst to use it in situations in which it is not truly applicable.

This temptation is probably never greater than in cost benefit analysis. Many alternative programs in areas such as public health, education, water resources, public transportation, and land usage have been compared by the use of this technique.[1] For a single objective function to be constructed it is necessary that a common measure of achievement of the multiple objectives be established. This measure must reflect the concerns of those who are affected by the programs in question. Measurement of benefits of the programs in terms of dollars comes readily to mind. This measure is often chosen on the grounds that the usefulness of an alternative can be judged by the amount that people concerned are prepared to pay for it. However, as noted in Chapter 3, there are many benefits such as health, comfort, social responsibility, personal well-being, and security that are not readily represented in monetary terms. Furthermore, the use of dollars as a measure of the value of these benefits can lead to distortion of the characteristics of the decision situation being considered. This distortion can lead to a situation in which individuals who are not familiar with the details of the analysis are seriously misled by the results of an apparently logical process of comparison of alternatives.

Use of Utility Assessments

The use of utility assessments appears to be attractive in multiple objective decision situations in that it allows the benefits of alternatives in different areas to be assessed in the same units of measurement. In theory, for example, an individual can express his or her preferences in the areas of two dissimilar objectives such as salary and working conditions, in the same units of utility. The utilities relating to each of the objectives can then be used to construct a single objective function expressing the individual's composite utility for an alternative across all of his or her multiple objectives. However, the serious reservations expressed by many authors with regard to the feasibility of measuring utility in this form have been discussed in Chapter 3. At the present time, these reservations essentially rule out the reduction of many multiple objective decision situations to the consideration of a single objective function.

Weighted Score Techniques

This often-used technique consists of establishing an arbitrary scale of, say, 0 to 10 to measure the performance of each of a number of alternatives against each member of a multiple set of objectives. In addition, a numerical weight is assigned to each of the objectives to represent its importance relative to the others. The alternatives are then judged in terms of the sum of the weights times the performance measure on the scale of 0 to 10 over all of the objectives. Suppose for example that three firms A, B, and C are bidding on a contract to supply steel pipe to a company engaged in constructing, operating, and maintaining a gas pipeline. The company's objectives in the decision situation involved with the choice of supplier are:

1. To have the least possible technical problems with the pipe in its construction, operation, and maintenance.
2. To pay the least possible price for the pipe consistent with 1 above.
3. To receive the pipe according to a delivery schedule with minimum delays in supply throughout the delivery period.

The bids submitted by Firms A, B, and C are to be assessed according to criteria derived from these objectives. The relative importance of the criteria are judged to be expressed by weightings of 3, 5, and 4 respectively. These details of the decision situation and the scores awarded by the company team assigned to select the supplier are shown in Table 5-2. On the basis of the highest weighted score, the contract would be awarded to Firm B.

TABLE 5-2. Criteria, Weights, and Scores in a Multiple Objective Decision Situation

Criteria Based on Company Objectives	Numerical Weightings	Company Assessment		
		Firm A	Firm B	Firm C
Technical competence	3	8	7	7
Cost	5	6	9	5
Capability of meeting schedule	4	7	5	8
Weighted score		82	86	78

This method has several apparent advantages for the decision maker faced with the choice between alternatives in a multiple objective situation. It is not complex; it is simply applied and it is apparently logical. The analysis results in what appears to be a basis for unequivocal choice in the form of performance scores for each of the alternatives. The method is widely used in proprietary decision methodologies such as the Kepner-Tregoe technique.[2] However, there are serious reservations about the employment of this method as the sole basis for choice between alternatives in a multiple objective situation. These reservations concern the assumptions implicit in the use of the method:

1. That the performance of the three firms in three different areas can be assessed on an arbitrary scale of 0 to 10.
2. That the priorities between the three areas of assessment can be expressed in terms of the numerical weightings used.
3. That the weighted score summing performance in the three areas represents a valid assessment of the bids by the three firms in the light of the company's multiple objectives.

Those in favor of the weighted score technique might argue that it presents a realistic representation of the views and preferences of the individuals involved in the assessment. They might add that the process of producing the weighted score provides an opportunity for discussion and thought during which individual opinions are formulated and clarified. The danger remains, however, that weighted score methods may be used as a superficial means of comparing alternatives that replaces the more comprehensive considerations required in the treatment of many multiple objective decision situations.

MINIMIZING DEVIATIONS FROM TARGETS

There is a significant class of multiple objective decision situations in which progress toward each of the objectives can be measured in quantitative terms, but in which the units of measurement for the individual objectives are different. Suppose, for example, that a manufacturer of stereo equipment has three objectives which can be stated in order of importance: (1) to minimize the underutilization of his production facilities; (2) to meet sales goals for each of two types of stereo equipment (S_1 and S_2) produced at the plant; and (3) to minimize overtime operation of the plant to the greatest extent possible. The units of measurement appropriate to the first objective is dollars, for the second objective it is numbers of units of stereo equipment, and for the third objective, it is hours of operation.

The units are not the same for the three objectives, nor is there necessarily a direct relationship between all of these units of measurement. Conversion of these units into one common measurement such as dollars may therefore not be possible. Situations of this nature can be treated by techniques that allow deviations from targets set in relation to each of the individual objectives to be minimized.

The stereo manufacturer's decision situation can be formulated in the manner shown in Exhibit 5-1. In this formulation, the objective function is represented by an expression involving the amounts of the deviations from the goals set with respect to the three objectives each qualified by a priority factor (P_1, P_2, and P_3). Note that the amounts of deviation are taken as being positive whether the deviation is an amount less than the goal or in excess of a goal. An amount less than a goal is shown thus: d_1^- and an amount in excess of a goal is shown thus: d_1^+.

The expression shown as the objective function in Exhibit 5-1 is not a true sum because the component amounts are not measured in the same

---

EXHIBIT 5-1.   Formulation of a Multiple Objective Decision Situation for Goal Programming

---

Objective Function   Minimize $Z = P_1 d_1^- + P_2 d_2^- + P_2 d_3^- + P_3 d_1^+$

Subject to $S_1 + S_2 + d_1^- - d_1^+$ = normal production capacity in units

$S_1 + d_2^-$ = maximum number of S_1 units that can be sold in period

$S_2 + d_3^-$ = maximum number of S_2 units that can be sold in period

where d_1^- = under utilization of production capacity

d_1^+ = amount of utilization of production capacity over the norm

d_2^- = underachievement of sales goals for S_1 units

d_3^- = underachievement of sales goals for S_2 units

P_1 represents the highest priority objective, that is minimization of the underutilization of production facilities

P_2 represents the next highest priority objective, that is meeting the sales goals for S_1 and S_2 units

P_3 represents the third highest priority objective, that is minimization of overtime operation at the plant.

All of d_1^-, d_2^-, d_3^-, d_1^+, S_1 and S_2 are positive.

units. Thus the objective function cannot be minimized in the strict fashion used for example in linear programming. Instead, the process consists first of minimizing the deviation related to the highest priority objective (denoted by P_1). When no further improvement is possible in these highest priority deviations, those associated with the second highest priority objective are minimized, and so on. The whole process is carried out within the conditions represented by the constraints shown in the formulation. In the example described in Exhibit 5-1, assuming that each stereo unit consumes 1 hour of production capacity and that the sales goals for S_1 and S_2 and 6 and 8 respectively in the period, it can be shown that all goals can be met (i.e., $S_1 = 6$, $S_2 = 8$, $d_1^- = d_2^- = d_3^- = 0$) as long as 4 hours overtime can be provided (that is $d_1^+ = 4$).

The technique by which situations of the above type can be analyzed is called *goal programming*.[3, 4] It is emphasized that this technique does not provide an overall optimum solution in terms of all the objectives expressed in the situation; nor does it necessarily determine an optimum solution in terms of any one of them. Goal programming is a method by which deviations from preset goals associated with multiple objectives can be minimized. This minimization of deviations, however, is not simultaneous. It is, instead, progressive, starting from the highest priority objective and proceeding step by step to the lowest priority objective. Note that the procedure requires that the priority between objectives can be expressed in terms of preferences on an ordinal scale. If no such preferences are available, the order of minimization of deviations can be chosen arbitrarily or objectives can be assumed to be of equal priority. The technique loses some of its effectiveness in such circumstances.

ELIMINATION METHODS

There are many practical decision situations in which the measures of progress towards objectives (and possibly some of the costs) cannot be expressed entirely in quantitative form. In these circumstances, there is no direct relationship between the ways in which the degree of achievement of the various objectives are assessed. Nor are there, in many cases, numeric weighting factors available to express the priorities between the achievement of objectives. These priorities can often be represented only by a preference between objectives expressed on an ordinal scale. In situations of this nature, none of the methods and techniques described to this point in the chapter can be of assistance to the decision maker in his task of choosing between alternatives. However, a series of techniques under the general title of *elimination methods*[5] offers some capability of placing a number of alternatives in an order of preference. These techniques can be used if each alternative can be ranked in terms of its contribution to the achievement of a number of objectives and if some ordering of priority of these objectives can be expressed.

Sequential Elimination

Suppose, for example, that an agency of a state government is engaged in a highway development and that there are six alternatives that have been proposed to meet the needs expressed for this project. The objectives of the agency as far as this development is concerned can be expressed as follows. These objectives are shown in decreasing order of priority as seen by the agency:

1.   To minimize the accident hazard on the new portion of highway.
2.   To minimize the cost of the development.
3.   To maximize convenience for traffic on the new highway.
4.   To minimize the expropriation of valuable farmland.
5.   To minimize the aesthetic impact of the development on the communities and regions through which the highway passes.
6.   To provide maximum service to industry from the new highway.
7.   To provide maximum access to recreational areas via the new highway.

Some of these objectives may be in conflict with others on the list. Reducing the accident hazard on the highway to a minimum may, for example, conflict with the objective of minimizing the cost of the development. Minimizing the expropriation of farmland may conflict with maximum service to industry, and so on.

Not all of these objectives are such that well defined quantitative measures can be used as a means of assessing the six alternative proposals against them. Dollars can probably be used with respect to the objective relating to cost, and acres is a likely measure of the loss of valuable farmland. Proxy measures, however, are required with respect to accident hazard, service to industry, and access to recreational areas. The proxy measure for accident hazard might be the number of injuries and/or the cost of property destroyed in the accidents expected in a given period after the highway is in service. Proxy measures with respect to service to industry and access to recreational areas might be in terms of time or miles saved by various classes of traffic. Possibly, convenience to traffic could be represented in the same manner, although a measure in units of time would not represent the aspects of convenience related to reduction in driver aggravation and increase in enjoyment during a trip. The objective concerning the minimization of aesthetic impact on the region may defy representation in any numeric terms.

Suppose that the alternative highway proposals can be evaluated against each of the objectives in terms of the factors shown in Table 5-3. Suppose, further, that when evaluation is possible on an ordinal scale only, each alternative evaluated against an objective is awarded a letter grade in the range: A, very good; B, good; C, average; D, fair; and E, poor. Extensions of this letter grade scale are possible by adding a plus or a minus to the letter: for example C+ or A−. The evaluation of alternatives in terms of all the factors related to objectives might then be as shown in Table 5-4. The task for the decision maker is to place the alternatives in an order of preference taking into account this evaluation.

The task of ordering the alternatives is simple if one of them is outstanding from all the others in the evaluation. Let us suppose that one alternative is better than all the others in terms of one of the factors evaluated and at least equal with respect to all the other factors. That alternative is said to *dominate* the others and the dominant alternative is a clear choice over the others in those circumstances. However, the condition of dominance cannot be expected to exist in many practical decision situations. It is much more likely that one alternative is found to be good against one factor and another alternative provides best results in terms of another factor. In the situation illustrated in Table 5-4, for example, the alternative showing least cost has a high accident hazard and the most unfavorable aesthetic impact. In order to place the alternatives in an order of preference we need a method that takes into account the evaluation of each of them against the factors related to objectives and the priority assigned to the objectives. One such method is based on the establishment of minimum performance levels for each of the factors.

Suppose that minimum performance levels have been established in the

TABLE 5-3. Sequential Elimination Method of Evaluating Alternatives against Objectives in the Highway Development Project

Objective	Evaluated in Terms of
Minimize accident hazard	Number of deaths and serious injuries expected in a given period
Minimize cost	Total project cost in dollars
Maximize convenience for traffic	Evaluation of alternatives on an ordinal scale only
Minimize expropriation of farmland	Acres expropriated
Minimize aesthetic impact	Evaluation of alternatives on an ordinal scale only
Maximize service to industry	Total miles saved in a given period
Maximize access to recreation	Total miles saved in a given period

TABLE 5-4. Evaluation of Alternatives in the Highway Development Project

Factors Related to Objectives	Alternatives					
	1	2	3	4	5	6
Minimize accident hazard (deaths and serious injuries)	300	120	84	140	780	135
Minimize cost (thousands of dollars)	1,700	4,400	1,600	2,800	1,000	1,200
Maximize convenience for traffic	A	B	B+	D	B	C
Minimize expropriation of farmland (acres)	7,600	8,600	6,600	3,600	5,400	5,600
Minimize aesthetic impact	B	D	B	C+	E	A
Maximize service to industry (thousands of miles saved per year)	5,200	3,600	1,800	7,600	7,500	4,900
Maximize access to recreation (thousands of miles saved per year)	3,600	14,800	3,100	7,100	13,800	6,100

highway development project as shown in Table 5-5. A cross (X) in this table denotes that the minimum performance level is not met by the alternative against the factors indicated. The most preferred alternative can now be determined in the following way. Start with the highest priority objective and eliminate alternatives 1 and 5 as not meeting the required performance level. Move to the next highest priority objective and elimi-

TABLE 5-5. Performance of Alternatives against Acceptable Levels of Factors Related to Objectives in the Highway Development Project

Factors Related to Objectives	Alternatives					
	1	2	3	4	5	6
Accident hazard not greater than 150	X				X	
Cost not greater than $2 million		X		X		
Convenience to traffic B+ or better		X		X	X	X
Expropriation of farmland not greater than 5000 acres	X	X	X		X	X
Aesthetic impact B or better		X		X	X	
Service to industry not less than 5 million miles		X	X			X
Access to recreation not less than 8 million miles	X		X	X		X

nate alternatives 2 and 4 from those remaining in a similar fashion. Only alternatives 3 and 6 remain: 6 is eliminated at the third level of priority, leaving alternative 3 as the most preferred alternative by this method of ranking. In practical situations, it is wise to allow some minor variation in the performance levels so that an alternative is not eliminated by being only very slightly under the required performance. This allowable variation can be achieved by allowing a small band of acceptance about the levels specified in each case.

The method of ranking illustrated in Table 5-5—*sequential elimination*—is noteworthy in that it allows an order of preference to be established in situations in which some factors can be measured in quantitative terms and others can be assessed only on a letter grade scale of evaluation. The final evaluation in such cases is done therefore on a combination of quantitative and nonquantitative evaluations. The process of ranking alternatives is not, however, always as well ordered as illustrated in Table 5-5. Suppose, for example, that the convenience to traffic for alternative 3 had been rated as B rather than B+. Alternatives 3 and 6 would then have been tied at the third stage of elimination. In such cases, further analysis is required to break the tie. It might be noted, for instance, that alternative 3 has much superior performance to 6 in the first priority accident hazard area and this superiority would no doubt be taken as reason to place alternative 3 ahead of 6 in the final ranking. In more general terms, a finer definition of the minimum performance levels is often needed to discriminate between alternatives that are tied in a first attempt at ranking them.

Conjunctive, Disjunctive, and Conditional Criteria

The sequential elimination procedure just described requires that an alternative be dropped from consideration if it does not meet the criterion associated with the highest priority objective, regardless of its performance with respect to the other objectives. Alternative 1 was eliminated in Table 5-5 because its accident hazard evaluation was greater than the maximum acceptable figure of 150 even though its cost and convenience to traffic evaluations were superior to many of the other alternatives. In the circumstances prevailing in the highway development project, elimination on the grounds of high accident hazard is probably justified. In other cases, however, superior performance relative to the second and third priority objectives might be taken to compensate to some extent for a poor evaluation in terms of the first priority objective.

One means of trading off performance between objectives is by the use of criteria linking the factors describing performance relative to the objectives. These criteria can be of three types:

1. A *conjunctive* criterion, characterized by "and."
2. A *disjunctive* criterion, characterized by "or."
3. A *conditional* criterion, characterized by "if . . . then."

The use of these types of criteria can be illustrated by an example.

Let us consider the case of a company engaged in manufacturing a range of products at an existing plant. The company has operated profitably for many years and it has accumulated a substantial amount in retained earnings. However, the manufacturing facilities at its plant are becoming outdated and inefficient. The company's objectives can be stated briefly as follows:

- To maintain an overall return on investment at a level as high as possible and in no circumstances below 12%.
- To engage in new ventures both related and unrelated to its present activities, but only in those ventures in which the risk is at an acceptable level.
- To diversify its activities to some extent from its present concentration on the existing product line.

The company has identified five possible activities each of which would contribute to achievement of the above objectives. These activities are:

1. To acquire a company engaged in activities compatible to its own and located in an area which would allow expansion of the combined companies' markets.
2. To invest a proportion of the retained earnings in oil and gas exploration.
3. To re-equip the main plant for more efficient operation.
4. To expand marketing of its products to Europe and possibly other off-shore areas.
5. To launch a major new product line.

The company wishes to place these possible future activities in an order of preference based on an evaluation of each of them that has just been completed. The results of this evaluation are summarized in Table 5-6. Minimum performance levels have been set in each of the areas of evaluation. These levels are shown in order of priority in Table 5-7. The judgments as to whether each of the alternative future activities meets the required minimum performance levels are also shown in this table.

Using the sequential elimination technique, the acquisition is ruled out at the first level: investment in oil and gas and expanding operations to Europe are eliminated at the second level of priority. Of the remaining two possible activities, launching a new product line is eliminated at the third level so that re-equipping the plant emerges as the most preferred activity.

TABLE 5-6. Evaluation of Five Possible Future Activities for a Manufacturing Company

	Activities				
Factors	Acquire Compatible Company	Invest in Oil and Gas	Re-equip Plant	Expand Operations to Europe	Launch New Product Line
Return on investment (%) (average over 5 years)	10.6	16.7	14.1	12.6	12.8
Risk	B	C	B+	C+	B
Capital required ($ millions)	8.5	21.6	11.6	7.5	14.1
Diversification	B	A	C	C+	B+
Ease of entry	C+	B	A	C+	C+
Ease of exit	C+	C+	C	C+	C
Human resources required (man years per year)	20	10	210	420	274

TABLE 5-7. Peformance of Possible Future Activities against Acceptable Levels for a Manufacturing Company

	Activities				
Factors	Acquire Compatible Company	Invest in Oil and Gas	Re-equip Plant	Expand Operations to Europe	Launch New Product Line
Return on investment at least 12%	X				
Risk B or better		X		X	
Capital required not more than $12M		X			X
Diversification B or better			X	X	
Ease of entry B− or better	X			X	X
Ease of exit B+ or better	X	X	X	X	X
Human resources not more than 200 man years per year			X	X	X

NOTE: a cross (X) in this Table denotes that the performance level is not met.

It might be argued, however, that the acquisition proposal was eliminated only because its estimated return on investment was 10.6% as compared with the required level of 12%. Furthermore, the acquisition proposal met the next three minimum performance levels including the fourth level, which the activity selected as most preferred did not meet. In circumstances such as these, there may be reason to replace the factors representing minimum performance levels with criteria in conjunctive, disjunctive, or conditional forms.

These criteria should be constructed to represent the views of management with respect to the linkages between the factors represented in Table 5-7. For example, if an activity that allowed a considerable amount of diversification is judged acceptable even though its return on investment is lower than others, a criterion in the disjunctive form such as "Return on investment must be greater than 14% *or* Diversification must be B or better" could be introduced. If two factors are important when taken together, the conjunctive form is used. For example, if management wished to maintain flexibility in its operations, the criterion "Ease of entry *and* Ease of exit must both be C+ or better" might be used. The conditional form allows a direct link between two factors. For example, a linkage between capital required and risk could be represented by a criterion such as "If capital requirements are greater than 12 million dollars, risk must be B or better."

The criteria to be used in any particular situation are usually selected finally only after considerable discussion among the managers concerned. In some cases, this process of discussion serves to clarify the issues considerably. It is often at least as valuable in reaching a conclusion as the analytical procedure itself.

Criteria chosen by management in the case of the manufacturing company are shown in Table 5-8 in the agreed order of priority. The evaluation against these criteria using the sequential elimination technique shows the acquisition of the compatible company to be the most preferred future activity.

Critics of sequential elimination point out that it is possible to manipulate the process in such a manner as to make a particular proposal appear to be the winner. If this is the case, the manipulation is nothing more than often happens in managerial discussions regarding the choice between alternatives. The key to use of sequential elimination is a thorough exploration of the views and opinions of those concerned and the incorporation of those views and opinions into the criteria in an accurate and concise manner. Some of the value of the technique undoubtedly lies in the clarification of objectives and required performance levels that occurs during the discussions preceding the setting of criteria. Additional value is obtained from the capability of placing alternatives in an order of preference that is available from the use of the method.

TABLE 5-8. Use of Criteria in Selecting a Possible Future Activity in the Case of the Manufacturing Company

| | Activities | | | | |
Criteria	Acquire Compatible Company	Invest in Oil and Gas	Re-equip Plant	Expand Operations in Europe	Launch New Product Line
1. Return on investment must be greater than 14% *or* Diversification B or better				X	
2. Ease of entry *and* Ease of Exit must be C+ or better			X		X
3. *If* Capital requirements are greater than $12 million, Risk must be B or better		X			
4. Risk must be B+ or better *or* Ease of Exit must be B or better	X	X		X	X
5. *If* Return on investment is less than 12%, Risk must be B+ or better	X				
6. *If* Risk is C+ or worse, Ease of Exit must be B or better		X		X	

NOTE: a cross (X) denotes that the criterion is not met.

TRADE OFF BY SURVIVING ATTRIBUTE

A method that provides some measure of trade off between performance against various objectives can be used in certain situations with special characteristics. Suppose that the performance of the alternatives can be assessed over a wide range of conditions. It may then be possible to compare the alternatives in terms of one factor or criterion related to one objective when their levels of performance against factors or criteria related to all the other objectives meets or exceeds a certain fixed level. In this technique, the factors or criteria for which performance of the alternatives meets or exceeds certain fixed levels are called the *base set*. The remaining single factor or criterion in terms which the final comparison is made is called the *surviving attribute*. The procedure consists of the following steps:

1. Choose the surviving attribute. It is usually best to choose the factor or criterion relating to the most important objective as the surviving attribute.

2. Choose the base levels for each of the factors or criteria in the base set. These levels may be selected as a basic minimum performance required against each of the factors or criteria involved.

3. Determine the performance in terms of the surviving attribute for each alternative under the condition that the performance levels in the base set are met.

4. Choose the alternative having the best performance in terms of the surviving attribute under the conditions described in 3 above.

Suppose, for example, that in the case of the manufacturing company described in Table 5-6 only the first three of the factors (return on investment, risk, and capital required) were considered. Suppose, in addition, that risk could be determined for a capital investment of $8 million and a return on investment of 13% for each of the possible future activities. The comparison between the activities might then appear as in Table 5-9. In this table, the base set consists of return on investment and capital required. The surviving attribute is risk. In terms of the evaluation shown in Table 5-9 the alternative of re-equipping the plant would be declared the

TABLE 5-9. Comparison of Five Possible Activities at Fixed Levels of Capital Investment and Return on Investment

	Activities				
Factors	Acquire Compatible Company	Invest in Oil and Gas	Re-equip Plant	Expand Operations to Europe	Launch New Product Line
Return on investment % (average over 5 years)	13	13	13	13	13
Risk	C−	C	B	C+	D
Capital required ($ millions)	8.0	8.0	8.0	8.0	8.0

most preferred by virtue of its superior performance in terms of the surviving attribute.

This technique has many limitations. First, it may be very difficult, if not impossible, to make an evaluation of alternatives at fixed levels of all but one of the factors or criteria involved. It may be, for example, that the investment in oil and gas is possible only if $21.6 million is available for this activity. In these circumstances, an evaluation at the level of $8 million invested is meaningless. Second, it may be very difficult to perform an evaluation if factors that are evaluated only in terms of qualitative ratings are required to be included in the base set. It may not be possible, for example, to evaluate all alternatives at a fixed level of risk. Third, the process of evaluation becomes very complex if more than two or three factors or criteria are to be taken into account. The procedure is recommended therefore only in situations in which alternatives can be evaluated over a wider range of conditions with respect to factors and criteria than can be measured in quantitative terms.

For those who hanker after some form of trade-off procedure there is yet hope. Advice is available in a letter from Benjamin Franklin to Joseph Priestley written in September 1772. This letter quoted by MacCrimmon[6] and contained in a collection of Benjamin Franklin's papers[7] reads as follows:

London, Sept. 19, 1772

Dear Sir,

In the affair of so much importance to you, wherein you ask my advice, I cannot, for want of sufficient premises, advise you what to determine, but if you please I will tell you how. When those difficult cases occur, they are difficult, chiefly because while we have them under consideration, all the reasons pro and con are not present to the mind at the same time; but sometimes one set present themselves, and at other times another, the first being out of sight. Hence, the various purposes or inclinations that alternately prevail, and the uncertainty that perplexes us. To get over this, my way is to divide half a sheet of paper by a line into two columns: writing over the one Pro, and over the other Con. Then, during three or four days consideration, I put down under the different heads short hints of the different motives, that at different times occur to me, for or against the measure. When I have thus got them all together in one view, I endeavor to estimate their respective weights; and where I find two, one on each side, that seem equal, I strike them both out. If I find a reason pro equal to some two reasons con, equal to some three reasons pro, I strike out the five; and thus proceeding I find at length where the balance lies; and if, after a day or two of further consideration, nothing new that is of importance occurs on either side, I come to a determination accordingly. And, though the weight of reasons cannot be taken with the precision of algebraic quantities, yet when each is thus considered, separately and comparatively, and the whole lies before me, I think I can judge better, and am less liable to make a rash step, and in fact I have found great advantage from this kind of equation, in what may be called moral or prudential algebra.

   Wishing sincerely that you may determine for the best, I am ever, my dear friend, yours most affectionately.

B. Franklin

SUMMARY

The methods available to assist decision makers in multiple objective decision situations are determined by whether or not the following conditions apply:

1. Quantitative measures of progress towards the achievement of each objective are available.
2. A direct relationship exists between the units in which these measures are expressed.
3. Numerical weighting factors or ordinal preferences exist to express priorities between objectives.

If each of these three conditions are satisfied, weighting methods are available by means of which performance of alternatives can be aggregated into a single objective function. The choice between alternatives can then be made in terms of the greatest or least value of this objective function. The simplicity of this method provides a considerable source of temptation to the analyst to use the technique in situations in which the above conditions do not truly apply. It has given rise to methodologies in which utility assessments have been used in situations in which true quantitative measures of performance are not available. It has provided the basis for methods involving the arbitrary assignment of numbers on a numeric scale to represent relative evaluations between alternatives. There are serious reservations about the validity of these methods in many practical situations.

If quantitative measures of performance relative to each objective are available, but not necessarily in terms of the same unit, and if at least a rank ordering between objectives can express priorities between them, methods for minimizing deviations from targets may be useful. These methods provide a means by which the deviations from target levels of performance can be minimized for each objective in turn, starting from that with highest priority. It is noteworthy that the methods, known as goal programming, do not provide an optimum solution to a decision situation in the same way as for example, in linear programming.

In many practical decision situations, no truly representative quantitative measures of performance can be found with respect to some of the objectives: nor are numeric weightings available to express priorities between objectives. In these situations, elimination methods offer some capability of placing a number of alternatives in an order of preference. These methods involve the evaluation of the alternatives against a factor or a criterion related to each objective in turn, starting with that with highest priority. Alternatives not meeting a specified level of performance are eliminated until only one is left that has satisfied all the tests to that point. Ties are resolved by making the levels of performance or the criteria used more discriminating. These methods are known under the general heading of sequential elimination.

There is a general desire amongst decision makers to trade off performance of alternatives against one objective with performance in terms of another. In this way, a poor evaluation in one area can be compensated by much superior performance in another. Trade offs can be calculated accurately only if quantitative measures of performance for each objective can be expressed in the same units and if numeric weightings can be found to represent the priorities between objectives. A method related to trade offs consists of evaluating alternatives in terms of one surviving factor or criterion when performance of the alternatives against all the others has been reduced to the same level.

PRACTICAL DECISION SITUATIONS

5.1 The United Oil Company

The United Oil Company of California has options on drilling permits in four areas. These areas can be developed over a period of twenty years. Estimates of the amount of crude oil reserves that could be made available by these developments in four five-year periods are as follows:

	Crude Oil Reserves (millions of barrels)			
Area	Period 1	Period 2	Period 3	Period 4
A	36	54	210	196
B	115	264	182	32
C	164	142	121	81
D	216	248	132	63

The prime objective of the company is to build its reserves of crude oil. However, it is judged by management to be twice as important to build reserves in Period 2 than in Period 1, four times as important in Period 3 than in Period 1 and 1½ times as important in Period 4 than in Period 1. The cost of developing each of the areas is about the same. On the basis of the above figures, which area should the company develop? If the company could afford to develop two areas, which two should it choose?

5.2 Unique Apparel Incorporated

Unique Apparel Incorporated makes two sorts of ladies' garments at its production plant, namely suits and coats. The number of man hours required to make a suit is 40 and those needed to make a coat is 20. The goal of the company is to use exactly 32,000 man hours in the next week. The maximum number of suits that can be made in that week is 600 and the maximum number of coats that can be made is 800. How can the company arrange its production so that there is the minimum deviation from the goal of 32,000 man hours of effort?

5.3 Acme Furniture Manufacturing Company

The Acme Furniture Manufacturing Company is a small family operation that makes two major products, armchairs and chesterfields. Each unit of the two products requires 10 hours of production time and the plant has a capacity of 80 hours of production time per week. The market is limited for the company's products. A maximum of only fourteen armchairs and nine chesterfields can be sold every two weeks. The unit profit for an armchair is $75 and for a chesterfield it is $45.

At a management conference held recently, the following objectives were set. These objectives are shown in descending order of priority:

1. To avoid any underutilization of production capacity.
2. To limit the overtime operation of the plant to 10 hours per week.
3. To achieve the sales goals of 14 armchairs and 9 chesterfields in every two-week period.
4. To minimize the overtime operation of the plant to the greatest extent possible.

How can production be arranged so that there is minimum deviation from these objectives?

5.4 United Oil Company Revisited

The company has now decided that objectives other than building reserves of crude oil should be taken into account in choosing between the four development possibilities. The complete list of objectives to be considered in descending order of priority is as follows:

1. To maximize crude oil reserves over a twenty year period, weighted in each of the four five-year periods as in Situation 5.1.
2. To maximize total net revenue from the developments over the twenty year period.
3. To add a development area that best complements the existing development activities of the company.
4. To select an area with a low risk factor with respect to the required development program and activities.
5. To minimize the number of skilled persons required to exploit the area selected.
6. To minimize the amount of new technology required to carry out the development in the area selected.

The four areas have been evaluated in terms of the objectives as shown in the following table:

Objective	Area A	Area B	Area C	Area D
Weighted crude oil reserves (millions of barrels)	1278	1419	1053½	1334½
Total net revenue (millions of dollars)	2474	2553	1914	2162
Complement existing developments	B	B−	C	B+
Risk factor in development	C−	D	B	C+
Number of skilled persons required	81	127	173	117
Amount of new technology required	B+	B	C+	B

The company has decided that the following criteria must be met by the area selected for development:

1. Weighted crude oil reserves must be greater than 1300 millions of barrels.
2. Total net revenue must be greater than $2000 millions.
3. Complementing of existing developments must be better than C+.
4. Risk factor in development must be better than C+.
5. Number of skilled persons must be less than 100.
6. Amount of new technology must be B or better.

Which area of development would be selected on the basis of the above minimum acceptable levels of performance? Would the use of conjunctive, disjunctive, or conditional criteria affect the choice of area?

5.5 Company Personnel Selection

A company is searching for a new Vice-President Marketing. There are six candidates remaining on a short list who must be evaluated before a final interview. The President's committee has evaluated the performance of these candidates against eight factors. These factors and the performance of the candidates are shown in the following table:

Factors	Candidates					
	A	B	C	D	E	F
Years of experience in marketing	12	18	23	18	16	17
Demonstrated initiative	B	B+	A	A	C+	A
Capability of working with others	A	B	A+	A	B−	A
Skill in directing staff	C+	C+	B+	B	B+	B+
Knowledge of the industry	A+	C+	A	C+	B+	B+
Salary requested (dollars)	80,000	78,000	95,000	90,000	75,000	80,000
Calibre of personal recommendations	B+	B+	A	A	A−	B
Impressions on first interview	C+	B+	A	A	B+	B

Management has laid down levels to be observed in the case of each of the factors, as follows:

1. At least 16 years of progressive experience.
2. Demonstrated initiative B+ or better.
3. Capability of working with others A or better.
4. Skill in directing staff B or better.
5. Knowledge of the industry C+ or better.
6. Salary requested not greater than $85,000.
7. Caliber of personal recommendations B+ or better.
8. Impressions on first interview B+ or better.

Assuming the above levels are listed in descending order of importance, which two candidates would you choose for final interview? Would you obtain a different result if conjunctive, disjunctive, or conditional constraints were used?

5.6 The Local Bookstore

The manager of a local bookstore employs four full-time and three part-time sales persons. Normal working hours per month for a full-time salesperson are 154 and for a part-time salesperson 88. Average sales are four books per hour and two books per hour for full-time and part-time sales staff respectively. The average profit from the sale of a book is $2.10. The average hourly rates are $5 and $3.50 for full-time and part-time staff.

The manager has set the following objectives for the store listed in decreasing order of priority:

1. Achieve sales of 4800 books per month.
2. Limit the total overtime of full-time salespersons to 100 hours per month.
3. Utilize fully the normal working hours of the full-time and part-time salespersons.
4. Minimize the sum of the monthly overtime of the full-time and part-time salespersons taking into account the net marginal profit ratio between them.

How should the manager formulate his problem?

DISCUSSION TOPICS

1. What are the conditions in practical decision situations that in many cases prevent evaluation of alternatives in terms of a single objective function?

2. What are the characteristics of situations in which weighting methods are applicable?

3. What are the reservations concerning the use of weighted scores in the evaluation of alternatives in multiple objective situations? Why do people use techniques involving weighted scores in situations in which many factors need to be decided arbitrarily in order that the technique can be used?

4. Why does goal programming not provide an optimum solution in a decision situation in a manner similar to linear programming?

5. How do you view sequential elimination as a technique to be used in evaluating alternatives in a decision situation? Does use of this technique

involve risk in terms of dismissing an alternative that has less performance in the highest priority category and superior performance in all the others? If so, what can be done to overcome this possibility?

6.   What are the uses of conjunctive, disjunctive, and conditional criteria in sequential elimination? Can the views of management be represented effectively by such criteria?

7.   Under what circumstances do you think trade-offs are possible in the evaluation of alternatives in multiple objective decision situations?

8.   Why does there appear to be an instinctive desire among decision makers to make trade-offs between alternatives? Is this desire in your opinion linked to the attraction many decision makers feel for the concept of utility?

9.   If you were involved in a multiple objective decision situation, which of the methods described in this chapter would you choose to assist in selecting among alternatives? Give reasons for your selection of a method or methods related to the characteristics of the decision situation that you have in mind.

10.   If weighting methods have such limited application, why do you think cost-benefit analysis has had such wide appeal in recent years? Has use of this method of analysis been the cause of many wrong decisions in your view? If so, what could have been done to prevent these wrong conclusions?

REFERENCES

1.   Prest, A. R. & Turvey, R., "Cost-Benefit Analysis: a Survey," *The Economic Journal*, Vol LXXV, No 300, Dec 1965, pp 683-735.
2.   The Kepner-Tregoe method is a proprietary technique, based in part on Kepner, C. H. and Tregoe, B. B., *The Rational Manager*, McGraw Hill, 1965.
3.   Charnes, A. & Cooper, W. W., *Management Models and Industrial Applications of Linear Programming*, Wiley, 1961.
4.   Lee Sang, M. & Moore, L. J., *Introduction to Decision Science*, Petrocelli/Charter, 1975, Chapter 6.
5.   MacCrimmon, K. R., "An Overview of Multiple Objective Decision Making" in Cochrane, R. L. and Zeleny, M. (eds), *Multiple Criteria Decision Making*, University of South Carolina Press, 1973, pp 18-46.
6.   MacCrimmon, K. R., *op cit*, p 27.
7.   Franklin, B., "Letter to Joseph Priestly" reprinted in *The Benjamin Franklin Sampler*, Fawcett, 1956.

 *Chapter Six*

Joint Decisions by Two or More Parties

INTRODUCTION

The discussion of decision making to this point in the text has been in the context of a single individual faced with the unilateral resolution of a decision situation. The decision situations have involved uncertainty, nonquantifiable measures of benefits and costs and multiple objectives. However, the task of choice between alternatives has rested entirely with the single individual involved. We now turn to discussion of the decision situations (placed in category 5 in Table 1-1) in which there is more than one participant engaged in the choice between alternatives.

These multiparticipant decision situations cover a wide range of circumstances. In one sort of situation, two or more individuals wish to cooperate in a venture that involves risk. These individuals seek an arrangement by which they can share that risk. In doing so, they hope to divide the rewards amongst themselves if the venture is successful. In another sort of situation, individuals are members of a group that is faced with a choice between alternatives. In many situations of this type the group members do not have exactly the same objectives. Their perceptions of the situation may not be identical and their assessment of the benefits and costs of alternative courses of action and outcomes may not necessarily be the same. Situations of this sort arise in the management group of a company, in committees elected to oversee the affairs of a community, and in a number of other similar circumstances. The members of the group wish to further the achievement of its objectives, but they do not necessarily agree upon the manner in which this desire should be accomplished. A third type of situation is that in which two or more participants are in open or implicit conflict for the benefits that can be obtained in a particular environment. Examples of this type of situation occur throughout the activities of businesses and communities and in our personal lives. The participants each have some power to influence the outcome of the situation in which they are engaged. Each wishes to bring about an outcome he or she most prefers, but the actual and ultimate outcome must be one that is eventually agreed upon by all the participants concerned.

These three types of situation have much in common. They will therefore be dealt with in a discussion that develops progressively over this and the following two chapters. In this chapter, the discussion starts with a treatment of risk sharing between individuals. It then develops into a more general treatment of decision making in groups. Chapter 7 is devoted to description of some basic situations that can arise when two or more participants in a decision situation are in competition. The content of Chapter 8 refers entirely to the resolution of situations in which two or more participants seek to persuade or coerce each other into accepting a particular outcome of the circumstances in which they are mutually involved.

RISK SHARING

Suppose that two individuals are contemplating a joint venture which (for the sake of simplicity) can be thought of as having only two outcomes: a gain x or a loss y. Suppose further that the two individuals agree on an estimate of the probability of a gain and that of a loss. The acceptability of the venture to each individual is not necessarily the same. It depends in each case on his or her attitude to risk. For example, one individual might well accept a joint venture in which his or her share was a possible gain of $10,000 with a possible loss of $5000. A more risk-averse individual might feel able to accept only a venture providing a smaller possible loss and possibly a smaller potential gain.

The attitude of one individual can be represented (following Raiffa's exposition[1]) in a diagram such as Fig. 6-1. In this diagram, each point (x, y) represents a possible share of a venture for the individual. The space is divided into two parts. The lower part, which is labeled "acceptable,"

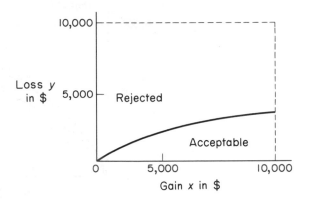

FIG. 6-1.   Acceptance and rejection sets for a particular individual in a venture
giving a 50% chance of a gain $x and a 50% chance of a loss $y.

contains all those risks that the individual concerned would be inclined to
undertake. The upper part of the diagram consists of risks in which the
possible loss outweighs the possible gain and which therefore might be
rejected by the individual to which the diagram refers. The line shown in
the diagram divides the ventures or shares of ventures that would be acceptable to the individual from those that would be rejected, according to
that individual's attitude to risk. For example, the $10,000/$5000 venture
referred to earlier is clearly not in the acceptable region of an individual
whose acceptance and rejection sets are as shown in Fig. 6-1. On the other
hand, a $5000/$1750 venture would fall just inside the acceptance set of
such an individual. He or she might therefore be interested in finding a
partner with whom to share the risk in such a way that each person involved found the share of the risk available to be acceptable.

Let us consider the situation shown in Fig. 6-2. In this diagram, the dividing line between the acceptance and rejection sets of the individual of
Fig. 6-1 is shown as the lower curve. A similar line for a second individual
is shown as the upper curve. The two individuals have different attitudes
to risk and therefore different acceptance and rejection sets. However, the
$10,000/$5000 venture is acceptable to neither of them.

There are two ways in which this venture might be shared between the
two individuals. The first is that in which each takes a *proportion* of the risk,
thus maintaining the same ratio of possible gain to loss for each. It can be
appreciated with a moment's thought that all *proportions* of the original
venture lie on the dotted line joining the origin (in Fig. 6-2) to the point
representing the ($10,000/$5000) venture. Most of these proportions are
within the acceptance set of individual 2, although only those involving up

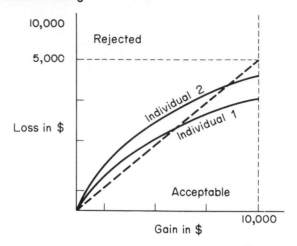

FIG. 6-2. Sharing of a venture by two individuals.

to about 50% of the venture are acceptable to individual 1. In these circumstances some arrangement for sharing the venture proportionally could no doubt be worked out. For example, for the case shown in Fig. 6-2, the situation in which each partner assumes half of the risk (that is each assumes a chance of a $5000 gain or a $2500 loss) would lie in the acceptance regions of both of them.

Suppose, however, that the acceptance sets of the two individuals are shown in Figure 6-3. In these circumstances, no proportional share of the venture is acceptable to individual 1. It may be possible, however, to share the venture in a *nonproportional* fashion. For example, it can be seen from Fig. 6-3 that the risk $5000/$1750 falls within the acceptance region of

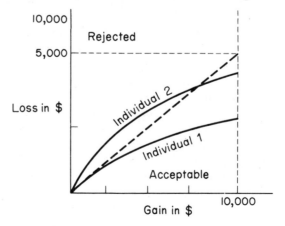

FIG. 6-3. Nonproportional sharing of a venture by two individuals.

individual 1 and the complementary risk \$5000/\$3250 falls within that of individual 2. A nonproportional sharing of a venture in this manner always involves a payment from one individual to the other. The effect of this side payment is that each individual assumes a percentage of the venture while remaining within his region of acceptable risks.

The relationship between the parameters in the sharing of a venture can be expressed in the form of the following equations:

gain for individual 1 = side payment received by 1 + percentage of risk assumed by 1 × total gain in venture;

loss for individual 1 = side payment received by 1 + percentage of risk assumed by 1 × total loss in venture.

Similar equations can be written for individual 2. The equations can be extended also to represent sharing between more than two individuals.

We can apply these equations to the case of the \$10,000/\$5000 venture that was to be broken by individuals 1 and 2 into two parts (\$5000/\$1750 and \$5000/\$3250) in the following way. If the side payment paid from individual 2 to individual 1 is s and the percentage of the risk assumed by individual 1 is p; then

$$5000 = s + p \times 10,000$$
$$-1750 = s - p \times 5000$$

These simultaneous equations can be solved to show that the side payment in this case is \$500 (from individual 2 to individual 1) and that individual 1 assumes 45% of the whole venture. Corresponding equations for individual 2 show the same side payment (in the reverse direction) and the assumption by that individual of 55% of the overall venture.

It may seem incongruous at first sight that one individual could enter a partnership and assume a \$5000/\$3250 share of the possible benefits and costs while the other partner enjoys a \$5000/\$1750 share. Note, however, that the total venture is outside the acceptance set of each of the partners, whereas the nonproportional shares are within each of these sets. It may be that one partner can afford to lose only \$1750. In these circumstances, the choice for the other partner is to assume the \$5000/\$3250, 55% share of the venture or to give up any idea of sharing the venture with this particular partner. Undoubtedly, the exact share of the risk assumed by the partners in any particular circumstances would be the subject of some negotiation. The basis for this negotiation is explored in the following example.

Example of Risk Sharing

Two individuals would like to enter a joint business venture. This venture would give them the opportunity of a \$500,000 profit, but it requires

TABLE 6-1. Sharing of a $500,000/$250,000 Venture with Individual 1's Investment Limited to $100,000 (including side payment)

Individual 1 (possible loss $100,000)			Individual 2 (possible loss $150,000)		
Percentage of venture assumed	Side payment received (-ve if paid)	Potential gain	Percentage of venture assumed	Side payment received (-ve if paid)	Potential gain
20	−50,000	50,000	80	50,000	450,000
30	−25,000	125,000	70	25,000	375,000
40	nil	200,000	60	nil	300,000
50	25,000	275,000	50	−25,000	225,000
60	50,000	350,000	40	−50,000	150,000
70	75,000	425,000	30	−75,000	75,000

an initial investment of $250,000. Both individuals agree that the chances of the venture being successful are good. However, individual 1 can afford to invest only $100,000. Individual 2 can afford to invest $150,000, but he wishes to investigate the range of possible shares of the opportunity and the side payments that will be necessary. Analysis of the situation is shown in Table 6-1.

Sharing and side payment arrangements at the top of this table are unlikely to be acceptable to individual 1, who stands to gain only $50,000 for an investment of $100,000. Individual 2, on the other hand, would gain $450,000 for an investment of $150,000 at this point in the table. Conversely at the bottom of the table, the 70/30 sharing is likely to be unacceptable to individual 2. In all probability, the actual sharing agreed would be between these two extremes, at a point that represented a sharing of the venture that falls within the acceptance set of the two individuals. Note that the 40/60 sharing is proportional and results in no side payment being necessary.

JOINTLY PREFERRED SOLUTIONS AND PARETO OPTIMALITY

In risk sharing situations, such as that just discussed, a large number of ways of sharing the venture are available to the participants. These arrangements can be regarded as feasible solutions to their problem of sharing the venture. Any one of these feasible solutions would probably be preferred by both the participants to the alternative of not engaging in the venture at all. However, one of the sharing arrangements that are available may be more favorable to one of the participants while another may be considered preferable by one or more of the other participants. There is no prescription given to this point in the text that can be used to determine which of the possible risk sharing arrangements is jointly preferred by all the participants.

This situation is illustrated in Fig. 6-4. In this diagram, the status quo prior to a risk sharing agreement between two participants is shown as the origin. The horizontal axis ("east") is the direction of increasing benefit to participant 1 and the vertical axis ("north") a similar direction for participant 2. A point in the quadrant shown represents a risk sharing arrangement between the two participants. A point that is further to the east than to the north is relatively more favorable to participant 1. Similarly, points that are further to the north than to the east are relatively more favorable to participant 2. Points that are to the north-east of the status quo represent positions that are to the benefit of both participants as compared with the status quo. The example chosen is limited to two participants in order that the diagram can be drawn in two dimensions. The discussion can be generalized intuitively to cases involving more than two participants.

In practical circumstances, there is a limit to how far to the north-east the two participants can go. This limit is set by restrictions on the sharing arrangements that are available to the participants. Consider, for example, the case of negotiations between management and a labor union during a strike in which the issue is limited to monetary matters. Certain increases in rates of pay for the union members are to the joint advantage of the

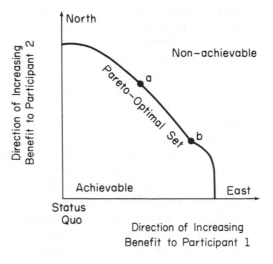

FIG. 6-4. Pareto-optimal set for risk-sharing between two individuals.

participants in that the strike is ended, giving management the benefit of resumed production, and workers more money for their efforts. Payment of too high a wage increase might, however, result in the bankruptcy of the enterprise, a development that would be to the disadvantage of all concerned. There is a practical limit therefore to settlements that are achievable. This factor is illustrated in Fig. 6-4 by the division of the diagram into achievable and nonachievable regions. This diagram is far less complex than conditions experienced in real situations of this type. However, it serves to illustrate the basic features of the relationship between the participants.

The point at issue in the negotiations between management and the union is which position in the achievable region will be chosen as the settlement. Clearly, both participants will wish to choose a point as far to the northeast as possible. With this in mind, the boundary between the achievable and nonachievable regions represents the set of best achievable arrangements for both participants between north and east. This boundary is called the *Pareto-optimal set*. Whereas the Pareto-optimal set consists of the best achievable arrangements between the individuals for all directions from the status quo, any point in the achievable region is an improvement with respect to the status quo for at least one of the participants. In general practice, therefore, any move from the status quo from which one participant gains and none loses is called a Pareto-improvement.

Individual points in the Pareto-optimal set are more or less attractive to the individual participants. For example, point *a* in Fig. 6-4 would be more preferred by participant 2 than point *b*; and vice versa for participant 1. In practice, the negotiations may not lead to a settlement that is in the Pareto-optimal set. The participants may agree to a point that is in the achievable region rather than on the boundary between the regions. However, in all cases, the crucial point in the negotiations is whether the settlement point is further to the east (favoring, say, management) or further to the north which is relatively more favorable to the union.

In negotiations of this sort, one or both of the participants may have a level of improvement from the status quo below which a settlement is regarded as unacceptable. This lowest limit of acceptability is called the *security level* of the participant. The security levels of the participants restrict the region in which outcomes that are jointly acceptable can be found, as illustrated in Fig. 6-5. In this diagram, the group of outcomes in the achievable region that are more preferred than the security levels of both participants is called the *negotiation set*. The negotiation set represents the group of possible outcomes that can practically be discussed in negotiations at any one time. In actual situations, the security levels of participants often change with time, so that the negotiation set may vary during the course of the discussions leading to a settlement.

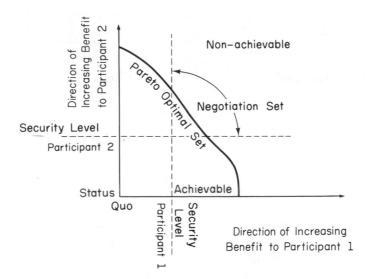

FIG. 6-5. Negotiation set for risk sharing between two participants.

The Nash Solution

It is interesting to consider how two participants who are eager to agree on a settlement might arrive at a division of the benefits of a venture. Let us suppose that each of the participants is anxious to agree to an outcome that can be considered "fair" by all the parties concerned. A similar situation faces an arbitrator who is appointed to suggest an outcome that can be accepted by all participants involved in the negotiation of an issue.

A specific approach to this situation has been proposed by Nash for the case in which the benefits to the participants are measurable in quantitative terms.[2, 3] Suppose that the benefits to two participants at a proposed settlement point can be represented by u_1 and u_2 and suppose further that each of the two participants assesses these benefits in exactly the same terms. Let u_1 and u_2 be the corresponding benefits at the status quo. Nash proposes that an outcome that can be considered "fair" occurs when the product $(u_1 - \bar{u}_1) \times (u_2 - u_2)$ is a maximum. A slight modification of this proposal in which the values $\bar{u}_1$ and $\bar{u}_2$ are the benefits at the security levels of the participants is called the *Shapley procedure*.

As an example of the application of the Nash procedure let us consider the case in which two participants must divide $100 between themselves. The status quo is that each participant has no benefit and this situation maintains until they agree on a settlement. Suppose that the participants' ultilities for money are identical and also that these utilities are linear with the amount of money received. The Nash procedure leads to a 50/50 split

TABLE 6-2. Split of a $100 Benefit between Two Participants with Identical Utilities That Are Linear with Money

Benefits Received		Utilities		Product of Utilities
Participant 1	Participant 2	Participant 1	Participant 2	
$ 0	$100	0.00	1.00	0.00
$ 25	$ 75	0.25	0.75	0.19
$ 50	$ 50	0.50	0.50	0.25
$ 75	$ 25	0.75	0.25	0.19
$100	$ 0	1.00	0	0

of the $100 under these conditions, as illustrated in Table 6-2. Most people would support this split of the $100 as "fair."

If the utilities of the participants are not identical, the Nash procedure provides a basis for a division of benefits based on these utilities. In the situation shown in Table 6-3, for example, Participant 1 can be regarded as rich with a utility function that is linear with money in the region 0 to $100.[4] Participant 2, on the other hand, is poor and has a relatively higher utility for smaller amounts of money. If Participant 1 were selfish, he could argue for a ($75, $25) split of the benefits on the grounds that the $25 gain to participant 2 was at least as great as the $75 gain to himself on the basis of utility evaluations. On the other hand, if participant 1 were altruistic, he might modify his utility function and accept a division of the benefits much more favorable to participant 2 in monetary terms.

The Nash procedure has, in addition, a number of more technical characteristics that recommend it for the resolution of situations in which the participants are eager to agree. For example, the "solution" obtained from the procedure leads to benefits to all participants and is therefore Pareto-

TABLE 6-3. Split of a $100 Benefit between Two Participants with Different Utilities for Money

Benefit Received		Utilities		Product of Utilities
Participant 1	Participant 2	Participant 1	Participant 2	
$ 0	$100	0.00	1.00	0.000
$ 25	$ 75	0.25	0.98	0.245
$ 50	$ 50	0.50	0.90	0.450
$ 75	$ 25	0.75	0.73	0.548
$100	$ 0	1.00	0.00	0.000

optimal. Participants in a situation that is symmetric (that is, it looks the same from the point of view of each of them) receive equal benefits. The solution procedure is not affected if additional possible outcomes arise in the situation. In this case, either the previously recommended outcome or one of the new outcomes appears as the solution. The solution procedure is not affected by the addition of irrelevant outcomes nor by arbitrary linear transformation of utilities.

The procedure does not have any direct application, however, if numeric estimates of the utilities of the participants are not available. There are many situations in management in which benefits to the participants cannot be expressed comprehensively in these terms. In these circumstances, other procedures may need to be used to arrive at an outcome that is jointly acceptable to the participants. Nevertheless, there is some evidence that the Nash procedure is at the basis of many settlements in which a direct representation of utilities is not available to the participants. For example, Fouraker and Siegel conducted experiments in which two participants were required to bargain over a contract.[5] One of the participants played the part of the sole manufacturer of a product and the other played the part of the sole distributor. Bargaining concerned the quality of goods that the distributor would take and the price per unit that he would pay. The experiment was designed to find out what sort of contracts the participants would agree on. The experimenters found that over a number of pairs of participants, the mean tendency was to split the profit arising from the negotiated contract evenly between the buyer and seller, confirming to some extent the Nash "solution." Differences in the split within bargaining pairs were greatest when the information available to the participants was least and vice versa. However, experiments of this nature are not conclusive. At best they can be used to support or reject conclusions reached in other independent studies.

Jointly preferred outcomes of a negotiating situation can be obtained in another way if the participants know that a situation similar to that in which they are involved will occur between them at some later time. For example, management and union leaders may be involved in essentially similar negotiations each time a contract has to be renewed. Suppose, in these circumstances, that two possible outcomes exist, one of which is more favorable to one participant and the other more favorable to the other participant. This situation is illustrated by the points a and b in Fig. 6-4 (and also in the two equilibria of the Battle of the Sexes controversy discussed in Chapter 7). It might be possible to arrange between the participants, either implicitly or explicitly, that one of the outcomes be chosen in the present circumstances on condition that the other be chosen in the next occurrence of the situation. The average of the outcomes of the two situations might then represent a combined benefit to each participant that would be unachievable in each of the situations independently.[6]

GROUP DECISION MAKING

We have discussed to this point in the chapter the basis for a joint choice between alternatives by two participants who wish to cooperate in a venture. We now wish to expand this discussion to the case of a group of participants who may have different preferences for outcomes of a situation but who nevertheless wish to arrive at a choice between outcomes on behalf of the group. Suppose, for example, that a group of 24 persons must make a choice between two alternatives. Seventeen of the 24 prefer alternative A and seven prefer alternative B. A seemingly natural way of making the choice on behalf of the group is by adopting the alternative most preferred by a simple majority. In the example quoted above, 17 of the members would see their more preferred alternative adopted by the group. However, 7 of the members would, if they remained in the group, have to accept a less preferred alternative. Those members that stayed in the group after the adoption of this less preferred alternative would presumably do so because it was more important or beneficial for them to remain as group members than to seek their more preferred alternative elsewhere.

Simple majority rule is often the most readily acceptable method of choice between alternatives in a group. Other decision rules are often adopted in practice, however, to meet special circumstances. For example, it may be seen as desirable that any choice made should represent the preference of a major proportion of the members of a group. In such a case, a "three-quarters majority" rule might be used. In the above example, a group making decisions by a three-quarters majority would not accept alternative A even though 17 of the 24 members of the group accepted it as their most preferred outcome. In other cases, very different and even more arbitrary decision rules are often adopted. In the Security Council of the United Nations for example, a motion cannot pass if one of the permanent members votes against it, even if all 14 other members are in favor. In democratic countries, we elect a small number of representatives to make decisions on behalf of the group (the nation) often by simple majority of these members of a legislature. This practice sometimes results in measures being adopted on behalf of the nation that are clearly not preferred by a majority of the members of the population. Legislation passed in the late 1970s resulting in abolition of the death penalty for murder in many jurisdictions provides recent examples of this phenomenon.

The situation becomes much more complex if a group has to decide between three alternatives rather than two. Suppose, for example, 9 members of the group of 24 prefer alternative A, 8 prefer alternative B, and 7 prefer alternative C. Simple majority rule would select alternative A as the group choice even though 15 of the 24 members (over 60%) did not have this alternative as their first preference.

TABLE 6-4.   Preferences of Individuals in the Voting Paradox

Individual 1	Individual 2	Individual 3	Group Preferences Based on Simple Majority
A to B			A to B
B to C	B to C		B to C
therefore			but
A to C	C to A	C to A	C to A
	therefore		
	B to A	A to B	
		therefore	
		C to B	

In certain circumstances, the use of majority rule can lead to an even more paradoxical result. Consider a group of three individuals which has three available alternatives, A, B, and C. Suppose that individual 1 prefers alternative A to B and B to C. Assuming that transitivity is maintained, this individual therefore prefers A to C. Individual 2 prefers B to C and C to A and therefore B to A. Individual 3 prefers C to A and A to B and therefore C to A. The situation is illustrated in Table 6-4. It can be seen from this table that the majority of the individuals in the group (2 out of 3) prefer A to B and B to C. If the simple majority rule were adopted, the group could be said to prefer A to B and B to C. Assuming transitivity is preserved by the group, it then must prefer A to C. However, a majority of its members (2 out of 3) do, in fact, prefer C to A. This famous paradox was apparently first discussed in a paper published in 1882 on the subject of voting procedures in elections.[7]

Search for a Basis for Group Choice

It seems from the above examples that the simple majority rule does not provide a universally applicable method of formulating group preferences. This being the case, we may ask if there are any other methods of deriving group preferences from those of the individual members that do not encounter similar problems. Several such methods have been suggested in the recent literature. Many of these methods involve the adoption by the group of a quantitative utility function derived from the utilities of the individual members for the alternatives before them. Assuming for the moment that these utilities can be measured in quantitative terms, it is interesting to explore the form that the group utility function might take.

The simplest form of group utility function that has been generally discussed is the sum of the utilities of the individual members for an alternative.[8] While a function of this nature may be intuitively appealing, there seems to be no compelling reason why the sum (rather than some other combination) of the individual utilities should be chosen to make up the group utility function. Why, for example, should not the sum of the squares of the individual utilities be chosen instead? Note, however, that the function selected automatically determines the relative weight that is to be given to any one individual's preferences.

One other difficulty must be surmounted before a meaningful group utility function can be constructed. It is only possible, at best, to measure individual utilities on an interval scale. In such a measurement, the zero point and the unit of utility can be chosen arbitrarily for each individual. These choices have an effect on the group utility function. For example, suppose that the group function is made up of the simple sum of the individual utilities and that one member measures preferences on a scale of 0 to 10 and another on a scale of 0 to 100. In these circumstances, preferences of the second member automatically have a much greater weight on the simple-sum group utility function that those of the first member. Steps must therefore be taken to establish the relationship between the zero points and units of measurement relating to all members of the group before any meaningful group utility function can be constructed. A form of standardization of this relationship is often achieved in organizations by the establishment of policies that are followed by members involved in group decision making.

In actual practice, it is often not possible to represent the preferences of members of a group in terms of quantitative utilities. In many cases, only the order of preference of the members for the available alternatives can be established. Suppose, therefore, that each member of a group can express a consistent order of preference between the available alternatives and that each member remains transitive in stating this order of preference. Is it possible to define a unique rule for choice between the alternatives that is based on the preferences of the members of the group?

The search for such a rule was the subject of a paper published in 1951 by K. J. Arrow that has become one of the basic modern contributions to group decision theory.[9] Arrow was interested in the methods by which "social" choices can be made by members of a group acting collectively, when all members of the group do not have the same preference orderings between available alternatives. He observed that suggestions for a rule of collective choice had been seen in previous work to be based on certain value judgments. He laid down what he considered to be five necessary conditions that a group decision rule should satisfy. He derived these conditions from a study of practical methods of group choice, such as voting, establishment of a convention for decision making among the members, and the imposition of choice by a dominant member of the group.

He sought a rule of collective decision making that has been called a *social welfare function,* because it is primarily involved with the economic problem of social welfare.

Arrow's five conditions that he thought were "apparently reasonable" can be stated as follows:[10, 11]

Condition 1:   The group decision rule should give a true group ordering for a sufficiently wide range of individual orderings.

Condition 2:   If one available option rises or remains constant in the value scale of each member of the group, then it must rise or remain constant in the group ordering.

Condition 3:   If the individual orderings for any subset of the available options are unchanged, then the group ordering for that subset should be unchanged also. This must be true even if there are changes in the individual orderings of the remaining options. The group ordering must be unaffected by the absence or presence of other options beyond those under consideration. This is referred to as the *Condition of Independence of Irrelevant Alternatives.*

Condition 4:   For any two available options under consideration, the group ordering must not be independent of the individual orderings. This is known as the *Condition of Citizen's Sovereignty.*

Condition 5:   The group ordering must not coincide with the ordering of one individual, regardless of the orderings of the other members of the group. This is the *Condition of Nondictatorship.*

Arrow constructed a theorem by means of which he was able to prove that it was impossible to propose a criterion of collective choice based on the preferences of group members that met all of these five conditions simultaneously. In other words, Arrow's "impossibility theorem" states that any proposed criterion for collective choice must break one or more of the above conditions. This startling conclusion dictates that any criterion for group decision making that meets the apparently reasonable conditions 1, 2, and 3 must either be imposed on some members of the group so that it contravenes condition 4; or that it must coincide with the ordering of one individual regardless of those of the other members, so that it contravenes condition 5. Furthermore, by virtue of this theorem no one group decision rule can be regarded as uniquely "best" over a wide range of circumstances. Criteria of collective choice may have to be devised to meet the requirements of particular cases as they arise.

The publication of this theorem in 1951 was followed by a great deal of research, publication, and attempted rebuttal, from which Arrow's work emerged relatively unscathed. Some authors attempted to establish that the conclusion was not important under certain specific conditions. For example, if the preferences of all the members of the group coincide, the fourth condition (nondictatorship) is not applicable. All the other conditions would be satisfied if the orderings of one individual were taken to represent those of the group. In the general case, however, where there is no restriction on the orderings of members of the group, the conclusion that no group criterion can satisfy the five stated conditions survives. Blau put forward some counter examples that seem at first sight to disprove Arrow's theorem; but these counter examples are close to conditions of dictatorship, so that little harm is done to Arrow's original conclusion.[12, 13]

Detailed proposals of methods by which Arrow's conclusion might be circumvented have been given by Luce and Raiffa[14] and by Rothenburg.[15] These proposals center on one or both of (1) means of rejecting or relaxing one of the conditions and (2) imposition of additional restrictions on the group members' orderings of options in order to find areas in which a group decision criterion *can* be constructed.

The condition most often selected for discussion is number 3, the independence of the group ordering to the introduction of irrelevant alternatives. Procedures have been suggested for incorporating *strengths of preference* into the analysis. However, these procedures require that some means of relating the preference orderings of the members of the group be introduced, in terms, for example, of establishing a common unit of utility and/or a basic utility scale to be used by all. Much of the work has concentrated on the formulation of restrictions on the individual orderings of alternatives necessary in order that a group decision rule can be established. For example, Luce and Raiffa discuss restrictions to be placed on the profiles of individual rankings, such that the simple majority rule always leads to a consistent group ordering.[16] However, many of the restrictions imposed in these proposals are difficult to relate to practical group decision making: some appear to be unnatural and arbitrary in relation to the everyday problems of making group decisions in business, government, and industry.

In other work on this subject, Raiffa has described a set of axioms that would allow a group of individuals, who are all dedicated to maximization of expected utility, to combine their utility functions and subjective probabilities in such a way that the group could act as a maximizer of group utility.[17] He shows, for example, that if each member of the group has a utility function that can be represented in exponential form, then the group utility function is also in exponential form. However, he points out that under conditions of risk sharing, a group utility function that depends on the individual members' utility functions cannot always be assumed to exist. Furthermore, he shows that there is no generally applicable method of combining individual subjective probability estimates to arrive at a group decision making procedure, even if the members of the group agree on utilities for available options. This conclusion is reached also by Fishburn in a study of various group choice functions that are generalizations of the simple majority rule.[18] In this work, he finds no satisfactory way of establishing a consistent group utility function.

The Group Decision Making Process

The group decision process is similar to that used by an individual decision maker, but it is much more complex. The additional complexity arises from the presence in the decision making process of a number of group members, each of whom may have somewhat different information about the situation under consideration and also different past experience in situations of the same general nature. These differences amongst the members may cause them to have varying perceptions of the alternative courses of action available to the group and also different initial preferences for such alternatives as have been identified. In these circumstances, the first task undertaken by a group faced with a decision situation is often an exchange of information among the members. The purpose of this exchange is to increase the individual members' awareness of different appreciations of the situation in which they are involved. Individual members of the group may present different versions of information relating to the same subject. Different sets of data may be brought forward, each purporting to be the true representation of the phenomena or events to which it refers. Discussion of such discrepancies can often produce agreement on the data or the interpretation that will be used by the group in the decision making process. Discussions of this nature however, can take up a great deal of time. Furthermore, there is no guarantee that a true consensus will be reached as a result of the discussions.

The second major constituent of group decision-making activity is a process of interaction in which the purpose of some members of the group is to influence the opinions of others. The interaction serves to inform members of the group of the preferences of others for alternatives and also of the strength of these preferences. Pressure is often used on some members of the group to align their views and preferences with those of others who are in favor of a particular course of action. Coalitions between some members of the group may be proposed in which possible benefits are offered to those participating in return for support of a particular course of action. Sometimes the interaction results in the emergence of a consensus among the members of the group. A consensus often results from the efforts of a dominant member or subgroup that spends much time and effort in recruiting other group members to a particular point of view. In such cases, much of the interaction and negotiation may take place outside the actual decision making group, in lobbying sessions or in side conversations. If no consensus arises in a group, it may be that two or more subgroups form, each of them putting forward proposals that are in conflict with each other. In such cases, the amount and nature of the conflict that arises in the group is a major factor in determining the manner in which the decision situation is eventually resolved.

Much of the group decision process is often concerned with the establishment of a rule for choice between alternatives on the part of the group. Some of the information exchange and a great deal of the interaction in a decision making group may be directly or indirectly related to the question of how this choice is to be made. In effect, the group has to decide how to decide before it can reach a conclusion on the choice between alternatives. Sometimes, the decision on how to decide is introduced into the group indirectly by a dominant member proposing a course of action to be adopted by the group and working towards acceptance of this course of action by all concerned. If the dominant member succeeds in this strategem, the group's ordering of alternatives eventually coincides with that of one member and Arrow's fifth condition is not met. A consensus of some sort is obtained, however, and this consensus may lead to a rapid resolution of the decision situation. In other circumstances, the subject of which decision rule to adopt may be debated at length in the group, before a decision on how to decide is arrived at.

The adoption of a decision rule for the group may have considerable effect on the alternative chosen. For example, in the original European Economic Community there were six member nations. It was agreed that these nations should have an influence in the Minister's Council overseeing the affairs of the community that reflected in some fashion their relative populations and gross national products. Furthermore, it was agreed that to pass in the Council, a proposal would require a total of at least 12 votes. The apportionment of votes (on proposals received from the Commission) in the Council that was eventually agreed upon is shown in Table 6-5.

The effect of these decision rules was as follows.[19] A proposal supported by all three of the larger nations could pass in the Council irrespective of the view of the other three nations. A proposal supported by two of the larger nations and the two middle-sized nations could also pass.

TABLE 6-5.

	Votes
France	4
Germany	4
Italy	4
Belgium	2
Netherlands	2
Luxembourg	1
Total	17

Luxembourg's one vote, however, had no significance at all in the Council. There is no grouping of nations in which the 1 vote held by Luxembourg would be decisive, as long as 12 votes (not 11 or 13) are required for a proposal to pass. One is led to wonder if the delegates appreciated the uselessness of the one Luxembourg vote at the time at which the decision making rule was formulated. If so, the one vote was possibly a means of persuading the Luxembourg population (completely incorrectly) that their nation could influence the decision as to whether a proposal received from the Commission would pass in the Council.

The nature of the decision making rule to be used by the group is therefore one of the most important considerations at the outset of a group decision process. Choice of a particular rule may have a considerable influence on the eventual choice between alternatives. Furthermore, a particular decision making rule may be supported by some farsighted members of a group as a means of ensuring that a particular alternative course of action is eventually chosen by its members. To avoid manipulation of the decision process and to ensure that all available alternatives are given due consideration, it is necessary, therefore, that a decision rule be adopted that does not automatically eliminate or relegate certain of the choices before the group. In addition, it is most desirable that ample time is allowed for the two major components of group activity, information exchange and interaction between the members, before the ultimate decision is made.

Types of Decision Making Groups

The internal structure of a decision making group provides some light on the manner in which the members act together in arriving at a choice between alternatives.[20] For example, some groups exhibit a degree of cohesiveness and internal solidarity that typifies them as teams. In such cases, there is considerable identity of purpose amongst the members. Group objectives and preferences are very close to those of the individual members. Any member's objectives that might be in conflict with those of the team are kept in the background at least for the time being. Team behavior of this nature is often observed in the early days of a new organization or when an older organization has been substantially reorganized. The sense of purpose in a group operating as a team is usually very strong. In newly formed businesses, for example, the direction of the enterprise is often in the hands of a group of people who work together single mindedly to promote its success. Tasks are delegated to subordinates who are similarly inspired and who, in essence, form part of the team.

Decision making groups acting as teams approach a choice between alternatives in much the same manner as an individual. Each of the group members identifies very closely with the objectives and preferences of the total entity. The degree of conflict among group members is very low. Team members are often willing to agree to choices suggested by a leader in the group with a minimum of discussion and examination of the alternatives.

In contrast, many decision making groups behave as a much less cohesive coalition. In such cases, the objectives of the members are often divergent and much less closely related to those of the group as a whole. For example, many employees have no strong loyalty to the organization in which they work, especially if employment elsewhere is reasonably easy to get. For the time being, however, they are prepared to perform services for the organization in order to further its objectives. They do so because they receive benefits from the organization that are useful to them in achieving their own objectives. For the most part the satisfactions of such employees are obtained outside the organization in which they work. Time spent working in the organization is regarded as a necessary means of achieving these satisfactions, but this achievement is postponed temporarily while the employee is on the job. Groups of employees engaged in a loose coalition of this nature do not display the high degree of group purpose that is evident in a team. The possibility of conflict amongst the members' objectives and preferences is likely to be much greater than in a team, especially if matters that affect the achievement of individual group members' objectives are raised.

There is a wide range of structural characteristics demonstrated by decision making groups between that observed in teams and in loose coalitions. Conditions within a group may change with time, sometimes quickly and possibly, unexpectedly, depending on the circumstances under which the group is operating. Any particular group may contain subgroups that have different types of structure. It is entirely possible to find a group consisting of a loose coalition of closely knit teams. The make-up of the subgroups may vary as conditions in the overall group change with time. Certain subgroups may break up at any time and new alignments may emerge. The factor most often causing such realignments is frustration and dissatisfaction regarding the rewards gained or to be expected from the existing arrangements.

DECISION MAKING BEHAVIOR OBSERVED IN GROUPS

It has been said that a committee is a group of people who individually can do nothing, but who can meet together and decide that nothing can be done. This is perhaps a little cynical, but it reflects a widespread disillusionment with group decision making. These feelings of frustration on the part of committee members are succinctly expressed in a lighthearted but penetrating article by Bruce Old on the mathematics of committees, boards, and panels.[21] In a calculated example of the worst type of analytical approach, Old reviews evidence of decision making behavior in a number of types of committees and assigns quantitative measures to the ability of a committee to perform work. His conclusions are most entertaining. For example, his analysis shows that "whereas elastic bending occurs under stress, no work is performed by certain types of committee." Perhaps the most significant result in the whole of this tongue-in-cheek article is the "finding" that the relation between the efficiency of output from a committee and the number of persons on the committee reaches a maximum at a committee size of seven tenths of a person. Old's conclusions may be closer to the truth than even he would have claimed for the results of his analysis.

Experiments on Group Decision Making

Turning to more serious studies, it has long been recognized that the degree of conflict between the objectives, preferences, and opinions of the individual members is a basic factor influencing the group decision making process. A series of experiments have been conducted by Bower to investigate and document the effect of conflict on the manner in which decisions are reached in a group.[22] He thought it possible that the effect of an increase in conflict between members of a group would be a decrease in the quality of group decision making performance. If this were so, the performance of a closely knit team in decision making would be superior to that of a less cohesive coalition. Bower sought evidence of this effect in experiments with groups of subjects faced with investment decisions characterized by profit, sales, and risk.

He found that the process of group decision making differed according to the internal relationships among the members of the group. For example, the activity with highest priority in a very cohesive group is sharing of information. Once the members of such a group have a common appreciation of the factors involved in the decision, the choice between alternatives is usually made very quickly. In a less cohesive coalition, however, the individuals are more reluctant to share information. They are also much more likely to enter into a process of bargaining with the other members before a group decision can be made.

Bower discovered also that the process of search for information was improved in both quality and quantity when conflict was present in the group. The results of his experiments suggest that the quality and quantity of the search process is related directly to the degree of necessity felt by each individual member to present to the group information in support of his point of view. Bower also found that the quality of analysis in a group appeared to increase with the degree of conflict. When conflict was present, each member of the group was careful to evaluate a position thoughtfully before presenting it for discussion and possible criticism. His experiments indicated, however, as might possibly be expected, that the probability of the group reaching an agreement on a choice between available alternatives decreased as the amount of conflict within the group increased. He concluded generally, therefore, that some degree of conflict within a group was beneficial to the group decision process. However, he felt that too much conflict would eventually be detrimental to group decision making.

Much of the research and experimental work concerning group decision making has necessarily been done using easily available groups (such as students) and simplified decision problems. Conduct of experiments under these conditions can be criticized as being one or more stages removed from the reality of actual decision making in real life situations. On the other hand, it is possible in this way to provide a controlled environment in which situations can be studied and a thorough and repeated examination can be made of certain phenomena. A summary of much of the basic work in this area has been written by Shaw.[23] In this account, he puts forward a series of "plausible hypotheses" concerning the difference between the individual and the group decision processes. He then tests these hypotheses using the available experimental data. Shaw comes to some interesting conclusions. For example, one of his hypotheses is that judgments made by a group are generally more accurate than those made by individuals. Data from a number of the studies reported show that groups arrive at a wider range of alternatives in a decision situation than do individuals. Many of these alternatives are judged to be more appropriate than those put forward by individuals working alone in the same decision situation. This phenomenon may possibly be due to the wider range of knowledge that is brought to bear on the situation in the group. Shaw notes, however, that groups usually require more time to arrive at a set of alternatives and to choose between them than do individuals working alone.

Shaw quotes from studies that support the hypothesis that groups learn faster than individuals. On the other hand, he notes that experienced individuals working alone may be more efficient in many decision making situations than groups of less informed persons. Groups are more effective than individuals on tasks requiring the combination of a number of steps in a definite order or where a number of different contributions or a number of areas of experience must be combined. Groups are generally more effective where solution of the problem requires learning, but not necessarily where the task requires the use of judgment. In summary, the question of whether groups or individuals are more effective in problem solving is seen to depend upon the type of task involved, the past experience of the individuals taking part, and on how the term "effective" is interpreted. In all cases, however, the use of a group in decision making or problem solving is found to be less efficient in terms of the amount of effort expended per problem resolution.

One other phenomenon that has been observed under experimental conditions is known as *risky shift*. This term refers to the fact that decisions made by groups are generally more risky than those that would be advocated by the individual members prior to group discussion of the problem. Research workers studying this effect conclude that the sharing of risk within a group contributes to the shift to alternatives that involve more risk. Individual members tend to feel less personally responsible for outcomes when the consequences are to be shared by all of the individuals in the group. Latent attraction toward gambling may also be brought to the fore when support from other group members is available.

Other experiments concern the leadership and influence relations that emerge in a group engaged in a decision situation. Some of the results of these experiments suggest that a dominant member tends to emerge in a group if a consensus does not develop after some period of time.[24, 25] This dominant member is often one of the more conservative individuals in the group. The role of this member increases in importance as the variation in individual opinions and choices increases. The dominant member sometimes instills a greater degree of cohesiveness in a group, which results in a consensus forming around the views of this member. Some groups formed to consider a decision situation are merely facades behind which a proposal of a dominant member is presented. In such cases, the members of the group become aware that the purpose of the group is to approve a course of action that has been selected in advance by a dominant member. The proceedings of the group are then concerned with the manner in which the members can adopt that course of action while preserving a semblance of individual independence.

Experimental Evidence from within Real Life Decision Making Groups

It is usually very difficult to obtain experimental evidence on decision making procedures in groups engaged in real life situations in the day-to-day world. Members of such groups may sympathize with the need for research into these procedures. However, the pressure of activities in the decision making groups and the need to reach conclusions as soon as possible often combine to provide such research only the lowest of priorities. The confidentiality of the matters confronting many groups also reduces the opportunity for observation of the proceedings.

Argyris, however, was able to conduct a comprehensive study of the behavior of 165 senior executives in six major companies in a large number of group decision making meetings.[26] The proceedings of the meetings were recorded on tape for later analysis and in most of the sessions an observer was present to take notes. The subjects covered in the meetings were investment decisions, introduction of new products, manufacturing problems, marketing and pricing strategies, and administrative and personnel issues. The results quoted by Argyris are a compendium of antagonism and distrust. He noted, for example, that the activities of executives in the decision making groups studied did not coincide with their individually stated views about effective managerial behavior. The activities of these executives tended to create interpersonal barriers to openness and trust that restricted effective decision making.

A more optimistic view of executive behavior is reported by Spetzler in a study of the development of a corporate risk policy for capital investment decisions.[27] Spetzler interviewed 36 executives of a particular company, each of whom was either a senior officer, a line manager, or a staff member involved with major capital expenditures. In a first set of interviews, the attitude to risk of each of the individuals (when acting on behalf of the firm) was investigated on the basis of reactions to a standard set of decision situations. The results of this first set of interviews were reported in general terms to the managers involved in order that the group could follow the development of the project. In a second stage, the managers were again interviewed and their reactions to a corporate utility function to be used on a trial basis were sought. As a result of these discussions, an agreement was reached on a policy for risk taking in capital investment decisions in quantitative terms.

Spetzler found that the group decision function derived by this process was markedly different from the average of those of the group members. At all levels of investment, the group consensus was in favor of more risk taking than the average of the individuals involved. This appears to confirm the risky shift phenomenon noted in a number of other studies. Unfortunately, Septzler does not report what benefits were obtained by the company from the exercise, except in general terms such as increased awareness of the need for risk policies on the part of executives. If actual results were obtained, however, they would probably have been confidential and not suitable for publication in the open literature.

Janis has pointed out that deficiencies in group decision making behavior are often due to faulty leadership of the group.[28] This faulty leadership may result in a situation in which individual members are subjected to subtle constraints (often unconsciously reinforced by leaders) that prevent them from bringing contrary information to bear on a decision process once the others in the group appear to be approaching a consensus. He calls the situation that arises in such circumstances by the Orwellian term "group-think," describing it as a mode of thinking that occurs "in a cohesive ingroup, when the members' striving for unanimity overrides their motivation to realistically appraise alternative courses of action." He has provided a number of prescriptions for avoiding group-think. These prescriptions have some application in providing for a broad based gathering of information relevant to a decision problem. They can be summarized as follows:

- The leader of an inquiry or of a decision making group should give high priority in discussion to the airing of objections and doubts.
- The leader should be impartial at the outset and not advocate the specific courses of action he would like to see adopted.
- More than one group should work on a complex problem, with each group having a different leader; if only one group exists, it should break up into subgroups under different chairmen from time to time and then reform and exchange information.
- Members of the group should discuss its proceedings on occasion with trusted associates and report their views and reactions to the group as a whole.
- One or more outside persons with expert knowledge should be invited to meetings of the group on a staggered basis and their views on proceedings to date solicited.
- At least one member should be assigned to act in the role of devil's advocate in each meeting.
- Significant amounts of time in the group sessions should be spent examining information on other participants' actions, preferences, and available courses of action, and details of natural and quasi-natural events that have occurred or might occur in the future.
- Once a consensus is reached, it should be reconsidered and confirmed or rejected at a later meeting held after time has been allowed for members to collect their doubts and reservations.

Janis has discussed each of these prescriptions in detail and the reader is urged to refer to his book for a comprehensive review of the advantages and possible undesirable side effects of these methods of approach to information gathering and group decision making.

One other form of behavior that has been observed in decision making groups has been called *logrolling*.[29] This term refers to an arrangement between two or more individuals or groups by which one agrees to support the other's position in one decision situation in return for similar support in another situation. Arrangements of this sort are often made implicitly in the course of group discussions rather than by an explicit and negotiated agreement. Those who have studied logrolling in decision making groups point out that such behavior arises from the fact that single decision situations are seldom considered in isolation. There is normally more than one decision situation under consideration in which some of the same participants are involved. It is natural therefore that some type of trading of support among participants in these situations would occur if this arrangement was to benefit all the participants involved.

SUMMARY

Decision making groups are formed when two or more parties decide to cooperate in a risky venture. The composition of such a group may be a two-person partnership, the employees of a large organization, or even two organizations involved in a cooperative arrangement. Each party in a venture has a set of risks that can be accepted and a set that cannot be accepted. The boundary between these risks may be known explicitly or may be only vaguely appreciated. A risk that is outside the acceptance sets of all participants in a joint venture may be partitioned in such a way that each individual undertakes a share of the risk that is acceptable to him or her. The process of partitioning the risk among the individuals engaged in a joint venture may involve side payments among the members to compensate for disproportionate sharing of the total risk.

In practical situations, there may be many risk sharing arrangements available to the participants in a joint venture. Some of these arrangements may favor some of the participants and some may be more preferred by others. The choice of one arrangement by which at least one participant gains and none loses is called a "Pareto-improvement." Sometimes an arbitrator is asked to decide on which of the Pareto-improvements should be adopted by the participants. A specific approach to finding a "fair" arrangement in such circumstances has been proposed by Nash.

Members of a group involved in decision making can be viewed in the same way as participants in a joint venture. These participants need to select a means by which they can make choices between alternatives on behalf of the group. Simple majority rule is often regarded as a natural way of making a decision in a group. A theorem by Arrow shows that no decision rule, however, can be regarded as uniquely best or most correct for group decision making over a wide range of circumstances. In practice, a group must construct a rule by which the members arrive at a decision. The decision rule in a group is often agreed before the choice is made between alternatives. Sometimes, however, there is no explicit discussion of the rule to be used for this choice. In such cases, the tasks of deciding how to decide and of choosing between alternatives are intermixed.

The group decision making process consists of several activities which do not necessarily take place in any given order. The first of these activities is an exchange of information among the members of the group. The second activity is a process of interaction among the group members during which some members of the group may try to influence the opinions and preferences of others. Sometimes this interaction results in the emergence of a consensus. In other cases, opinions in the group may polarize and subgroups may form with views that are in conflict with those of others. The amount and nature of this conflict is a major factor in determining how the group will choose between alternatives.

The internal structure of a group is often a factor in its decision making activity. Groups demonstrating a high degree of cohesiveness often act as a team with a strong sense of common purpose. Consensus is common in such groups. However, where there is a much less cohesive coalition, the conflict of interests and objectives in the group may make the achievement of consensus much more difficult. A wide range of structures is found in practical decision making groups. A series of experiments has shown that conflict in a group often improves the quality and quantity of information search and analysis done in connection with a decision. However, the chance of a group reaching a decision decreases markedly as the amount of conflict increases. In other experiments, groups have been found to be more efficient than individuals in some aspects of decision making (such as information gathering) and less efficient in others. Groups have been found to tend towards more risky choices than individuals. Leadership in the group is often a major factor in group choice. Sometimes a dominant individual emerges and a conclusion is reached on the basis of his views. Over-zealous leadership in a group can lead to the stifling of contrary opinion and a consequent lack of breadth in the choice between alternatives.

PRACTICAL DECISION SITUATIONS

6.1 The Father-Son Consultant Company

A good friend has asked you for advice with regard to a business venture that he would like to undertake with his son. He wants to set up a firm of management consultants. He estimates that the venture might make a profit of $100,000 or it might make a loss of $60,000. The father would like to share the venture in such a way that if the venture is successful, his son should make a profit of $30,000. However, if it is unsuccessful, the son should suffer a loss of only $10,000.

What risk sharing arrangements would you advise? In particular, what proportion of the risk would the son assume under your recommended sharing arrangement and what amount of money would he pay or receive as side payment?

6.2 A Development Corporation

A development corporation has been set up to assist entrepreneurs to engage in risky ventures. The corporation has the following policy with regard to ventures offering a 50% chance of complete success and a 50% chance of complete failure. It accepts ventures in which it might lose more than $40,000 only if the ratio of its possible gains to its possible losses is 3 to 1 or better. It accepts ventures in which it might lose more than $25,000 but less than $40,000 only if its gains-to-losses ratio is 5 to 2 or better. It accepts ventures in which it might lose up to $25,000 only if its gains-to-losses ratio is at least 2 to 1. The corporation is considering the following situations at the present time:

1. It has been offered a $10,000 side payment if it takes a 50% stake in a venture with an even chance of making an overall gain of $110,000. What should be the maximum necessary investment for the venture if it is to be acceptable to the corporation?

2. An entrepreneur is considering a venture offering a 50% chance of a gain of $90,000 and a 50% chance of a loss of $40,000. It is desired to determine whether the corporation would be willing to enter a proportional risk sharing arrangement without side payments, given that the entrepreneur is willing to carry a potential loss of $20,000.

3. For the same venture as under 2, it is required to determine whether the development corporation would be willing to pay a $4,000 side payment to the entrepreneur in return for a 40% stake in the venture.

6.3 The Council of Ministers of the European Community

The example in the text refers to the original Community, which had 6 member states. Three new members (Denmark, Ireland, and the United Kingdom) were admitted after the original Council of Ministers was established. A new Council was formed in 1973 in which the 9 members had votes in rough proportion to their population and gross national products. A comparison of the 1958 and 1973 Councils is as follows:

Member	1958	1973
France	4	10
Germany	4	10
Italy	4	10
Belgium	2	5
Netherlands	2	5
Luxembourg	1	2
Denmark	—	3
Ireland	—	3
United Kingdom	—	10

Proposals of the Commission required 12 of the 17 votes in the 1958 Council to pass. This requirement was changed to 41 of the 58 votes in the 1973 Council.

Comment on the effect of the change in the Council of Ministers and in the votes allocated on the power of each of the members of the Council in group decision making.

6.4 The Shareholders' Meeting

You are the Chairman of the Board of a Corporation. A shareholder's meeting is to be held at which three proposals A, B, and C are to be considered. One of the proposals must be chosen by a vote of the shareholders. You have made some enquiries and you find that the following is an accurate representation of the voting preferences of the shareholders:

45% prefer proposal A to B and proposal B to C
25% prefer proposal B to C and proposal C to A
30% prefer proposal C to B and proposal B to A.

You are considering how the crucial vote will be conducted in the meeting. If a simple majority rule is used to make the decision, proposal A will win, assuming the shareholders vote for their first preference in all cases. You are certain, however, that either proposal B or C would be more to the benefit of the corporation. In addition, you note that 55% of the shareholders have proposal A as their least preferred alternative.

Can a voting procedure be adopted that will ensure the defeat of proposal A? Which proposal would emerge as a winner in each case that you consider?

DISCUSSION TOPICS

1.   In some risk sharing situations, a partner who assumes a greater proportion of the venture pays a side payment to one who assumes a lesser proportion. Why is this so? What role does the side payment play in the sharing of the risk?

2.   In a Pareto-improvement, no member of the group loses and at least one gains. Where does that gain come from? For example, when management and a union agree to a resolution of an industrial relations dispute that is Pareto optimal, is there a third participant who pays the bill for the settlement?

3.   Do you think the Nash procedure is a "fair" approach to arbitration between participants in a risk sharing venture? What are its major advantages? Can you propose a procedure that you think is preferable to that suggested by Nash?

4.   Simple majority rule is a procedure that is often readily acceptable to members of a decision making group. Can you think of practical situa-

tions in which this rule has led to paradoxical outcomes? What alternative rule would you suggest for these situations?

5. Do you think that Arrow's five "apparently reasonable" conditions are in fact reasonable? What are the implications of Arrow's proof that these five conditions cannot all be met simultaneously?

6. Arrow considered the possibility of constructing a "social welfare function" for use in group decision making. Do you think it would be possible to construct such a function from the utility functions of the individual group members? What would be the practical conditions under which such a group utility function could be used?

7. Under what conditions does consensus arise in a decision making group?

8. Do you think that the introduction of contrary opinions should be allowed in a group that is moving quickly towards a consensus? Are there any conditions in which you as leader of the group would move to exclude such opinions?

9. Why does the phenomenon known as risky shift occur in a decision making group? Is this an aspect of decision making behavior that should be resisted by members of a group?

10. Suppose that you were the only member of a group who was opposed to choice of a particular alternative. Under what conditions would you continue your opposition? What factors might cause you to join a consensus?

11. Give some examples of log rolling in decision situations with which you have had experience. Do you consider that log rolling is a useful procedure in the resolution of group decision situations?

12. Under what conditions does group decision making become a conflict situation between two or more components of the group? How would you deal with a situation in a group in which extreme polarization had taken place and the degree of conflict seemed to be inhibiting a resolution?

REFERENCES

1. Raiffa, H., *Decision Analysis—Introductory Lectures on Choices Under Uncertainty*, Addison-Wesley, 1968, pp 188–205.
2. Nash, J. F., "The Bargaining Problem", *Econometrica* Vol 18, 1950, pp 155–162.
3. Nash, J. F., "Two-Person Cooperative Games", *Econometrica* Vol 21, 1953, pp 128–140.

4. Example quoted from Luce, R. D. and Raiffa, H., *Games and Decisions*, Wiley, 1957, p 129.

5. Fouraker, L. E. and Siegel, S., *Bargaining Behavior*, McGraw Hill, 1960.

6. Raiffa, H., *op cit*, p 197.

7. Paper by E. J. Nanson in *Transactions and Procedures of the Royal Society of Victoria*, Vol 19, 1882, pp 197–240.

8. A function of this nature has been discussed in Marshall, A., *Principles of Economics*, 8th Ed., MacMillan, 1949, pp 130–134 and pp 467–470.

9. Arrow, K. J., *Social Choice and Individual Values*, Cowles Foundation for Research in Economics at Yale University, published by Wiley, 1951.

10. *Ibid*, p 59.

11. Bergson, Abram, "On the Concept of Social Welfare," *Quarterly Journal of Economics*, Vol 68, May 1954, pp 233–252.

12. Blau, Julian, "The Existence of Social Welfare Functions," *Econometrica*, Vol 25, April 1957, pp 302–313.

13. Rothenberg, Jerome F., *The Measurement of Social Welfare*, Prentice Hall, 1961, pp 26–30.

14. Luce, R. D. and Raiffa, H., *Games and Decisions*, Wiley, 1967, pp 340–370.

15. Rothenberg, J. F., *op cit*, p 44–52.

16. Luce and Raiffa, *op cit*, pp 353–357.

18. Fishburn, P. C., "A Comparative Analysis of Group Decision Methods," *Behavioral Science*, Vol 16, 1971, p 538.

19. Example adapted from Brams, S., *Paradoxes in Politics*, Free Press, 1976, pp 184–185.

20. Marschak, J., "Elements for a Theory of Teams," *Management Science*, Vol 1, 1955, pp 127–137.

21. Old, Bruce S., "On the Mathematics of Committees. Boards and Panels" *Scientific Monthly*, August 1946, reprinted in Brown, R. G. (ed) *Source Book on Production Management*: The Dryden Press, 1971.

22. Bower, J. L., "The Role of Conflict in Economic Decision-making Groups: Some Empirical Results," *Quarterly Journal of Economics*, Vol 79, 1965, pp 263–277.

23. Shaw, M. E., *Group Dynamics: The Psychology of Small Group Behavior*, McGraw Hill, 1971, pp 59–83.

24. Clarkson, G. P. E., "Decision Making in Small Groups: a Simulation Study," *Behavioral Science*, Vol 13, 1968, pp 288–305.

25. Leavitt, H. J., "Collective Problem Solving in Small Groups," *Journal of Abnormal Social Psychology*, Vol 46, 1951: reprinted in Alexis, M. and Wilson, C. Z., *Organizational Decision Making*, Prentice Hall, 1967, pp 40–55.

26. Argyris, C., "Interpersonal Barriers to Decision Making," *Harvard Business Review*, March/April 1964, pp 84–97.

27. Spetzler, C. S., "The Development of a Corporate Risk Policy for Capital Investment Decisions," *IEEE Transactions on Systems Science and Cybernetics*, SSC-4, September 1968, pp 279–300.
28. Janis, I. L., *Victims of Group-Think*, Houghton Mifflin Company, 1972.
29. Tullock, G., "A Simple Algebraic Logrolling Model," *American Economic Review*, Vol 60, June 1970, pp 419–426.

 *Chapter Seven*

Competitive Situations With Two or More Participants

INTRODUCTION

In Chapter 6, the discussion centered on situations in which individuals were contemplating joint ventures or were members of a group faced with a choice between alternatives. In all the situations treated in that chapter, the assumption was made that, despite some differences in objectives, the participants placed considerable value on their joint participation in a venture or on their membership of a group. Whereas some conflicts might arise between the interests of the participants, the emphasis was on a co-operative resolution of the decision situation rather than on the competition between them.

We must now turn to the analysis of decision situations in which the competition between the participants is the major factor. The simplest of these situations are those in which there are two participants and in which one participant gains what the other loses. These situations are called two-person, zero-sum games in the basic language of game theory. They are also known as strictly competitive situations because of the direct relationship between one participant's gains and the other's losses. A much broader class of situations is known as *n*-person, non-zero-sum games. In these situations, two or more participants may be involved. However, the gains and losses of the participants in situations of this nature do not necessarily balance each other. One participant may gain more or less than the sum of the losses of the others. Hence the term non-zero-sum. Situations of this latter kind are known as "non-strictly-competitive" because of the more indirect nature of the competition between the participants.

The theory of games and competitive situations was first described by von Neumann and Morgenstern.[1] A more recent summary of classical game theory has been provided by Luce and Raiffa.[2] These works of reference will be the basis of the discussion in this chapter. This discussion will start with the treatment of strictly competitive situations, and pass from there to more complex situations that are not strictly competitive. The aim throughout the chapter is to review how a decision may be resolved when the interests of the participants are in direct or indirect conflict.

STRICTLY COMPETITIVE DECISION SITUATIONS

Suppose that two participants, A and B, are engaged in a situation in which any loss to A becomes a gain to B and vice versa. A two-person, zero-sum situation of this nature can be represented by a matrix as in Table 7-1. In this table, each of the participants is shown as having four available courses of action (A_1, A_2, A_3, and A_4, for A and B_1, B_2, B_3, and B_4 for B). The elements of the matrix indicate the results of a simultaneous choice of a course of action by each participant. Where the result shown is positive, it denotes a gain to A. A negative figure, on the other hand, denotes a gain for B. Because the situation is zero-sum, a gain to A means a corresponding loss to B and vice versa. For example, if A chooses A_2 and B chooses B_3, the table shows that A makes a gain of 3. In these circumstances, B would suffer a loss of 3. The question is which of their alternative courses of action should A and B choose taking into account the outcomes shown in Table 7-1?

B would naturally be attracted to B_3 or B_4 if maximization of gain was an objective. However a choice of A_3 by A would be costly to B if B_3 or B_4

TABLE 7-1.   Simple 2-Person, Zero-Sum Situation

		B's Available Courses of Action			
		B_1	B_2	B_3	B_4
A's Available	A_1	+14	+1	−9	+8
Courses of Action	A_2	− 2	+2	+3	−7
	A_3	+ 7	+3	+8	+9
	A_4	+17	−2	+4	−6

were chosen. Similarly A might argue that A_1 or A_4 would offer more reward than A_3 unless B chose B_3 or B_4 respectively, in which cases A would be faced with a loss. Both participants might, however, notice a particular characteristic of the situation in which they are mutually engaged. This characteristic concerns the choice of strategy A_3 by A and of B_2 by B. The outcome of this pair of choices A_3, B_2 is a gain of 3 to A and a corresponding loss of 3 to B. Note, however, that the outcome of A_3, B_2 is both the minimum in its row and the maximum in its column in Table 7-1. By choosing A_3, A can be assured of a gain of at least three whatever B chooses. Similarly B can limit A's gain to three by choosing B_2. The outcome from the joint choice A_3, B_2, represents a maximum of the minimum gains to A over all the available courses of action. It also represents the minimum of B's possible losses. The pair of choices A_3, B_2 is, therefore, simultaneously the maximin strategy for A and the minimax strategy for B.

The outcome A_3, B_2 is also called an *equilibrium*. A two-person, zero-sum decision situation may have more than one equilibrium. However, the value to the players at each of the equilibria in such a situation is the same. An outcome that is an equilibrium has the unique characteristic that no participant can move away from it and gain by doing so, as long as the other participants remain at the equilibrium outcome. For example, if B remains with the choice B_2, A cannot gain by moving away from A_3. Similarly B cannot gain by moving from B_2, as long as A remains at A_3. Von Neumann and Morgenstern regarded the equilibrium position as the "solution" of the two-person, zero-sum game. It is perhaps better described as a position of stability that two risk-averse participants might care to adopt in order to ensure a certain minimum gain or to limit losses to a particular figure. In this respect, the equilibrium provides what might be called a security level for the participants. Those with other attitudes to risk might adopt other strategies. Note that a participant using the equilibrium strategy can reveal this choice in advance to an opponent. Foreknowledge of this choice of strategy cannot be advantageous to the opponent in situations of this kind.

The figures representing gains and losses in Table 7-1 were chosen deliberately to illustrate the concept of an equilibrium in a competitive situation. Not all such situations have a readily identifiable equilibrium point. For example, no such point can be detected in the situation illustrated in Table 7-2. However, a major contribution of the von Neumann-Morgenstern theory is that the equivalent of a single strategy choice equilibrium (for example A_3, B_2 in Table 7-1) exists in all situations in which such an equilibrium is not readily identifiable. This equivalent equilibrium situation involves the use of a mixture of choices of courses of action in repeated resolutions of the same decision situation. Von Neumann and Morgenstern called this equivalent equilibrium a *mixed strategy equilibrium*

TABLE 7-2.   Two-Person, Zero-Sum Situation without a Readily Identifiable Equilibrium

		B's Available Courses of Action		
		B_1	B_2	B_3
A's Available	A_1	2	−3	4
Courses of Action	A_2	−3	4	−5
	A_3	4	−5	6

in contrast to the single (or pure) strategy equilibrium illustrated in Fig 7-1. In a mixed strategy situation, a participant achieves the equilibrium position by selecting from his available courses of action according to a predetermined pattern. The characteristics of this pattern can be calculated for each participant. Furthermore, each participant can reveal the choices that are included in the mix to an opponent. However, the method of selection from the mix for any one encounter with the decision situation cannot be revealed without risking a reduction in the results from those guaranteed by the equilibrium point.

The method of determining the correct mixture of strategies is given in Exhibit 7-1. Note that this method also determines the *value* of the situation to both participants. This is the *expected* payoff to each party in the situation, assuming that courses of action are chosen in repeated encounters with the decision situation in the manner required to ensure that the equilibrium is maintained. In such situations, the average result for each participant approaches more and more closely the value of the situation as the number of encounters increases.

Example of a Strictly Competitive Decision Situation

Situations such as those represented by Tables 7-1 and 7-2 do not occur very often in real life. However, some competitive situations do have the characteristics of a zero-sum game. Consider, for example, two retail outlets that are the sole suppliers of a certain product to a community. They compete by offering special prices every week in the Thursday night paper. It is assumed that the two competitors disclose their price and learn of the other's price simultaneously. The price may be either high or low. What A gains in sales, B loses and vice versa. If the prices offered by each outlet are the same (i.e., both high or both low) outlet A gains 10 units from B, because it is more conveniently located. If A's price is high and B's low, B gains 15 units from A. However, if B's price is high and A's low, B still gains 5 units from A, because customers suspect A is selling off old stock. The payoff matrix describing this somewhat contrived situation is illustrated in Table 7-3, with gains to A being shown as positive.

Application of the method outlined in Exhibit 7-1 shows that A should

EXHIBIT 7-1. Determination of the Mixed Strategy
for a Two-Person Zero-Sum Game.[3]

Consider a two-person, zero-sum game, where A has m strategies and B has n. Let the payoff matrix have elements a_{ij}, $i = 1 \ldots m$ and $j = 1 \ldots n$. Suppose A and B play their respective strategies with probabilities p_i and q_j respectively where $\sum_{1}^{m} p_i = 1$ and $\sum_{1}^{n} q_j = 1$. We need to find sets of mixed strategies $S_A^* = (A_i, p_i)$ and $S_B^* = (B_j, q_j)$ such that S_A^* guarantees A a payoff of at least v (the value of the game) for any of B's strategies and equal to v for his optimal strategy S_B^*; and similarly for B.

The average payoff for A's optimal strategy S_A^* against any strategy (Bj) of B is:

$$a_j = a_{1j}p_1 + a_{2j}p_2 + \ldots . a_{mj}p_m$$

The requirement that a_j be not less than v gives the following n conditions:

$$a_{11}p_1 + a_{21}p_2 + \ldots . + a_{m1}p_m \geqq v$$
$$\vdots \qquad \qquad \vdots$$
$$a_{1n}p_1 + a_{2n}p_2 + \ldots . + a_{mn}p_m \geqq v$$

Since A wishes to maximize v, the value of the game, the solution amounts to the following formulation:

Minimize $\quad \sum_{i=1}^{m} \quad p_i/v$ (i.e., *maximize* the value, v)

Subject to $\quad \sum_{\substack{i=1 \ldots m \\ j=1 \ldots n}} \quad a_{ij}p_i \geqq v$

This can be recognized as a simple linear program and solved accordingly. The values p_i thus obtained provide the proportion of times that the ith strategy should be played in terms of the matrix elements a_{ij}. A similar analysis can be conducted for B.

select "High" 3/8 of the time and "Low" 5/8 of the time. B should select "Low" 3/8 of the time and "High" 5/8 of the time. The value of the situation is +5/8. The *expected* value to A of a single encounter is 5/8. The situation is therefore disadvantageous to B in some respects. If A uses a correct mixed strategy and does not reveal the method of choice of a course of action for any particular encounter, the outcome in the long run is a gain for A. If, on the other hand, A does not follow a correct mixed strategy, B may

TABLE 7-3. Strictly Competitive Situation Involving Two Retail Outlets

		B's Courses of Action	
		High	Low
A's Courses	High	10	−15
of Action	Low	−5	10

have the opportunity to gain in spite of the inherent bias in the situation in favor of A.

Procedures in a "Single-Play" Strictly Competitive Situation

The Von Neumann-Morgenstern theory shows us that the use of a mixed strategy is appropriate if an equilibrium is sought in repeated encounters with the strictly competitive decision situation. The question remains of what strategy to employ in a single encounter with such a situation. Suppose, for example, that a merchant ship must supply a beachhead in enemy territory. To get to the beachhead, the ship must pass either to the north or to the south of a large island. A warship lies in wait for the merchant ship and has the same alternative courses of action of steaming to the north or south of the island. The situation is illustrated in Fig. 7-1. The rules of the situation are that if the two ships meet, the merchant ship is sunk. The sinking is of course less preferred by the merchant ship than evasion of the warship by steaming north of the island while the warship goes south or vice versa. The preferences of the warship are the reverse. The situation is essentially two-person, zero-sum although the consequences to the warship and to the merchant ship are not exactly equal. Such situations are often referred to as constant sum, rather than zero-sum, situations.

The preferences of the participants in this situation are shown in Table 7-4 on a mutually ordinal scale. For any pair of strategy choices, such as Warship/North, Merchant Ship/South, the preference of the Warship is written first and that of the Merchant is written second. A larger number indicates a higher preference. Thus outcome 2, 1 represents a situation in which the Warship gets its more preferred outcome (sinking the Merchant

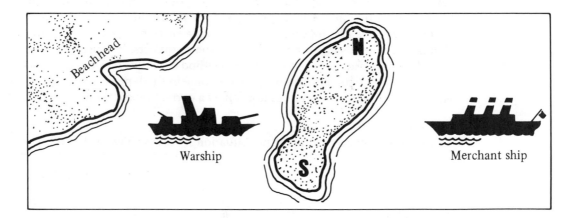

FIG. 7-1. Warship-merchant ship situation.

TABLE 7-4. Preferences in the Warship-Merchant Ship Situation

		Merchant Ship	
		North	South
Warship	North	2, 1	1, 2
	South	1, 2	2, 1

Ship) and the Merchant Ship gets its less preferred outcome (being sunk).

A mixed strategy would dictate that the Merchant Ship should go to the north of the island half of the time and to the south half of the time. The same mixed strategy is appropriate for the Warship; but these strategies are not helpful in a single encounter between the two ships. The Merchant Ship captain must choose between a northerly and a southerly path in a single encounter. In either case, he has a 50 percent chance of losing his ship. Luce and Raiffa have suggested that the mixed strategy can be implemented in such a situation by selecting a pure strategy for each encounter by means of a simple physical experiment such as tossing a coin or throwing dice.[4] Provided that the experiment has the same number of alternatives and the same probabilities of outcomes as the situation under consideration, it is suggested that the choice of strategy be made on the basis of the experiment alone. This procedure may be acceptable in a multi-encounter situation. It is, however, very difficult to accept that it should be used in real life decision making in a single encounter. In any case, a manager who is convinced that he should decide between two alternatives in such a situation by tossing a coin would be well advised to do it in the privacy of a locked office.

An alternative procedure in a single encounter with a strictly competitive decision situation without a pure strategy equilibrium is to try to gain knowledge of the other participant's strategy before choosing one's own. However, even if both players try to do this, one of them *must* eventually make the wrong decision. There is no equilibrium that provides a security level to each participant in a single encounter with this type of situation.

It is interesting to note that a situation similar to that of the Warship and Merchant Ship was described by Conan Doyle in an adventure of Sherlock Holmes entitled *The Final Problem*.[5] Holmes is being pursued by Moriarty and catches a train from London to Dover with a view to escaping to the Continent. The train has one stop (at Canterbury). As it leaves the station, Moriarty catches a glimpse of the departing Holmes who sees Moriarty arrive at the station in pursuit. Holmes reasons that if Moriarty catches up with him he will kill him and deduces that Moriarty will charter a train in pursuit. Holmes now has the choice between getting off at Canterbury or going on to Dover. Moriarty presumably has the same choices. The situation is summarized in Table 7-5. In the book, Holmes

TABLE 7-5. Preferences for Outcomes in Holmes vs. Moriarty

		Holmes	
		Canterbury	*Dover*
Moriarty	*Canterbury*	2, 1	1, 2
	Dover	1, 2	2, 1

gets off at Canterbury and watches Moriarty pass through on his way to Dover. The outcome was no doubt chosen because of the necessity of continuation of the confrontation.

It is interesting, also, that the mixed strategy is entirely appropriate in repeated encounters of the same situation. A Commander-in-Chief with 10 supply ships sailing at different times should send 5 to the north of the island and 5 to the south. Five of the ships could then be expected to survive. An outcome of this nature might be acceptable to a commander in time of war. However, it might be of little solace to the captains of the ships that were sunk to know that the mixed strategy was the appropriate policy in the repeated encounters with the situation.

Do Strictly Competitive Situations Occur in Real Life?

Very few of the decision situations encountered by managers in modern organizations are of the strictly competitive, zero-sum type. Managerial decisions are seldom as clear cut as the simple examples that can be constructed in the zero-sum category. Many other factors not contained in the strictly competitive model impinge upon most decision situations. There may be a tendency in some persons to perceive competitive situations in terms of the zero-sum approach because it is thought to be hard headed, tough minded, and realistic.[6] It may be that this tendency arises because of the strictly competitive nature of games and sports that are used in some instances to train people from the earliest age in conflict behavior. Experienced managers faced with a strictly competitive situation, however, often introduce alternative courses of action not included in the original formulation, specifically to reduce the possibility of direct conflict and the attendant risks. For example, in the case of the two stores advertising in the Thursday night's paper discussed earlier, it is most unlikely that both participants would remain in the situation described unless there was absolutely no alternative. One or both of them would almost certainly seek to change the situation by the introduction of another course of action such as advertising in a different medium (say, television) once the other store's announcement had been made. The Commander-in-Chief would no doubt equip his merchant ships with radar or helicopters, if this were

possible, in order to change the decision situation in his favor. The Warship commander would no doubt try to adopt a similar policy.

There may, however, be a small number of types of situations in which
the participants choose to remain in a strictly competitive state and in
which they seek the security against major losses in that situation that an
equilibrium position offers. In such circumstances, the choice of a pure or
a mixed strategy that brings about an equilibrium in the situation is clearly
a good policy. In a number of experiments conducted in a research environment, participants in strictly competitive decision situations were in
fact found to search for, and move towards equilibrium positions using
both pure and mixed strategies.[7] These observations tend to confirm that
the approach to two-person, zero-sum situations suggested by the theory
is likely to be adopted by participants in practical circumstances that conform closely to the strictly competitive model.

DECISION SITUATIONS THAT ARE NOT STRICTLY COMPETITIVE

Strictly competitive, two-person, zero-sum games have the following
characteristics:

1. Nothing is lost nor is anything gained by disclosing to an opponent
the pure or mixed strategies to be employed to obtain an equilibrium outcome in the decision situation.

2. If there is more than one equilibrium point in the situation, the
value to each participant is the same at all such points.

3. The maximin strategy for one participant and the minimax strategy
for the other are an equilibrium pair. Conversely, the strategies that lead
to an equilibrium are maximin and minimax strategies for the participants.

Situations that are not strictly competitive do not generally have these
characteristics. In such situations, it may be to the advantage of one participant to declare a strategy in advance of the choice of the others. These
situations may have more than one equilibrium point but the values of
these points to the participants may be different. The strategies that form
an equilibrium pair are not necessarily maximin and minimax. The maximin and minimax strategies do not therefore provide a level of security in
the decision situation. In fact, the choice of a maximin or minimax strategy
in a non-strictly-competitive situation may produce the opportunity for
another participant to move to an optimal strategy against this choice.

These characteristics of situations that are not strictly competitive are illustrated in the following descriptions of typical situations.

The Battle of the Sexes

A simple example of a non-strictly-competitive decision situation has been described in the literature under the somewhat distracting title of "Battle of the Sexes." In this situation, a man (participant 1) and a woman (participant 2) each have two available options, to go to a prize fight or to a ballet. The man prefers to see the fight and the woman the ballet, but they both prefer to go out together, rather than go alone to a more preferred entertainment. The preferences of the participants are illustrated in Table 7-6. In this table, the most preferred outcome for both participants (going together to the more preferred event) is indicated by a 2 on an ordinal scale of preference. The intermediate preferences (going together to a less preferred event) are indicated by a 1 on the scale. The least preferred outcomes (going separately to the more-or-less preferred events) are indicated by a −1 and −2 respectively.

The situation illustrated in Table 7-6 has two equilibria, which are indicated by circles around the preference orderings. To confirm that these positions are indeed equilibria, it is helpful to remember that the man's alternatives are listed vertically in the table and the woman's horizontally. Remembering also that the man's preferences are shown to the left of the pair in each case, it is clear that he would not wish to move vertically from point 2, 1 to point −2, −2. At the same time, the woman would not wish to move horizontally from point 2, 1 to point −1, −1. Point 2, 1 is therefore a point from which it is not to the advantage of either participant to move provided the other does not. This condition qualifies point 2, 1 as an equilibrium by definition. The reader can confirm that point 1, 2 is also an equilibrium by definition. It is interesting to note that the values of the two equilibria to the participants are different. Clearly the 2, 1 equilibrium is preferable to the man, while the 1, 2 equilibrium is preferable to the woman.

The choice that presents itself to the man and woman is therefore whether they go together to the fight or to the ballet. This choice can be

TABLE 7-6. Preferences for Outcomes in the Battle of the Sexes

		Woman	
		Fight	*Ballet*
Man	*Fight*	(2, 1)	−1, −1
	Ballet	−2, −2	(1, 2)

affected by a prior statement of intent by either the man or the woman. If, for example, the man says, "I am going to the fight and I will not change my mind," the woman would be forced to go to the fight as long as she retains her original preferences. She has in fact been forced by the prior declaration of the man to act in *his* interests while acting according to her own preferences. It might be that the prior declaration by the man would cause the woman to change her preferences. Such a change would alter the situation from that illustrated in Table 7-6. However, as long as the participants retain their original preferences, the prior communication between the participants benefits the one making the statement. The effect of the prior communication constitutes an *inducement* by one participant of the other.

In the case in which neither participant makes an initial statement, each of them may reason in the following way prior to a simultaneous choice between their two alternatives. The man may reason, for example, that he prefers to go to the fight with the woman (2, 1), but that if he chooses to go to the fight and she simultaneously chooses to go to the ballet they both will lose out (−1, −1). Would it not be better, therefore, to choose to go to the ballet, knowing that the woman prefers this outcome? If both participants go to the ballet, the man would at least experience his next-to-best preferred outcome 1, 2. Unfortunately, however, without prior communication, the women might reason the same way. If both choose the lesser preferred event under the impression that the other would choose the more preferred event, each would go alone to the lesser preferred event and the outcome would be the least beneficial to both, −2, −2. Furthermore, there is no security in a maximin strategy. The pair of maximin strategies is not in equilibrium.[8] It would therefore be to the advantage of each participant to react to the choice of a maximin strategy by the other by choosing a nonmaximin strategy.

The key to the resolution of situations like the Battle of the Sexes lies in communication between the participants. Each participant sees an equilibrium position which is beneficial to him or her, but which cannot be obtained without the cooperation of the other. Communication between the participants can lead to a negotiated outcome that is mutually satisfactory. For example, either participant can agree to a less preferred outcome in return for a side payment of some kind. Alternatively, in repeated encounters with the same situation, one equilibrium position can be chosen on one occasion, with the understanding that the other will be selected the next time the situation occurs.

Situations of this nature occur often in real life. Suppose, for example, that two ski resorts in the same general area are thinking about taking advantage of the new enthusiasm for cross-country skiing by building a large facility for the sport in their area of the country. There are two possible locations for the facility, one close to resort A and the other close to

TABLE 7-7. The Two Ski Resort Situation

		Resort B	
		Build Facility Near A	*Build Facility Near B*
Resort A	*Build Facility Near A*	(4, 3)	2, 2
	Build Facility Near B	1, 1	(3, 4)

resort B. The management of each resort would rather have the facility close to their own existing site, but each would rather share a single facility even if it were nearer to the other resort. This situation can be represented as in Table 7-7. The management of resort A might argue as follows: "If we believe that resort B is not yet committed to a site, we should provide evidence to B of our commitment to a site near Resort A. This commitment could be shown by the expenditure of money on the site; for example, by obtaining an option on the land, by hiring surveyors, contractors, and lawyers, and by other like measures. If, however, we believe that resort B is already committed to a site nearby, we should perhaps indicate to B our interest in a joint project, but at the same time endeavor to extract some concessions in return for our participation." The management of resort B could argue in similar fashion. The outcome of all such situations depends upon the results of a process of negotiation and bargaining between the participants during which the objective is to agree on the conditions surrounding a mutually acceptable outcome.

Prisoners' Dilemma

Prisoners' Dilemma is another type of situation discussed extensively in the technical literature of games and competitive situations.[9, 10, 11] In Prisoners' Dilemma, two men decide to commit a crime but are caught in the act and separated by police before they have an opportunity to communicate. They are placed in separate cells as shown in Figure 7-2 and are left

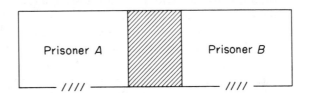

FIG. 7-2. Prisoners in separate cells without communication.

to consider their fate. After some time, a police officer enters one man's cell and discusses the situation with the occupant. He says that the prisoner has two available alternatives, to confess to the crime or not to confess. He adds that he is going to make (or has made) the same explanation to the other prisoner. If both prisoners do not confess, each man will receive a minor punishment on some other charge. If both confess, they will be prosecuted on a major charge, but the police will recommend leniency. However, if one prisoner confesses and the other does not, the prisoner who confesses will receive a very light sentence, whereas the other will be treated very severely. The essence of each prisoner's dilemma is that he does not know how his partner will react (or has reacted) to the approach by the police officer.

The situation is summarized in Table 7-8. This table shows the preference orderings for outcomes for the two participants. A larger number indicates a more preferred outcome. Prisoner A, acting without the benefit of communication with Prisoner B, can argue as follows: It would be best for me (4, 1) to confess if only I could be sure that B would not confess. However if we both confess, the outcome we receive is only (2, 2). The outcome if we both did not confess (3, 3) would be better than 2, 2. However, if I do not confess and B does then I shall receive my least preferred outcome 1, 4. Consequently, although I would like to achieve 3, 3, I must confess. By so doing, I safeguard myself from the 1, 4 outcome, I may obtain 4, 1 and the worst I can receive is 2, 2. Prisoner B can argue in exactly the same way.

The paradox of Prisoners' Dilemma centers around the fact that if each man seeks his most preferred outcome (4, 1 or 1, 4), the outcome each receives is the much less preferred 2, 2. Furthermore, the jointly rational strategy of both men not confessing is not stable. Note that the outcome 3, 3 in Table 7-8 is not an equilibrium point. Even if a prior arrangement had been made between the two men not to confess, it is to the advantage of each of them acting unilaterally to break that agreement in an endeavor to achieve the 4, 1 or 1, 4 outcomes. If both break the agreement, the outcome is 2, 2 which is less preferred than the jointly rational outcome 3, 3.

It would be comforting if situations such as Prisoners' Dilemma did not occur in real life; but, in fact, they do. Consider the competition between two firms, each supplying the same product, for which they must inde-

TABLE 7-8.   Prisoner's Dilemma

		Prisoner B	
		Not Confess	Confess
	Not Confess	3, 3	1, 4
Prisoner A	Confess	4, 1	(2, 2)

pendently choose a price, say for simplicity, high or low. Suppose that each firm would profit most by undercutting the other's price and would profit least by being undercut. Furthermore, let us assume that each firm would benefit from both charging a high price rather than each charging a low price, although the profit level in this situation would not reach that achieved by undercutting the other. The situation just described is exactly that shown for Prisoners' Dilemma in Table 7-8. The outcome most preferred by each participant is that in which he charges a low price while the other charges a high one. However, if both seek their most preferred outcomes, the result is the much less preferred outcome in which both charge low prices. Moreover, a situation in which both participants charge high prices (3, 3) is vulnerable to defection by either participant. It may also be illegal under legislation concerned with restraint of trade if there is collusion in setting the price.

One solution to the Prisoners' Dilemma is that the participants should enter into a binding pact before the expedition that they will not confess if arrested. However, even with such a pact the best course of action of each of the prisoners seeking to obtain an individual best possible outcome would be to confess. Moreover, the existence of the pact might increase the temptation to confess, because the chance that the other prisoner will not confess can be assumed to be greater. If a pact is arranged, therefore, it must contain a provision by which the penalty for breaking the pact is greater for each individual than the benefit which could be obtained by so doing. The existence of the penalty clause then changes the situation and the preferences of the participants to that shown in Table 7-9. The outcome 4, 4 is a stable equilibrium in this situation, guaranteeing that neither participant will defect from this outcome.

There are a number of variations of the Prisoners' Dilemma model which may have application to practical decision situations. For example, three or more participants may be in a situation where it is mutually beneficial for all the participants to conserve a scarce resource. However, as long as one participant conserves, the others may be better off if they consume the resource freely. It is possible also that participants in a Prisoners' Dilemma could be faced with repeated encounters with the same situa-

TABLE 7-9. Situation Derived from Prisoners' Dilemma in Which Participants Prefer Not to Break an Agreement Not To Confess

		Prisoner B	
		Not Confess	*Confess*
Prisoner A	*Not Confess*	4, 4	1, 3
	Confess	3, 1	2, 2

tion. The possibility of employing a mixed strategy in such circumstances should therefore be explored. Suppose, for example, that one of the participants made it clear implicitly or explicitly over a number of encounters with the same situation that he or she would not confess if the other participant did not confess. This participant could then defect from the understanding in a future situation of the same kind and obtain his or her highest preference as an outcome. Behavior of this sort is by no means ethical. In addition, a strategy of this kind is vulnerable to countermeasures by the other participant (such as by a confession on his part) in the early encounters with the situation.

A very large number of experiments have been conducted in the laboratory to study the reaction of subjects in a Prisoners' Dilemma situation.[12] It has been found that the subjects use both strategies of "confess" and "not confess" in the situation, but that the "confess" strategy typically predominates. Those involved in the experiments seemed relatively unaffected by the opponent's strategy and often found a great deal of difficulty in interpreting it.

Chicken

Chicken is a game that is played by two participants who drive cars towards each other at high speed. Each of the participants has the same two options, to swerve or to go ahead. The four possible outcomes are shown in Table 7-10. If neither of the participants swerves, the result is mutual destruction, which is indicated by the preferences 1, 1, and is least preferred by both participants. Each participant most prefers to go ahead while the other swerves. These outcomes are indicated by the outcomes 4, 2 and 2, 4. The outcome in which both participants swerve is the second most preferred by both participants as indicated by the preferences 3, 3. There are two equilibria in this game, indicated by circles around the 4, 2 and 2, 4 outcomes. These two equilibria have different values for the two participants.

The Chicken situation has some interesting characteristics. First, each participant can only obtain the most preferred outcome (4, 2 or 2, 4) by actually risking the least preferred outcome 1, 1. A participant must say "I

TABLE 7-10. Preferences for Outcomes in Chicken

		Participant 2	
		Swerve	*Go-Ahead*
Participant 1	*Swerve*	3, 3	2, 4
	Go-Ahead	4, 2	1, 1

am determined to go ahead at all cost" in order to obtain the most preferred outcome. The opponent may be persuaded to swerve by this show of determination and therefore be induced into the 4, 2 or 2, 4 outcome. However, the original participant risks obtaining the 1, 1 outcome if the opponent is not impressed by the show of determination. Second, if no participant is willing to risk the outcome 1, 1, a stable resolution of the situation is not possible. If each participant declares that he will swerve, the temptation immediately arises for the other to defect from the arrangement and go ahead instead, hoping to obtain the outcome 4, 2 or 2, 4. Third, a participant may benefit in a Chicken situation by bluffing. Suppose, for example, that a participant declares that he or she will never swerve while at the same time secretly preparing to do so. The display of determination never to swerve may have the result that the participant avoids being induced into a losing situation. The display may also induce the other participant into such a situation. The bluff can then be discarded at the last moment when disaster seems imminent and unavoidable.

Situations with characteristics like those of Chicken occur in real life. In the Cuban missile crisis for example, Russian ships were steaming towards U.S. naval vessels engaged in a blockade of Cuba. For each side to have remained determined to maintain its position was to risk disaster. In the event, the Russian ships turned back and the U.S. gained its most preferred outcome. In another similar situation, Mr. Chamberlain went to Munich in 1938 to meet Hitler declaring that he was going to save the peace. Hitler surmised correctly that Chamberlain had no intention or capability to risk war. The inability on Chamberlain's part to take that risk led him to be induced to Hitler's most preferred outcome during the negotiations.

In a more everyday situation, consider an oriental carpet merchant who has a particularly valuable Persian carpet for sale. The carpet, however, has been in the store for 4 years and it is beginning to deteriorate. The merchant is therefore anxious to sell. He has recently found a customer who is clearly interested in the carpet, but there is a considerable gap between the merchant's asking price and the amount the customer is apparently willing to pay. The merchant must decide whether he will lower his asking price. He knows that the customer is considering whether he should increase his offer. The situation and the preferences of participants for outcomes is illustrated in Table 7-11. In this situation, the merchant can declare his determination not to lower the asking price, hoping to induce the customer to buy at that price. The customer can head towards the door, hoping thereby to induce the merchant to lower the asking price. Neither participant can obtain the most preferred outcome without risking that no sale is made. The compromise outcome can be reached only through a process of negotiation and bargaining, after which the conditions leading to the 3, 3 position can be stablized in a contract.

TABLE 7-11. The Merchant/Customer Chicken Situation

		Merchant	
		Lower asking price	*Maintain asking price*
Customer	*Increase bid*	3, 3	2, 4
	Maintain bid	4, 2	1, 1

INDUCEMENT

The purpose of each participant in the negotiation and bargaining process is to persuade or coerce the other participants to an outcome that is more preferred rather than less preferred. The process of forcing another participant to an outcome that is more preferred by oneself is called inducement.[13] We have already seen inducement as a means of leading to more-preferred outcomes in the Battle of the Sexes and in Chicken.

Consider more generally the situation illustrated in Table 7-12. In this situation, the best outcome for both participants is 3, 3. If A is seen to be about to select a course of action A_2, B can indicate a choice of B_1. Such a move would induce A to choose A_1, so that both can proceed to the mutually preferred outcome 3, 3. Similarly, if B is thought to be contemplating B_2, A can induce B to choose B_1 by choosing A_1. No conflict exists between the participants in this situation. It is to the benefit of both to proceed to the jointly preferred outcome 3, 3.

In the situation illustrated in Table 7-13, however, A most prefers the outcome 4, 3. A may therefore indicate the choice of A_2 hoping that B will choose B_2 in order to avoid the least preferred outcome 1, 1. However, B may indicate choice of B_1 hoping to persuade A to choose A_1 in order to avoid the outcome 1, 1. Each participant must therefore risk the least preferred outcome 1, 1 in order to obtain a more preferred outcome, as in Chicken. The outcome 1, 1 is called the *conflict point* in the situation. It is

TABLE 7-12. Situation with No Conflict between Participants

		B's Possible Courses of Action	
		B_1	B_2
A's Possible Courses	A_1	3, 3	0, 0
of Action	A_2	0, 0	2, 2

TABLE 7-13. Situation with a Conflict Point

		B's Possible Courses of Action	
		B_1	B_2
A's Possible Courses	A_1	3, 4	2, 2
of Action	A_2	1, 1	4, 3

the outcome that neither participant wants, but which both may end up with unless a more preferred outcome can be established during the process of negotiation and bargaining between the participants.

Consider the situation in which a European car manufacturer is considering building a new assembly plant in Canada. Among the sites under consideration is one in Ontario and one in Nova Scotia. The Canadian Government is able to give certain tax incentives for such a venture. The manufacturer would prefer to build the plant in Ontario rather than in Nova Scotia. If a tax incentive were granted for the Nova Scotia site, however, this location would be preferable to one in Ontario without an incentive. The manufacturer has recently declared that in the absence of a tax incentive, the plant would be built either in Ontario or abroad. The company stated also that it would like to accommodate the government's desire for a site in Nova Scotia, but that it saw this as uneconomical without some financial support. This situation and the preferences of the participants are illustrated in Table 7-14. The car manufacturer's most preferred outcome is clearly 4, 2, but it considers that it has little chance of achieving that outcome. It does not want the outcome 2, 3. In these circumstances the manufacturer must try to induce the government to offer the tax incentive so that its second most preferred outcome 3, 4 can be brought about. The government on the other hand tries to induce the car

TABLE 7-14. The Assembly Plant Siting Problem

		Government	
		Grant no tax incentive	Give tax incentive
Car Manufacturer	Build in Ontario	2, 3	4, 2
	Without incentive build abroad; with incentive, build in Nova Scotia	1, 1	3, 4

manufacturer to build in Nova Scotia by providing the tax incentives for a plant in that province.

SUMMARY

Decision situations in which competition or conflict between the participants is a major factor can be divided into those that are strictly competitive and those that are not strictly competitive. The simplest of strictly competitive situations are called two-person, zero-sum games because they involve two participants and one participant's gain is the other's loss. These situations are interesting in that choices of courses of action by the participants can lead to an equilibrium outcome. An equilibrium is a position from which no participant can move and gain by doing so as long as the other participant maintains an equilibrium strategy. Equilibria can result from the choice of a single course of action in a single encounter with the situation (pure strategy) or from appropriate choice of different courses of action in repeated encounters with the same situation (mixed strategy). Two-person, zero-sum games have the characteristic that nothing is lost (nor is anything gained) by disclosing to an opponent the pure or mixed strategy that is to be employed to obtain an equilibrium position. If there is more than one equilibrium position in such a situation, the value to each participant of each equilibrium is the same. Furthermore, the strategies that lead to equilibria are maximin and minimax strategies for the participants.

Very few of the decision situations encountered in modern management are of the strictly competitive type. They are similar instead to n-person, non-zero-sum games. These games may have none of the characteristics of the two-person, zero-sum type. In n-person, non-zero-sum situations it may be advantageous to disclose a choice of a course of action in advance of negotiations. If more than one equilibrium position exists in such situations the value of these equilibria to each of the participants may be different. Furthermore, equilibrium strategies may not be minimax or maximin in these circumstances. Situations of this nature are normally resolved by an explicit or implicit process of negotiation between the participants.

A series of simple non-strictly competitive decision models serves to illustrate the characteristics of these situations. The Battle of the Sexes illustrates the existence of more than one equilibrium with different values to the participants and the ability of each participant to influence the outcome by statements of intent. Prisoners' Dilemma illustrates that an outcome that is more preferred by both participants can be obtained by joint agreement between the participants whereas pursuit of individual preferences may lead to a less preferred outcome. The game of Chicken and the Battle of the Sexes illustrate that participants may be induced to outcomes favorable to others by the appropriate choice of tactics governing communications and actions between the participants.

PRACTICAL DECISION SITUATIONS

7.1 The Company A Retailing Decision

Two companies compete by each manufacturing and marketing a similar product in the region of the United States east of the Mississippi. In some centers, Company A has set up its own retail outlets while in others it has entered into agreements with independent dealers to carry the retail trade. Company B has similar retail arrangements. Both companies do not set up their own retail outlets in centers in which independent dealers are licensed to market the product. The return to each of the companies is essentially the same whichever form of retail operation is used.

Company A is very interested in expanding its retail operations to the region west of the Mississippi. It suspects that Company B is planning a similar move. There is some evidence that the share of the market in an area both east and west of the Mississippi is dependent primarily on whether each company has its own retail outlets or uses independent dealers. Company A has therefore carried out extensive surveys and has found the following results. In centers in which both companies maintain their own retail outlets, Company A can expect to achieve 60 percent of the market. In centers in which A maintains its own outlets but B sells through dealers, A obtains only 30 percent of the market, due possibly to the strong promotional activities of B's dealers in such situations. In areas in which A uses dealers and B has its own outlets, A may expect to obtain 50 percent of the market. In centers in which both A and B use dealers, A can capture 55 percent of the market. The situation is summarized in Table 7-15 showing A's share of the market in each of four possible cases. Company A wishes to know the proportion of centers west of the Missis-

TABLE 7-15

		Company B	
		Own Outlets	Dealers
Company A	Own Outlets	60%	30%
	Dealers	50%	55%

sippi in which it should set up its own retail outlets and the proportion in which it should make agreements with independent dealers. Assume that both companies must select a strategy independently of the other and that no communication between the companies is possible prior to this decision. Assume also that maximization of market share is the objective of both companies.

7.2 Control of the Price Company

In 1974, the Abitibi Paper Company tried to take control of the Price Company by entering a bid for its shares on the Toronto Stock Exchange. The situation was complicated when the Power Corporation disclosed that it too was aiming for control of the Price Company and that it was considering making a counterbid. The Price shareholders could therefore sell their shares to Abitibi, sell them to the Power Corporation, or could not sell their shares at all. Neither bidder might therefore obtain the more than 50 percent of the shares necessary for control of the Price Company. Considering the courses of action available to Abitibi and the Power Corporation, can you suggest a simple model for this situation? Are there any equilibria in this situation?

7.3 Atlantic Fishing War

Two nations maintain fishing fleets off the East Coast of Canada. At the present rate of catch, fish stocks will be depleted to the extent that large scale fishing will become unprofitable in 5 years time. If the nations reduced their quotas to 70 percent of the present catch, then the fish population could be preserved over the foreseeable future. Suggest a suitable model for this situation, stating your assumptions. Should either or both of the nations continue to fish at the present rate?

7.4 Three-Farmer Irrigation System Problem

Three large farms share the water provided by a nearby reservoir. Each of the farmers installed extensive new irrigation systems during the past year. In the height of the season, they found that the continuous use of these irrigation systems exhausted the reservoir to the extent that they all had to haul in water by tankers at very high cost. Each farmer believes that if the other two were more judicious in their water consumption, a shortage could be avoided in the following year. However, each farmer would like to consume as much water as possible.

1. Suggest a model for the conflict, stating your assumptions.
2. Does this model have similar characteristics to any of the two-person models presented in the text? Which characteristics are they?

7.5 Blackmailer's Fallacy[14]

A blackmailer called B has obtained control of something that he knows is worth an amount X to another person called A. The blackmailer now thinks that he can demand and get up to an amount X from A in exchange for giving A control of the article or information in question.

1. Is the blackmailer certain to obtain any amount up to X from A or is his thinking incorrect?
2. Does this situation have similarities to Chicken or to the Battle of the Sexes?

DICUSSION TOPICS

1. Do you think that strictly competitive situations occur in modern business, government, and industry? If such situations do not occur often, what circumstances cause most encounters to be of the non-strictly competitive kind?

2. How does the concept of a "security level" brought out by the existence of an equilibrium outcome in a conflict situation relate to Simon's concept of "satisficing"?

3. The use of mixed strategies in strictly competitive conflict situations applies to decision situations that are likely to be repeated many times. Does it have any application to situations encountered in the same form only once? Would you toss a coin to resolve a single encounter of a situation of this type?

4. In situations that are not strictly competitive, the maximin strategies designed to provide a certain security level are not necessarily in equilibrium. What effect should this conclusion have on a manager who wishes to stabilize his position in such situations?

5. What assumptions are necessary if chess is to be regarded as, a strictly competitive game? If it were to be so regarded, are there any equilibria in the game? Can the appropriate equilibrium strategies be calculated?

6. In Prisoners' Dilemma, participants seeking the individually most preferred outcomes are likely to experience a less preferred outcome 2, 2. How can this outcome be avoided? What measures are necessary to ensure that the jointly preferred outcome 3, 3 can be stable?

7. Inducement is not a factor in two-person, zero-sum games or in Prisoners' Dilemma. Give detailed explanations of why this statement is correct.

8. How is inducement involved in Chicken, in the Battle of the Sexes, and in the Blackmailer's Fallacy?

9. What is the effect of bluffing on the outcome of a decision situation like Chicken? Can a practical strategy using bluffing be to the advantage of a participant in such a situation?

10. How does the concept of rationality apply to situations such as Prisoners' Dilemma and Chicken? What definition could be placed on rational behavior in these situations?

REFERENCES

1. von Neumann, J. and Morgenstern, O., *Theory of Games and Economic Behaviour*, 3rd ed., Princeton University Press, 1953.
2. Luce, R. D. and Raiffa, H., *Games and Decisions*, Wiley, 1957.
3. *Ibid*, Appendix 5.
4. *Ibid*, pp 86–87.
5. Sir Arthur Conan Doyle, *The Final Problem:* included in *The Complete Sherlock Holmes Short Stories*, John Murray, London, 1928, pp 536–556.
6. Howard, Nigel, *Paradoxes of Rationality*, MIT Press, 1971, p 152.
7. Wayne, Lee, *Decision Theory and Human Behavior*, Wiley, 1971, pp 282–286.
8. Luce, R. D. and Raiffa, H., *op cit*, p 92.
9. Luce, R. D. and Raiffa, H., *op cit*, pp 94–111.
10. Howard, Nigel, *op cit*, pp 44–48.
11. Rapoport, Anatol, *Two Person Game Theory*, University of Michigan Press, 1966, pp 128–144.
12. Lee, Wayne, *op cit*, pp 291–297.
13. Howard, Nigel, *op cit*, pp 168–198.
14. Harsanyi, John, "Measurement of Social Power, Opportunity Costs and the Theory of Two-Person Bargaining Games," *Behavioural Science*, Vol 7, No 1, 1962, p 74.

 *Chapter Eight*

Analysis of Complex Decision Situations

INTRODUCTION

The discussion in Chapter 7 centered around some models of decision situations in which there is direct or indirect competition between participants. These models provide a method of treatment of those situations that conform exactly to the conditions described in the formulations. However, many of the decision situations encountered in modern organizations are much more complex than the basic competitive situations that can be treated by the standard models. These complex decision situations often have many more than two participants. The participants have many alternative courses of action. There is usually a large number of possible outcomes of the decision situation, each of which results from a combination of courses of action adopted by the participants.

The process of resolution of complex situations of this nature can be represented by the simple model shown in Fig. 8-1. In this model, the participants are shown in a box at the top of the diagram. Time is unfolding down the page. Each of the participants is gathering information on the situation in which he or she is involved and forming perceptions of the various elements of the environment in which the decision situation exists. All participants consider, consciously or unconsciously, the courses of action that are available to each of the other participants and those open to the organization that he or she represents. They ponder the future and contemplate the outcomes that could result from combinations of these

215

courses of action. Each participant also establishes preferences among the outcomes that can be perceived. If all the participants prefer the same outcome, and if these preferences can be communicated among them, there is usually little difficulty in resolving the decision situation on the basis of a consensus. However, if the participants place the outcomes in different orders of preference (as indicated at the bottom of Fig. 8-1), no one outcome is clearly identifiable as that which all participants would accept as the basis of resolution of the decision situation. In such cases, resolution comes about only after a process of negotiation and bargaining among the participants. The objective of each of the participants in this process is to persuade or coerce the others to accept the outcome that he or she most prefers. Once an outcome has been agreed upon by the participants, measures such as signing an agreement or a contract are usually taken to reinforce its stability. The outcome then becomes an equilibrium because it is not normally to the advantage of the participants to move away from it as long as the others do not.

The process of resolution can be illustrated by the diagram in Fig. 8-2. In this diagram, a number of participants 1, 2. . . . . .n is depicted with time represented as unfolding down the page. Each participant considers the situation in which he or she is involved in a number of sessions represented by the larger rectangular boxes. These sessions are shown as occurring at irregular intervals for each of the participants. The input of information from the intelligence gathering activity of each participant is represented by the block arrows to the left of the rectangular boxes. The fact that the process is continuous is suggested by the dotted boxes at the top and bottom of the diagram. From time to time, the participants communicate with one another as part of their endeavors to persuade the others to accept a particular outcome. This interaction among the participants is shown in the form of smaller boxes interspersed between the larger ones. Participants do not necessarily communicate with each other after each session in which the present state of the decision situation is considered; nor do they necessarily communicate with all of the other participants in any one of the interactions.

There are two types of analysis that are useful to participants in this sort of decision process: (1) *strategic analysis,* in which possible outcomes are identified and the participants' preferences between them are assessed; and (2) *tactical analysis,* which forms the basis for choice of the tactics to be adopted by a participant in an immediately following interaction. These two types of analysis are now described in detail. The decision situations to which the analysis applies and which are used as examples in the text are from Category 5 of Table 1-1.

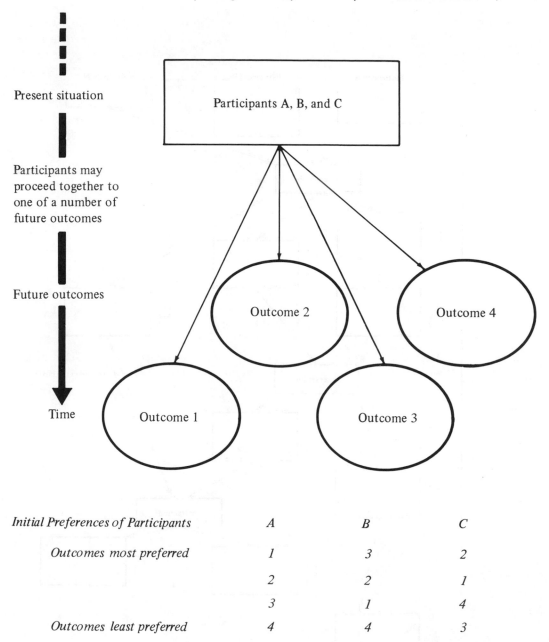

Present situation

Participants may
proceed together to
one of a number of
future outcomes

Future outcomes

Time

Participants A, B, and C

Outcome 2

Outcome 4

Outcome 1

Outcome 3

Initial Preferences of Participants	A	B	C
Outcomes most preferred	1	3	2
	2	2	1
	3	1	4
Outcomes least preferred	4	4	3

FIG. 8-1. Simple model of a complex decision situation.

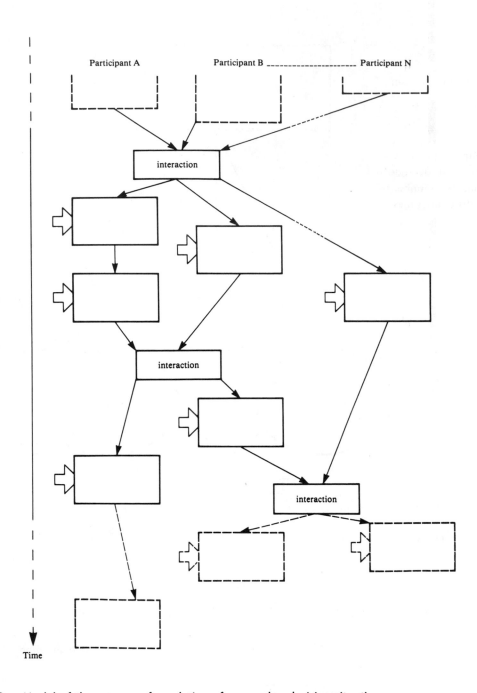

FIG. 8-2. Model of the process of resolution of a complex decision situation.

STRATEGIC ANALYSIS OF A COMPLEX DECISION SITUATION

The purpose of strategic analysis is to identify the possible future outcomes of the decision situation and the relative preferences of the participants for these outcomes. The analysis forms the basis for the choice of a strategy by a participant. In this context, a strategy is defined as a statement of the outcome that the participant wishes to see occur. Tactics refer to the manner in which the participant will act in order to bring about that outcome.

Strategic analysis is concerned with the manner in which the available courses of action of the participants impinge upon one another. It investigates courses of action that one or more participants may consider taking in order to obtain an improvement from the existing situation and the courses of action that other participants might take in order to deter or prevent these participants from attempting to achieve that improvement. The procedure for analysis consists of seven steps which are listed in Table 8-1. This procedure is based on the original Analysis of Options technique.[1,2,3] Minor changes to the original technique have been incorporated in the modified procedure as a result of experience with its use.

Step 1 of the procedure consists of listing the participants and their

TABLE 8-1.   The Modified Analysis of Options Procedure

Step 1	List the participants and their available courses of action.
Step 2	Indicate the participant from whose point of view the analysis is to be conducted.
Step 3	Choose the scenario to be analyzed.
Step 4	Consider improvements from the chosen scenario that may be available to the participant considered. If no improvements can be found, return to Step 1 or Step 2.
Step 5	Determine courses of action by other participants that may be supportive of the improvements in Step 4.
Step 6	Consider course of action by other participants that may deter the participant from attempting to achieve the improvements (i.e., *sanctions* by other participants). If the sanctions are inescapable, return to Step 1 or Step 2.
Step 7	Determine outcomes that can be achieved irrespective of the actions of other participants (i.e., *guaranteed improvements*). Return to Step 1 or Step 2 and repeat for other participants and scenarios.

available courses of action. This step is closely akin to activities referred to in the technical literature as "scenario development."[4] The work involved in this step consists of a review of the environment of the decision situation to identify those organizations and individuals that have the power to influence the outcome. These organizations and individuals are listed as participants and the courses of action that are available to them are recorded. Step 2 consists of identifying the participant from whose point of view the strategic analysis is to be conducted. Note that this choice may affect the listing of participants and courses of action in Step 1, as the perceptions of the participant chosen in Step 2 must now be used exclusively in the analysis. Step 3 requires the scenario to be analyzed to be chosen. In most (but not all) cases, this scenario is that in which the participants find themselves at the present time, as indicated by the rectangular box at the top of Fig. 8-1.

In Step 4, improvements from the chosen scenario that may be available to the participant considered are investigated. These improvements may be brought about by unilateral action by the participant considered or by action in cooperation with one or more other participants. In other cases, the improvement may result from another participant taking a course of action or ceasing to take a course of action. If no improvements can be found, the procedure returns to Step 1 or Step 2 and the position of another participant is analyzed. Step 5 consists of determining courses of action by other participants that may be supportive of the improvements identified in Step 4. Step 6 considers the opposite possibility, that is, courses of action by other participants that may deter the participant considered from attempting to achieve the improvements. Such courses of action are called *sanctions*. If sanctions are such as to prevent any improvements, the procedure returns to Step 1 or Step 2. The final step is to identify any improvements that can be achieved irrespective of the actions of the other participants. These improvements are called *guaranteed improvements*. The procedure will now be illustrated by an example.

The Firm 1/Firm 2 Competition

Firm 1 is a company based in the west that markets a major product line. It holds a 63 percent share of the market in the west, but only 16 percent in the east. Firm 1 operates a very successful network of company owned stores in the west, but similar outlets have not yet been developed in the east. The company's competition is Firm 2, which holds 68 percent of the market in the east, but which has as yet made no significant penetration in the west. Firm 2 is thought to be planning an aggressive sales campaign to improve its market share in both the east and the west. Firm 1 is sure of its position in the west, but it considers that it needs a greater proportion of the eastern market. It has to decide how to proceed in this decision situation.

Combining Steps 1 and 2 of the analysis, the participants and their available courses of action as seen by Firm 1 are shown in Table 8-2. Note that Firm 3 is included in the listing because Firm 1 has been considering negotiating an arrangement with Firm 3 to improve its position in the east. In the right column, the present situation is indicated by placing a No against a course of action that has not yet been taken and a Yes against one that is already implemented. Reading down the list of Yes's and No's gives a description of the present situation in terms of whether the courses of action available to the participants has been implemented. Note that the symbols 1 and 0 can be used to represent Yes and No in tables of this sort.

Let us suppose (Step 3) that the present situation is that which Firm 1 wishes to analyze. Step 4 requires that Firm 1 identify improvements it might achieve in this situation. These improvements are defined as situations that Firm 1 would prefer to the present situation and that it might bring about by its own unilateral efforts or in cooperation with other participants. Improvements for Firm 1 from the present situation are shown in Table 8-3, Columns 1, 2, and 3. Reading down these columns, the first represents the situation in which Firm 1 opens company owned stores in the east without lowering prices and without cooperating with Firm 3. This column depicts the future scenario most preferred by Firm 1 neglecting for the moment any reactions by the other participants. The most preferred scenario is always shown to the left of those included under the "Preferred" heading. Column 2 represents the scenario second-most preferred by Firm 1, in which it cooperates with Firm 3 in order to improve its market position in the east. Note that this scenario requires that Firm 3 cooperate with Firm 1, not compete for markets in the east and not cooperate with Firm 2. Column 3 shows the least preferred of the scenarios preferred

TABLE 8-2. Participants and Courses of Action in the Firm 1/Firm 2 Situation (as seen by Firm 1)

Participants	Available Courses of Action	Present Situation ↓ (read down) ↓	
Firm 1	Lower prices in east.	No	0
	Open company-owned stores in east.	No	0
	Cooperate with Firm 3 in east.	No	0
Firm 2	Lower prices in east.	No	0
	Expand in west: low prices.	No	0
	Cooperate with Firm 3 in east.	No	0
Firm 3	Cooperate with Firm 1 in east.	No	0
	Compete with Firm 1 in east.	Yes	1
	Cooperate with Firm 2 in east.	No	0

TABLE 8-3. Improvements for Firm 1 from the Present Situation (as seen by Firm 1)

Participants	Available Courses of Action	Preferred by Firm 1			Present Situation	Not Preferred by Firm 1		Infeasible
Firm 1	Lower prices in east	0	0	1	0	1	1	—
	Open company-owned stores in east	1	0	0	0	1	0	1
	Cooperate with Firm 3 in east	0	1	0	0	0	1	1
Firm 2	Lower prices in east				0			
	Expand in west: low prices				0			
	Cooperate with Firm 3 in east				0			
Firm 3	Cooperate with Firm 1 in east	1			0			
	Compete with Firm 1 in east	0			1			
	Cooperate with Firm 2 in east	0			0			
	Column number	1	2	3	4	5	6	7

by Firm 1 to the present situation. This scenario is that in which Firm 1 lowers its prices in the east without opening company owned outlets or cooperating with Firm 3.

Columns 5 and 6 show scenarios that Firm 1 does not prefer to the present situation. These columns record the fact that Firm 1 does not wish to lower prices in the east in conjunction with the opening of company owned outlets there or with cooperation with Firm 3. Column 7 shows that it is infeasible to open company owned outlets and cooperate with Firm 3 in the east, whether or not prices are lowered. Note that the hyphen (-) against the first course of action of Firm 1 in Column 7 is interpreted as "whether-or-not" or "1 or 0." Since Column 7 represents two scenarios, Columns 1 through 7 record a total of eight scenarios. Firm 1 has three courses of action shown in Table 8-2 each of which it can take or not. The combination of two possibilities for each of three courses of action results in eight (2^3) scenarios, all of which are depicted in Columns 1 through 7. It is necessary at this stage of the analysis to ensure that all combinations of the courses of action of the participant being considered (Firm 1 in this case) are recorded in the Table.

Step 4 of the analysis has resulted in the recording of Firm 1's preferences for scenarios that could be brought about by unilateral actions on its part, provided that Firm 2 does not oppose these actions and that (in the case of Column 2) Firm 3 cooperates. The three preferred scenarios (Columns 1, 2, and 3) are shown in order of preference starting from the left. This order of preference is determined in practical cases from a combination of quantitative studies, such as sales and profit forecasts and managerial judgment. Step 5 requires that courses of action by other participants that would be supportive to any improvements for Firm 1 be recorded. It has already been noted that the improvement in Column 2 requires the support of Firm 3. No other supportive moves by Firm 3 or Firm 2 are apparent.

The next step in the analysis (Step 6) is to record courses of action that the participants other than Firm 1 might take to deter Firm 1 from realizing its improvements. These courses of action are known as sanctions. Possible sanctions against Firm 1 are shown in Table 8-4. Column 5 of this table records that an action by Firm 2 to lower prices in the east would be a deterrent to all three improvements for Firm 1 shown in Columns 1, 2, and 3. Furthermore, a move by Firm 2 to cooperate with Firm 3 (Column 6) would be a sanction against the second most preferred improvement for Firm 1 shown in Column 2. The analysis procedure now requires that each sanction and each combination of sanctions be assessed in terms of two factors: (1) the *force* of the sanction, and (2) the *credibility* of the sanction. The force of a sanction is a measure of its preventive or deterrent effect. The credibility is an estimate of whether the participant or participants involved will take the actions necessary to invoke the sanction.

TABLE 8-4. Sanctions against Improvements for Firm 1 (as seen by Firm 1)

Participants	Available Courses of Action	Preferred by Firm 1			Present Situation	Sanctions against Improvements for Firm 1	
Firm 1	Lower prices in east	0	1		0		0
	Open company-owned stores in east	1	0		0		0
	Cooperate with Firm 3 in east	0	1		0		1
Firm 2	Lower prices in east				0		1
	Expand in west: low prices				0		0
	Cooperate with Firm 3 in east				0		1
Firm 3	Cooperate with Firm 1 in east			1	0	0	
	Compete with Firm 1 in east			0	1	1	
	Cooperate with Firm 2 in east			0	0	1	
	Column number	1	2	3	4	5	6

The information recorded in Steps 4, 5, and 6 of the analysis can be put in the form shown in Table 8-5 for each of Firm 1's improvements. This form is useful for briefing those for whom the analysis is conducted. It also facilitates consideration of the force and credibility of sanctions against a specific improvement. Note that a supporting move is the opposite of a sanction and that a move by a participant may be recorded in either form in Table 8-5.

The last step in the analysis (Step 7) is to determine whether any improvement for Firm 1 is guaranteed. An improvement is said to be guaranteed if no sanction or combination of sanctions is judged sufficient to prevent the particular participant from achieving the improvement. In Table 8-4, all of the sanctions have some force and credibility, so that none of the improvements can be reckoned to be guaranteed.

The analysis performed in the seven steps does not produce new information nor does it result in any conclusions that could not be reached by a productive process of intuitive thinking. Its major value, however, is as a means of structuring the consideration of a decision situation that might otherwise appear to be completely unstructured. The identification of improvements and sanctions in specific stages of the analysis provides emphasis on these aspects and the opportunity to uncover opportunities for action that might otherwise be overlooked. The analysis is best used in support of active consideration of a decision situation by a team of individuals who have between them a broad range of experience of the matters that are at issue.

Once the analysis has been completed from the point of view of Firm 1, it is necessary to conduct a similar analysis from the standpoint of the other participants. In the Firm 1/Firm 2 decision situation, for example, an analysis from the point of view of Firm 2 might reveal improvements for that firm that Firm 1 might wish to counter. Representatives of Firm 1 might find some difficulty in analyzing the situation from Firm 2's point of view. This difficulty can be lessened somewhat by appointing a member of the analysis team to concentrate on Firm 2 and to prepare a detailed brief on the objectives, intentions, likely preferences, and courses of action of that participant.[5] The duties of that member are to present and promote views that might be held by Firm 2 and that might be contrary to positions currently favored within Firm 1 in order that these views not be neglected or ignored. Rotation of members of an analysis team through this position ensures that the widest possible range of views is brought to bear on the decision situation under consideration.

One further extension of the analysis may yield important conclusions. It is often revealing to list the assumptions made during the analysis procedure and to test the effect of variation of these assumptions on the results that have been recorded. The sensitivity of these results to the assumptions made can then be assessed in a manner similar to that described under the heading of sensitivity analysis in Chapter 4.

TABLE 8-5. An Improvement for Firm 1 and the Effects of Possible Moves by Other Participants

Participants	Available Courses of Action	Improvement for Firm 1		Possible Moves by Other Participants
		(Column 2 of Table 8-4)		
Firm 1	Lower prices in east	No		
	Open company-owned stores in east	No		
	Cooperate with Firm 3 in east	Yes		
Firm 2	Lower prices in east		Yes	Sanction
	Expand in west: low prices			
	Cooperate with Firm 3 in east		Yes	Sanction
Firm 3	Cooperate with Firm 1 in east		Yes	Supporting
			No	Sanction
	Compete with Firm 1 in east		No	Supporting
			Yes	Sanction
	Cooperate with Firm 2 in east		Yes	Sanction

The results of the strategic analysis of the Firm 1/Firm 2 decision situation can be illustrated in the format of Fig. 8-1 as in Fig. 8-3. In this diagram, the three possible future outcomes contained in Table 8-4 are shown in the ovals below the rectangular box representing the participants in their present decision situation. The preferences of Firm 1 and Firm 2 for these outcomes are shown at the bottom of the diagram. The question for Firm 1 that arises from this diagram is how to bring about the outcome it most prefers without precipitating the outcome that it least prefers. Consideration of that question is matter for the tactical analysis that follows the strategic analysis just described. Before proceeding to a description of the tactical analysis, however, certain other aspects of strategic analysis must be considered.

NATURE AS A PARTICIPANT

The outcomes of many decision situations are influenced by the occurrence of natural and quasi-natural events. Natural events are those such as hurricanes, drought, and crop failure that are caused by an intervention by Nature. Quasi-natural events are caused by the unintended consequences in a decision situation of intended actions by participants in unrelated decision situations. These events can be included in the analysis by the addition of a participant called "Nature." The occurrence of such an event is then considered as the equivalent of Nature selecting one of its available courses of action at some future time.

In this extension of the analysis procedure, Nature cannot be regarded as a true and full participant in the decision situation. It cannot, for example, be considered to have preferences for future events or for outcomes. Nor can Nature be allowed to enter into a coalition with another participant. On the other hand, Nature can have an important effect on other aspects of the analysis. The occurrence or nonoccurrence of a natural or quasi-natural event can, for example:

1. Affect the characteristics of the outcomes derived from combinations of courses of action of the other participants.
2. Affect the preferences of the other participants for outcomes.
3. Impose the equivalent of a sanction against improvements for other participants.
4. Reinforce or reduce the credibility and increase or decrease the force of a sanction by another participant.
5. Bring about an infeasibility, for example, when a course of action is dependent upon a natural or quasi-natural event such as a technological development and that event does not occur.

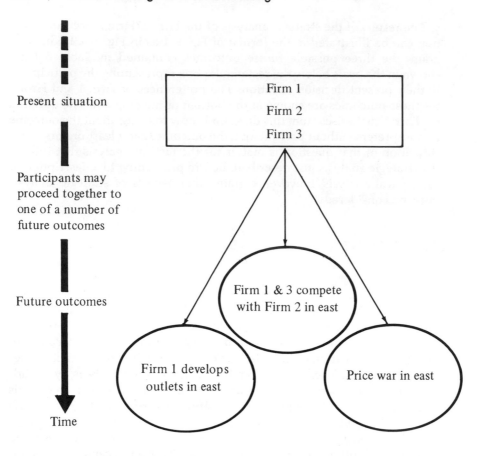

Present situation

Participants may
proceed together to
one of a number of
future outcomes

Future outcomes

Time

Firm 1
Firm 2
Firm 3

Firm 1 & 3 compete
with Firm 2 in east

Firm 1 develops
outlets in east

Price war in east

Initial Preferences	Firm 1	Firm 2
Highest	Firm 1 has company-owned outlets in east	Price war in east
	Firm 1 and Firm 3 compete with Firm 2	Firm 1 and Firm 3 compete with Firm 2
Lowest	Price war in east	Firm 1 has company-owned outlets in east

FIG. 8-3.   Possible outcomes and preferences in the Firm 1/Firm 2 decision situation.

To illustrate the inclusion of natural and quasi-natural events in the analysis, suppose that the possibility of two such events in the Firm 1/Firm 2 situation is represented as shown in Table 8-6. Nature is shown as a participant in this Table with two possible "courses of action." The first of these courses of action consists of a recession, leading to a reduction of consumer spending and a decrease in the overall market for the product line. This possible event is indicated as a sanction against all three improvements for Firm 1. The second course of action by Nature is the occurrence of a shortage of capital required for construction of the new, company owned outlets. The occurrence of the shortage of capital would also probably change the order of preference of the two improvements. In such an event, cooperation with Firm 3 would probably be more preferred than the program of development of company owned outlets.

The strategy adopted by Firm 1 in this decision situation would depend upon management's judgment of the probability of a recession and/or a shortage of capital. If these events were judged to be unlikely, the chosen strategy would no doubt be to develop a network of company owned outlets in the east in order to raise the company's market share in that region. This initiative by Firm 1 would probably be countered by Firm 2 lowering its prices in the east. This competition is likely to reduce the profitability of the company owned outlets somewhat in normal times. In the event of a recession, however, the drop in consumer spending would reduce the return on investment below that desirable for the project. In addition, if capital supply became short and if interest rates rose, the project probably could not be financed within company guidelines.

Since a recession and a shortage of capital seem to be likely events to the Firm 1 management, the best strategy would seem to be to reach a cooperative arrangement with Firm 3 to market the product line in the east. This strategy is not vulnerable to a reduction of consumer spending or to a shortage of capital. It is likely to meet with some opposition in the form of a reduction in prices in the east by Firm 2 or a competitive approach to Firm 3 by Firm 2. A less appealing strategy would be to lower prices in the east. This strategy is probably least vulnerable to countermeasures by Firm 2, but the expected gain in market share from such a course of action is likely to be minimal.

A standard format for recording the chosen strategy is shown in Table 8-7. This format shows the preferred outcome, a more detailed description of it, variations on the preferred outcome that are still acceptable, and sanctions that may be implemented by other participants. Also important in the implementation of the strategy is a statement of linkages between the decision situation to which the document refers and other situations currently under consideration by the Firm. Information on these factors is drawn from documentation of the detailed analysis on which the sheet summarizing the preferred outcome is based.

TABLE 8-6. Inclusion of Natural Events in Analysis of the Firm 1/Firm 2 Situation

Participants	Available Courses of Action	Preferred by Firm 1			Present Situation	Sanctions against Improvements for Firm 1			
Firm 1	Lower prices in east	0	0	1	0				
	Open company-owned stores in east	1	0	0	0				
	Cooperate with Firm 3 in east	0	1	0	0				
Firm 2	Lower prices in east				0	1			
	Expand in west: low prices				0				
	Cooperate with Firm 3 in east				0		1		
Firm 3	Cooperate with Firm 1 in east				0		0		
	Compete with Firm 1 in east				1				
	Cooperate with Firm 2 in east				0		1		
Nature	Recession				0			1	
	Shortage of capital				0				1
	Column numbers	1	2	3	4	5	6	7	8

TABLE 8-7.   Summary of Firm 1's Preferred Outcome to the Firm 1/Firm 2 Decision Situation

Preferred Outcome:	Firm 1 negotiates a cooperative arrangement with Firm 3.
Description:	The cooperative arrangement covers all details of a method for marketing Firm 1's product line in the east through facilities provided by Firm 3.
Variations:	Firm 1's product line is marketed by Firm 2 at reduced prices.

Sanctions:

	Force	Credibility
1. Competitive approach by Firm 2 to Firm 3	Strong	High
2. Reduction in prices by Firm 2	Medium	High

Time Factors:	The approach to Firm 3 should be made at the earliest possible time in order to forestall an approach by Firm 2.
Linkages:	*Facilitating:* A decision is about to be made to increase production at the main plant.
	Constraining: The cost of the cooperative arrangement with Firm 3 is likely to constrain other projects under consideration by the Firm.

COALITIONS

In decision situations in which many participants are involved, there is always the chance that two or more of them will form a coalition in order to achieve a common objective. Coalitions form naturally when participants perceive the opportunity to achieve more while working together than they could solely by their individual endeavors. However, coalitions are inherently unstable. When the members are motivated primarily by self-interest, the coalition is usually preserved only as long as there is mutual advantage in the arrangement. As soon as this mutual advantage diminishes, or when other more advantageous opportunities arise, there is a tendency for the coalition to break up.

Participants in complex decision situations should continually consider the possibilities and advantages of coalitions with any of the other participants. In analyzing these situations, each possible coalition must be treated as an additional participant. The courses of action available to the coalition are determined in the same way as for a single participant. In practice, because the number of possible coalitions that could be formed may be very high, only the more likely coalitions are considered. Care must be taken, however, not to neglect a coalition that appears to be most unlikely but that has considerable power to influence the outcome.

Let us consider as an example, the situation in which United Pipelines Incorporated is considering the acquisition of a majority interest in Transmountain Resources Incorporated of Denver, Colorado. This acquisition would represent a substantial diversification of activities for United as well as a means of putting an amount of retained earnings to good use. Tom Bailey was the founder of Transmountain Resources and he still owns 38 percent of the stock. He is approaching retirement, however, and he is in poor health. He is considering selling his interest in the firm prior to moving to Florida. Bailey's long-time friend, Bob Sanderson, is now President of Transmountain and holds 17 percent of the stock. Sanderson has been assuming more and more of the responsibility of running Transmountain in recent years and it is thought that he would not want to see the firm acquired by other interests such as United Pipelines. The remaining 45 percent of Transmountain stock is widely held, with just over two thirds of this stock in the hands of company employees.

The President of United Pipelines is considering approaching Bailey and suggesting that he sell his Transmountain shares to United for $14.75 a share, $1.75 above the current market price. United would then make a similar offer for the remaining 62 percent of Transmountain shares. Bailey has told United that he would like to sell his stock to United. However, he thinks that Sanderson would try to retain a controlling interest in the firm by buying shares on the open market. He would probably be assisted in this effort by company employees loyal to him. A listing of the participants in this decision situation and of their apparently available courses of action are shown in Table 8-8. Also shown in this Table is a scenario preferred by United to the present situation in which no offer has been made for the Transmountain shares. Note that this scenario requires the cooperation in supporting moves by Bailey (to cooperate with United), Sanderson (to sell to United), and by the Minority Shareholders (to sell to United), or by any combination of these participants that owns at least 51 percent of the stock. Each of these participants has a sanction against the scenario preferred by United in coalition with one of the other participants. Bailey and Sanderson can together deny United a majority interest in Transmountain, as can each of them in coalition with the Minority Shareholders. However, it may be that Sanderson will not be able to buy all of Bailey's shares, unless he can arrange substantial financing through another party.

Strategic analysis of this decision situation must include consideration of improvements for each of the possible coalitions treated as single par-

TABLE 8-8. Participants, Available Courses of Action, and Improvements for United Pipelines in the Transmountain Resources Decision Situation

Participants	Available Courses of Action	Preferred by United	Present Situation	Not Preferred by United			Infeasible	
United Pipelines	Offer $14.75 per share	1	0	0	0	1	1	0
	Seek a minority interest	0	0	0	1	1	–	1
	Increase offer for shares	0	0	1	1	0	1	0
Bailey	Cooperate with United	1	0					
	Sell shares to Sanderson		0					
Sanderson	Refuse to sell to United	0	0					
	Buy Bailey's shares		0					
	Buy shares from minority shareholders		0					
Minority Shareholders	Sell shares to United	1	0					
	Sell shares to Sanderson		0					
	Column numbers	1	2	3	4	5	6	7

TABLE 8-9. An Improvement for the Bailey & Sanderson Coalition and Possible Moves by Others Participants in the Transmountain Resources Decision Situation

Participants	Available Courses of Action	Improvement for the Bailey-Sanderson Coalition	Possible Moves by Other Participants
United Pipelines	Offer $14.75 per share		
	Seek a minority interest		
	Increase offer for shares	1	Sanction
	Offer Bailey a nonmonetary incentive to sell	1	Sanction
Bailey & Sanderson	Refuse to sell to United	1	
	Seek financing for part of Bailey's shares	1	
Bailey	Support Coalition		{0 Sanction, 1 Supporting
Sanderson	Support Coalition		{0 Sanction, 1 Supporting
Minority Shareholders	Sell shares to United		
	Sell shares to Sanderson		
	Join coalition with Sanderson		

ticipants, and possible sanctions against these improvements by other co-alitions or single participants. A typical part of the output of such an analysis is shown in Table 8-9. Note that the Bailey & Sanderson coalition is shown as an additional participant in this Table and that the available courses of action of the members of the coalition are shown only as "Support Coalition" in these circumstances. Sanctions by United Pipelines aimed at breaking up the coalition, or at least defeating its purposes are shown to the right of the table. Since the Bailey & Sanderson coalition controls 55 percent of the shares, the minority shareholders have no power to influence the outcome. Possible outcomes and the preferences of the participants for these outcomes are shown in Fig. 8-4.

LINKAGES BETWEEN DECISION SITUATIONS

Many complex decision situations encountered by modern organizations coexist with other situations of the same nature.[6] There is often a linkage between two or more of these decision situations. If the linkage is strong, events and outcomes in one decision situation can be expected to have a significant effect on those in the other situation; if it is weak, the effect is likely to be much less significant.

The effects of linkages between decision situations may be characterized broadly as "facilitating" or "constraining." Actions in one decision situation that support those in another bring about facilitating linkages. Linkages that restrict freedom of action in another situation are termed constraining linkages. The most common constraining linkage is the use of a scarce resource that limits the amount of the resource available in another decision situation.

Linkages among decision situations may affect the courses of action open to participants who are involved in some or all of them. A constraining linkage among situations may prohibit the use of a particular course of action in one of them. A facilitating linkage may provide the opportunity for a course of action to be used in a situation in which it was otherwise unavailable or inappropriate. Linkages may also affect preferences of the participants for outcomes. An outcome not much desired in one situation may appear to be preferable when considered in conjunction with an outcome in a linked decision situation.

Suppose, for example, that Firm 1 in the Firm 1/Firm 2 decision situation is a subsidiary of United Pipelines. There might be some conflict in these circumstances between the need of Firm 1 for capital to bring about its most preferred outcome of establishing company owned outlets in the east (Fig 8-3) and the requirements of the parent company for the capital needed to acquire control of Transmountain Resources. These competing needs for capital represent a constraining link between the two decision situations. On the other hand, if Firm 3 has an interest in acquiring some

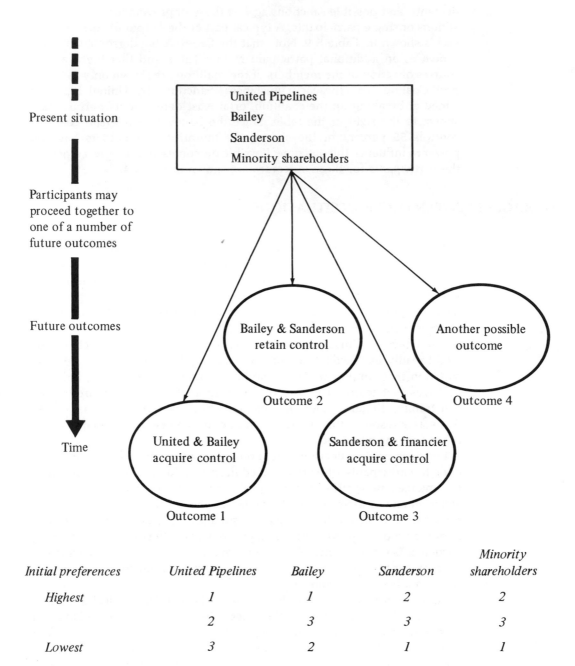

Initial preferences	United Pipelines	Bailey	Sanderson	Minority shareholders
Highest	1	1	2	2
	2	3	3	3
Lowest	3	2	1	1

FIG. 8-4.   Possible outcomes of the Transmountains Resources decision situation.

of the equity in Transmountain Resources, this interest might represent a facilitating link between the two situations. Arrangements might be made for Firm 3 to join the United & Bailey coalition to acquire Transmountain Resources. In these circumstances, the facilitating link between the two situations would cause Firm 1 to rank cooperation with Firm 3 as its most preferred outcome in the Firm 1/Firm 2 situation.

Consideration of linkages between coexisting decision situations is an important part of strategic analysis. It takes an additional significance with respect to the relationship between tactical and strategic analysis.

TACTICAL ANALYSIS

Complex decision situations are seldom resolved in a single, all-encompassing action in which the future outcome is decided for all participants. Instead, this outcome is determined in a series of "rounds" of analysis and interaction between the participants, as depicted in Fig. 8-2. Each participant takes part in a round with a basic strategy in mind. This strategy defines the outcome of the decision situation that the participant most wishes to bring about and also outcomes that would be acceptable if the most preferred resolution cannot be obtained. The strategy is either chosen implicitly by the individuals involved after thought and discussion of the decision situation with others or it is defined more explicitly after analysis of the type described in the previous sections of this chapter. The strategy of a participant may change as the sequence of rounds of the resolution process unfolds.

Some form of interaction among the participants takes place in each round. The interaction may consist of bargaining sessions among participants across a table as in many union-management decision situations. In these sessions, statements are made and positions are taken that are calculated to inform or misinform others of the intentions of a participant and possibly of a commitment to a particular outcome. In other cases, the interaction takes the form of a demonstration of intent in a much more open forum, such as by a statement to the press or a widely publicized action. The essence of the interaction in all cases is communication among the participants. The objective of each of the participants in the series of interactions is to persuade or coerce the others to proceed towards a most preferred outcome.

Each participant enters an interaction not only with an overall strategy in mind but also with a possible set of tactics. The strategy relates to the outcome that the participant wishes to bring about as the final resolution of the decision situation. The tactics are chosen as methods of achieving progress towards the desired outcome in the particular interaction for which they are designed. Tactics may be direct or indirect. For example, in some cases it may be judged desirable to make an open statement of intentions in order to persuade others of the virtues of a particular outcome. In other circumstances, it may be thought better to refrain from such statements, but to gather information on the intentions and attitudes of others. Whereas the strategy of a participant may remain essentially unchanged over a number of interactions, tactics are specific to each encounter. Furthermore, the choice of tactics in one interaction depends upon the participant's perceptions of likely developments in future interactions. The choice of tactics to be used in any one interaction may therefore be dependent on a chain of such choices related to the later interactions. The problem involved in the choice of tactics is to ensure that the tactics used in a sequence of interactions leads to the outcome specified as most preferred in the strategic analysis.

With these considerations in mind, the model of the resolution of a complex decision situation shown in Fig. 8-2 can be expanded from the point of view of one participant as indicated in Fig. 8-5. In this diagram, both information gathering and strategic analysis are shown as ongoing activities. A period of tactical analysis is indicated prior to each interaction. The purpose of this analysis is to assess tactics for the immediately ensuing interaction and to form a basis of choice of tactics for that interaction. The analysis is concerned with outcomes from the interaction which are labeled "Tactical Outcomes" in Fig. 8-5. Information with regard to those outcomes is passed both to the continuing strategic analysis and to the session of tactical analysis relating to the next interaction. A series of interactions is indicated by the dotted lines in the lower half of the diagram. The outcomes from the final interaction correspond to the strategic outcomes.

The Analogy with Chess

When searching for a methodology to be used in tactical analysis, a similarity emerges between the process of resolution of a complex decision situation, as illustrated in Fig. 8-5, and the play in the game of chess. Strategic analysis in our terms applied to chess consists of recognition that there are three outcomes: win, lose, and draw. The players no doubt have clearly defined preferences for these outcomes. A typical chess game consists of a number of moves by each player. A move by one player and a countermove by the other can be regarded as similar to an interaction in the illustration of Fig. 8-5. Before each move, a player makes a study of the existing situation and chooses a move from those available at the particular time. The move selected is chosen not only with respect to its effects on the existing situation, but also after consideration of possible effects on later moves. These aspects of chess can be likened to the tactical analysis and the choice of tactics in the resolution of complex decision situations.

The analogy between chess and the resolution of complex decision

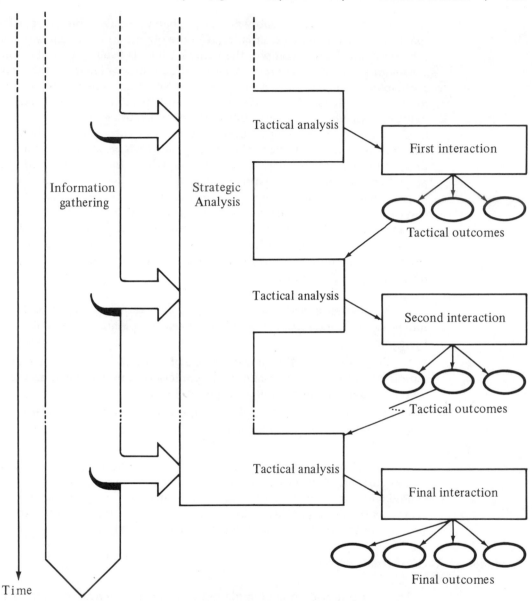

FIG. 8-5.   Resolution of a complex decision situation as seen by one participant.

problems is not complete. A typical chess game consists of between thirty and sixty interactions, far more for example, than the number of negotiating sessions in a typical industrial relations decision situation. The number of alternatives available to a chess player prior to an interaction may be very large, although possibly not larger than those available to a participant in a real-life decision situation. On the other hand, the real world is inherently much more complex than chess. Chess is usually a two-person, zero-sum game. Many complex decision situations involve more than two participants and the characteristics of the situations are not zero-sum. Real-life situations seldom exist in isolation from one another. Linkages between situations frequently introduce complications into their resolution not found in chess. In addition, the rules of chess are well defined, whereas the complex decision situations with which we are concerned are unstructured and only partial rules under which the "game" must be played are available to the participants.

The analogy is nevertheless interesting in one respect—that of the choice of tactics prior to each of a series of interactions. We are fortunate to have available in the literature a comprehensive analysis of the manner in which very competent chess players make these choices.[7] The conclusions of this analysis that may relate to the choice of tactics in a complex decision situation are as follows:

1. Most chess experts think on average a maximum of only 6 to 7 half moves (3 to 3½ interactions) ahead when selecting a move at any stage of the game.

2. Players who consider a wider range of possible moves in a given situation do not necessarily make better choices of a next move than those who consider a smaller number of possibilities.

3. The use of standard procedures appears to simplify the choice of a next move, but these procedures do not appear to be crucial prerequisites to a good choice.

4. Good chess players seem to place great weight on a good evaluation of the current situation when contemplating the next move. When presented with the need to choose a next move in a previously unknown situation, nearly all players began by giving a quick evaluation of the current position in terms of who had the better chance of winning.

A Model for Tactical Analysis

The first impulse on contemplating a model for tactical analysis is to construct a process by which the tactics leading to the desired outcome could be chosen for each of a series of interactions. Since the choice of tactics in one interaction depends upon that for the following interaction, which in turn depends upon these for further interactions, such a process would be very complex. It would need to take into account all possible combinations of tactics in all possible interactions. The complexity of this process is probably the reason why chess experts think only six to seven half moves ahead when selecting a move at any stage of the game. Taking a lead from the game of chess, therefore, it seems neither possible nor desirable to develop a comprehensive model directly associating all possible tactics throughout the chain of interactions in a complex decision situation.

The behavior of grandmasters in chess suggests that a model for tactical analysis should attempt to exploit a participant's apparent capability to reach intuitive evaluations of tactical choices when the path from the present interaction is highly uncertain. Furthermore, it suggests that participants in a complex decision situation should undertake detailed evaluation of the future consequences of tactical choices only to the point at which they feel able to assess in specific terms the effects of the alternatives available to them. This concentration in tactical analysis on the more immediate consequences of a choice has similarities to the process of disjointed incrementalism recommended by Braybrooke and Lindblom in another context.[8] The detailed analysis of the immediate consequences of tactical action must be complemented, however, by a much broader and more intuitive review of the effects of a choice of tactics on the overall decision situation.

The partition of the analysis model into two components has a number of advantages. Much more information is likely to be available to the decision maker for use in assessing the immediate consequences of a choice of tactics. This information is also likely to be much more reliable than that relating to events and conditions further into the future. The evaluation of immediate consequences of a choice is therefore likely to be much less affected by uncertainty. In addition, the individual involved deals with a manageable amount of information, comparisons, and decisions. He or she is not faced with a complex task of assessing a very large number of chains of decisions stretching some length of time into the future.

There is also some reason to believe that participants in real-life decision situations make a distinction between immediate and later consequences when deciding on a tactical course of action. For example, the union leadership undoubtedly considers the immediate consequences of strike action before it actually issues the call to the members to leave their jobs. Immediate consequences can be assessed with some certainty. Members will lose money. A certain amount of ill feeling will be generated. Some discontent may arise amoung the members if the strike is prolonged. There is also the possibility that a tactical action may have to be reversed at a later stage if it appears detrimental to the interests of the initiator. For example, a strike may have to be called off if it does not seem to be achieving the desired results, or if the immediate consequences to those involved are overly burdensome. The cost of such a reversal in financial terms and in other ways, such as a loss of face, must be evaluated in an assessment of the immediate consequences of a tactical action.

In the above example, the possibility that the strike will assist in bringing about the union's most preferred outcome in the strategic sense balances to some extent the adverse immediate consequences of the action. The longer term consequences of a strike are assessed intuitively by the union leadership, using their experience and judgment gained after many years in the environment of similar decision situations. The decision to strike or not as a tactical measure can be seen therefore to be a multiple objective problem in which more clearly defined disadvantages in the short term are weighted against less clearly defined benefits in the longer term.

The method by which the longer term benefits or disbenefits of a choice of tactics can be evaluated is much less clear. A method of evaluation in which all possible effects of all possible tactics are assessed throughout the chain of interactions seems impossible to design or to implement. One means of overcoming this dilemma that has some intuitive appeal is to attempt to assess the extent to which a tactic may contribute to the emergence of a particular outcome or act against this eventuality. In the language used earlier in this chapter in discussing linkages between decision situations, a tactic can be assessed to be facilitating to a particular outcome to some degree, or on the other hand constraining to that outcome. A facilitating link between a tactic and an outcome would make that outcome more desirable to all participants or more likely to be achieved in some other way. A constraining link would make an outcome less desirable or less likely to be achieved.

The method of establishing linkages between a choice of tactics and the possibility of achieving a strategic outcome corresponds closely to the manner of intuitive thinking of participants. Negotiators consciously present suggestions in a manner likely to make them more acceptable. The manner of justifying an argument often enhances or reduces its credibility. Furthermore, the method of linkage can lead to the establishment of a preference ordering for all contemplated tactics with respect to a particular strategic outcome. This preference ordering is another input into the assessment of alternative tactics in the framework of a multiobjective decision suggested above.

In summary, therefore, the tactical analysis is partitioned into two components. The first of these components is concerned with the immediate consequences of a choice of tactics. This component is pursued in as much detail as time and available information allow. The second component is concerned with the longer term effects of a choice of tactics. This second component consists of an assessment of the linkages between a chosen tactic and a desired strategic outcome. These linkages are classified as facilitating or constraining and this assessment is used to establish a preference ordering between available tactics in terms of their effect on the achievability of a desired strategic outcome.

Tactics in the Transmountain Resources Decision Situation

Let us consider the choice of tactics by United Pipelines in the Transmountain Resources decision situation described in Table 8-8. The strategic outcome desired by United in that situation is that it obtains a majority interest in Transmountain by paying $14.75 a share (Column 1 of Table 8-8). United cannot achieve that outcome without the cooperation of at least two of the three other participants. The question involved in United's choice of tactics is how to insure that these participants cooperate with United rather than set up a coalition in competition to them. An analysis of this tactical problem is shown in Table 8-10.

In the first column of this table, six possible tactics for United Pipelines are shown. The estimated immediate consequences of each of these tactics are shown in the central column of the table. The information in these columns indicates that United favors contacting Bailey with an offer to buy his shares and for help in influencing the minority shareholders to accept United's offer. This approach may not be accepted by Bailey, however, and it is thought that he may then contact Sanderson to arrange a coalition against the United offer. An initial approach to Sanderson (Tactic No. 2) is regarded as even less likely to succeed. A public offer of $14.75 a share (Tactic No. 3) is also not seen as useful at this stage. A fourth tactic of offering to buy Bailey's shares and at the same time offering him a nonmonetary incentive to sell, such as a continuing appointment to the Board of Directors is assessed as likely to be acceptable to Bailey. The degree of acceptability is thought to be dependent on the attractiveness of the nonmonetary incentive. The fifth tactic included in Table 8-10 is the offer of a similar incentive to Sanderson, but this initiative is regarded as unlikely to succeed. The last possible tactic, which is to gather information and await developments, is not attractive on any count.

The right-hand column of Table 8-10 shows the estimated effects of the tactics on the achievement of United's desired strategic outcome of obtaining control of Transmountain Resources. These effects are shown in terms of an estimate of whether use of a tactic facilitates or constrains the achievement of the desired outcome.

The conclusion of the analysis is that the best tactic in the first interaction is to offer to buy Bailey's shares and to suggest that a nonmonetary incentive will be available to Bailey if he sells all his shares to United. This tactic is judged to be attractive to Bailey because he wishes to dispose of his shares expeditiously. He also would probably be interested in a continuing and part-time association with Transmountain should United gain control of the company. The tactic is judged to be highly facilitating to achievement of the desired outcome. United's offer should probably be made in general terms in a first interaction with Bailey. More specific tactics, especially with regard to the nature of the nonmonetary incentive,

TABLE 8-10. Tactical Analysis in the Transmountain Resources Decision Situation

Tactic	Immediate Consequences	Effects on Achievability of Desired Strategic Outcome
1. Contact Bailey with regard to a United & Bailey coalition.	Bailey may agree. On the other hand, he may immediately contact Sanderson and influence minority shareholders against United's bid.	If Bailey agrees, *facilitating*. If Bailey does not agree and forms another coalition, *constraining*.
2. Contact Sanderson with regard to United & Sanderson coalition.	Sanderson may not agree, because he is thought to oppose a take-over bid. He may attempt to form a coalition with Bailey and to influence minority shareholders.	If Sanderson agrees, (but this is considered unlikely), *facilitating*. If Sanderson does not agree, *constraining*.
3. Make public offer of $14.75 per share.	Bailey and/or Sanderson may not sell and one and/or other may influence minority shareholders not to sell.	If less than 50% of shares tendered, *constraining*.
4. Contact Bailey offering to buy shares plus a nonmonetary incentive.	Bailey will probably agree if the nonmonetary incentive is sufficiently attractive. If it is not, Bailey's attitude to United may harden. Bailey will probably not contact Sanderson while negotiations are in progress.	If Bailey agrees, *facilitating*. If Bailey does not agree, *constraining*.
5. Contact Sanderson offering to buy shares plus a nonmonetary incentive.	Sanderson is not likely to agree, since he appears not to favor control of Transmountain by an outside company.	*Constraining*
6. Take no action but actively gather information on decision situation.	Bailey will seek other methods of disposing of his shares.	*Constraining*

would be appropriate to further interactions with Bailey. Once Bailey's co-operation had been secured, interactions with minority shareholders should be initiated in order to gain sufficient shares to exercise majority control of Transmountain.

SUMMARY

Many decision situations are considerably more complex than those which can be treated by the basic competitive models described in Chapter 7. The process of resolution of these complex situations consists of a series of rounds in which the participants negotiate an outcome. The process of negotiation is either explicit, as during bargaining sessions in an industrial relations dispute, or implicit, in which case the interaction between the participants is much more subtle and less direct. In all cases, the objective of each participant in the negotiation process is to persuade or coerce the others to accept the outcome that he or she most prefers.

There are two types of analysis that are useful to participants in this sort of situation: (1) strategic analysis, in which possible outcomes are identified and participants' preferences for them are assessed; and (2) tactical analysis, the basis for choice of tactics by a participant in an immediately ensuing interaction. Strategic analysis can be performed using a modified form of the Analysis of Options. In this analysis, improvements for each of the participants from a particular situation (usually the present situation) are identified. Actions that may be taken by other participants to deter or prevent these improvements (called sanctions) are also identified in the analysis. The analysis does not produce new information or result in any conclusions that could not be reached by a productive process of intuitive thinking. Its major value is as a means of structuring the strategic consideration of a situation that might otherwise appear to be completely unstructured.

The effect of natural events on the outcome of a complex decision situation can be investigated by representing these events as available courses of action of a pseudo-participant called Nature. In this extension of the analysis, Nature cannot be regarded as a full participant in the decision situation. It cannot, for example, be considered to have preferences for outcomes. However, it can have an important effect on other aspects of the analysis. In decision situations in which many participants are involved, there is always the chance that two or more of them will form a coalition. Another extension of the analysis provides for consideration of possible coalitions as additional participants in the decision situation. Many complex decision situations coexist with other situations of the same nature. Strategic analysis must take account of possible linkages between decision situations, their effect on the availability of courses of action and the possible effect on participants' preferences for outcomes.

Tactical analysis is conducted in two components. The first of these components is concerned with the immediate consequences of a choice of tactics. The second component is concerned with the strategic effects of a choice of tactics. It consists of an assessment of the linkages between a chosen tactic and a desired strategic outcome. These linkages are classified as facilitating or constraining. This assessment may be used to establish a preference ordering between available tactics in terms of their effect on the achievability of a desired strategic outcome.

PRACTICAL DECISION SITUATIONS

8.1 International Chemical Company Inc.

The International Chemical Company wishes to build a large plant at a site within 10 miles of a small town. The company has the support of the state government, which sees the large site as being an economic way of providing jobs in an otherwise depressed area. The local citizens are divided on the issue. Some fear that a large complex would take up many acres of valuable land and might also pollute the atmosphere, as well as destroy important recreational facilities. Others think that a medium or small plant would be more in keeping with the interests of the town. Local contractors, however, feel that a large facility will bring them more work, and will therefore benefit the area. An election is pending at both the local and state levels. A local citizens' committee is meeting to discuss actions designed to influence the outcome of this difficult situation.

You are hired by the citizens' committee to analyze the situation and to make recommendations. As you start work, a local politician suggests a compromise solution in which a medium size plant is built 30 miles to the southeast of town.

Describe how you would approach your task of analyzing this problem. Use your imagination to fill out details of the situation.

8.2 The Dealers' Association

An oil company has a number of service stations across the country operated by semi-independent dealers under a range of different types of agreement. It also operates wholly owned self service outlets and private brand stations. The dealers belong to an association that represents them in relationships with the company and with agencies of government.

The current issue is that the dealers feel their livelihood is being undercut by the operations of the self service outlets and the private brand stations. They have made representations to the Association, which is bringing pressure on the company to improve the lot of the dealers. Collective action against the company has been mentioned. The Association has asked for help from governments in their dispute with the company. It has proposed a compromise solution that it considers is midway between the more extreme demands of some of the dealers and the original offer of the company.

Analyze the structure of this decision problem in a manner that would assist the company representatives in their forthcoming meeting with the Association. What tactics would you recommend that these representatives follow at this meeting? Use your general knowledge of this sort of situation to fill in details not mentioned above.

8.3 The Roy Hawkins Situation

You are in charge of an operation that provides service to the public and your main concern is the quality of that service. Your chief assistant is Roy Hawkins. He has an excellent technical background and he seems to have a knack for going directly to the cause of systems problems. However, morale is low among the staff that report to Roy and there is considerable turnover. You are convinced that this is because of the way he deals with people. He is abrupt and abrasive. He conveys to the staff members that he has little respect for them. He seems to distrust them and they, in turn, distrust him. You recently overheard a conversation between Roy and Peter, one of his technicians. Roy was criticizing Peter harshly for careless workmanship. Peter disagreed that his work was careless. He accused Roy of carrying a grudge against him for a mistake that he (Peter) had made over six months ago. Roy responded, pointing his finger at Peter, "Listen, I've been carrying you for as long as I'm going to. From now on you're going to pay. The next time you goof off, I'll put you on suspension." Peter has now come to you asking that you intervene in the dispute.

Analyze the situation in a manner that will allow you to choose an outcome that you would like to bring about. What tactics would you use to ensure that you attain this outcome?

8.4 An Industrial Relations Situation

The local union has called a strike vote at the plant of which you are the manager and it seems that the membership will vote to go out. The issues are (1) wages, with the gap being between 5 percent and 9 percent over a one year contract; (2) safety in the plant; and (3) the impact of technological change. The union has the support of other organized labor in the plant and in the neighborhood. It has threatened to call a boycott of your product and to take action against other firms that do not observe the boycott.

A plant shutdown would not be damaging in the short term. In fact, the level of absenteeism and incidents that might possibly be due to minor sabotage suggest that a lock-out might be advantageous in some respects. A mediator has suggested a compromise between your position and that of the union that you could live with and that you suspect the union would agree to. However, this compromise would be costly and you think it might be more advantageous to hold off agreeing to it for a while in the hope of obtaining better terms of settlement.

You are meeting with the union leadership the day after tomorrow. Describe how you might analyze the situation prior to deciding on the tactics that you will use at this and subsequent meetings.

8.5 The House in Florida

You have a house in Florida that you wish to sell. A potential buyer has been found and you are considering how best you can entice this buyer to close the deal. You consider the strategic situation and conclude that there are only two likely outcomes: potential buyer actually buys the house or he does not. You naturally prefer the first of these. Your problem is to ensure that the buyer proceeds to your more preferred outcome.

You are meeting with the potential buyer tomorrow. You consider that you have two available tactical courses of action: (1) to show the buyer pictures of the house; and (2) to finance a trip to Florida for him to view the house. How would you conduct an analysis which could act as a basis for choice between these tactics? Do any other possible tactics occur to you? If so, how do these tactics fit into the analysis?

DISCUSSION TOPICS

1. A diagram representing the process of resolution of a complex decision situation is shown in Fig. 8-2. What is the purpose of the boxes marked "interaction" in this depiction of the resolution process?

2. Strategic analysis is said to be concerned with possible future outcomes of a decision situation and participants' preferences for them, whereas tactical analysis is concerned with tactics to be adopted by a participant in an immediately ensuing interaction. Is this distinction viable or are these two types of analysis one and the same thing?

3. How does the modified analysis of options procedure relate to the process of intuitive thinking used by many experienced managers? Does the analysis of operations provide any advantages over the intuitive approach?

4. What are the advantages in strategic analysis of representing natural events as available courses of action of a pseudo-participant called Nature? Are there any pitfalls to that approach?

5. What are the advantages of a coalition in a complex decision situation? Under what circumstances would you consider a coalition with another participant in such a situation.

6. Can the preferences of a coalition be different from those of its members? How can such differences be represented in a strategic analysis?

7. What are the possible effects of linkages between two or more decision situations on their outcomes? Can these effects be used to advantage by participants?

8. Do you consider the analogy with chess to be useful in considering tactics to be used in a complex decision situation? What are the most useful aspects of the analogy and what are the least useful?

9. Do you agree that people intuitively partition the analysis of the effects of tactics into immediate and long term categories? If this is done intuitively by most decision makers can you suggest a reason for this behavior?

10. Is the choice between tactics truly a multiobjective decision problem between immediate consequences and longer range effects on the achievement of strategic outcomes? Should a formal procedure be set up for resolution of this multiobjective problem?

REFERENCES

1. Howard, N., *Paradoxes of Rationality*, The MIT Press, 1971, pp 127–146.
2. Radford, K. J., *Managerial Decision Making*, Reston, 1975, pp 145–172.
3. Fraser, N. M. and Hipel, K. W., "Solving Complex Conflicts," *IEEE Transactions on Systems, Man and Cybernetics*, Vol SMC 9, No 12.
4. For example, see Ralph-MacNulty, Christine A., "Scenario Development for Corporate Planning," *Futures*, Vol 9, April 1977.
5. Herbert, T. T. and Estes, R. W., "Improving Executive Decisions by Formalizing Dissent: the Corporate Devil's Advocate," *Academy of Management Review*, October 1977, pp 662–667.
6. Radford, K. J., *Strategic Planning: an Analytical Approach*, Reston, 1980, Chapter 7.
7. De Groot, A. D., *Thought and Choice in Chess*, Mouton and Company, The Hague, 1965.
8. Braybrooke, D. and Lindblom, C. E., *A Strategy for Decision*, The Free Press, 1963, Chapter 5.

Index